What Teachers Need to Know About Children at Risk

Barry B Frieman
Towson University

Boston   Burr Ridge, IL   Dubuque, IA   Madison, WI
New York   San Francisco   St. Louis
Bangkok   Bogotá   Caracas   Lisbon   London   Madrid   Mexico City
Milan   New Delhi   Seoul   Singapore   Sydney   Taipei   Toronto

McGraw-Hill Higher Education

A Division of The **McGraw-Hill** *Companies*

WHAT TEACHERS NEED TO KNOW ABOUT CHILDREN AT RISK

1 2 3 4 5 6 7 8 9 0 DOC/DOC 0 9 8 7 6 5 4 3 2 1 0

ISBN 0-07-239070-0

Vice president and editor-in-chief: *Thalia Dorwick*
Editorial director: *Jane E. Vaicunas*
Sponsoring editor: *Beth Kaufman*
Developmental editor: *Cara Harvey*
Senior marketing manager: *Daniel M. Loch*
Senior project manager: *Kay J. Brimeyer*
Senior production supervisor: *Sandra Hahn*
Coordinator of freelance design: *Rick D. Noel*
Cover designer: *Jamie O'Neal*
Cover image: © *Tony Stone Images, Children with Self-Portraits by Ed Honowitz*
Senior photo research coordinator: *Lori Hancock*
Photo research: *Connie Gardner Picture Research*
Compositor: *Carlisle Communications, Ltd.*
Typeface: *10/12 Palatino*
Printer: *R. R. Donnelley & Sons Company/Crawfordsville, IN*

The credits section for this book begins on page 210 and is considered an extension of the copyright page.

Library of Congress Cataloging-in-Publication Data

Frieman, Barry B
   What teachers need to know about children at risk / Barry B Frieman.—1st ed.
     p. cm.
   Includes index.
   ISBN 0-07-239070-0
    1. Socially handicapped children—Education—United States.   2. Socially handicapped children—Education—United States—Case studies.   3. Effective teaching—United States.
I. Title.

LC4091 .F679   2001
371—dc21

                                              00-024635
                                             CIP

www.mhhe.com

Contents

Part Three
PHYSIOLOGICAL CONDITIONS

Part Four
SOCIAL CONDITIONS

Preface

ORIENTATION OF THE TEXT

This book is written for the classroom teacher in training or in practice. It is designed to give the learner practical, hands-on help in dealing with children in challenging situations. The book does not address school policy but instead focuses on things that can be done by the average classroom teacher without classroom aides.

The approach of this book is to view children at-risk as developmentally normal children who happen to be coping with a challenging situation. I present all of the children in this book as children and not as conditions. For example, I discuss "children who are homeless" rather than "homeless children" in order to reinforce this position.

CASE EXAMPLES

The book is filled with case examples. The examples have come from my own experience in working as a social worker with children and families, the stories that teachers have shared with me when I visited their classrooms, and the observations I have made while working in schools with children and teachers. Of course, all of the names and identifying circumstances of the children have been changed to ensure their privacy.

ORGANIZATION OF THE TEXT

The first chapter discusses the concept of at risk, noting that certain situations seem to be correlated with predictable challenges for children. The concept of correlation is explained. The second chapter looks at children who are resilient and notes how the classroom teacher can promote resiliency skills in all children. Subsequent chapters explore:

Psychological Conditions

- Children with behavioral problems
- Children who are alienated
- Children and father absence
- Children with disabilities
- Children who are gifted
- Children with incarcerated parents
- Children dealing with death

Physiological Conditions

- Children with chronic medical problems
- Children with Attention Deficit Hyperactivity Disorder

Social Conditions

- Children and poverty
- Children who are homeless
- Children and violence
- Children and divorce
- Grandparents raising children
- Children who are members of a racial, religious, or sexual minority
- Children new to the United States
- Children of substance-abusing parents

USE OF TEXT

This text can be used as a primary text in a course on Children At Risk, or as a supplemental text in an introductory education course. This text will supplement a growth and development text or introduction to education, or curriculum text by providing the learner with information necessary to meet the needs of a diverse student body.

FEATURES TO HELP THE STUDENT EXTEND THEIR THINKING

Each chapter has a series of research questions for the learner to ponder. These questions can be used as the basis for student research papers or class discussions. Websites of related interest are also noted after each chapter.

PEDAGOGICAL FEATURES

- Case Examples—throughout the text
- Chapter Objectives—learner objectives in behavioral terms are noted for each chapter
- Advance Organizers—each chapter has advanced organizers to help focus the reader
- References—are reported at the end of each chapter
- Research Topics and Related Websites—are reported at the end of each chapter
- Websites of General Interest—are noted at the end of the text
- Summary—each chapter has a complete summary

A NOTE ON CONTRIBUTORS

I would like to thank the following reviewers who provided feedback on the text:

William E. Davis, *University of Maine*

Joan Henderson-Sparks, *California State University—Fresno*

Kenneth W. Merrell, *The University of Iowa*

This text is enhanced by the contributions of three other scholars. My brother, Maury Frieman, a licensed clinical social worker, has spent many years counseling children and families. He works as a mental health counselor at Pinehill Elementary School in Massachusetts and has contributed his experience in dealing with alienated children.

My sister, Marcia Mindel, is a special education resource teacher working at Viers Mills Elementary School, a public school in Montgomery County, Maryland. She has shared her experience in working with children whose parents are immigrants.

Most important is the contribution of my wife, Joanne Settel, Ph.D., who is Professor of Biology at Baltimore City Community College, and the author of many science books for children. She contributed her science expertise to the chapter of children with medical problems. She also edited the entire book. Her support and encoragement are greatly appreciated.

About the Author

All of my life experiences have colored my view of children at risk. I am the child of first generation Americans. My grandparents were immigrants who faced discrimination and poverty. As a young child, I heard family survivors tell about how they witnessed others in the family exterminated as a result of ethnic hatred. From that point on I have worked to fight bigotry.

Being an active father to my two daughters has made me appreciate the need to be practical. I discovered as a parent that theory was only valuable if I could translate it into action.

I was trained at the Institute For Child Study at the University of Maryland, where I earned a Doctor of Education degree. My focus on a career in teacher education was decided after my contact with James Hymes, Jr., a most valued mentor. Later, I earned a Master of Social Work degree and have used that clinical training to work with children and their families.

I am a Professor in the College of Education at Towson University in Baltimore, Maryland where I teach both undergraduate and graduate students. Most of the articles that I have written in the scholarly journals have concerned various aspects of children at risk.

This book is dedicated to my father, Colman, who taught my brother, my sister, and me to care.

Who Are Children at Risk?

What Does "At Risk" Mean?

OBJECTIVE

After reading this chapter, you should be able to explain the concept "at risk" and note how teachers can use the label *at risk* to maximize children's educational experience.

CHAPTER OUTLINE

Through the Eyes of a Child
    The Wisdom of a Second-Grader
    Why Children Are Considered to Be at Risk
Definition of "at Risk"
Differential Experiences
The Label *At Risk*
Summary

THROUGH THE EYES OF A CHILD

The Wisdom of a Second-Grader

One day my second-grade daughter came home from school anxious to tell me about a presentation her class had heard on Handicapped Awareness Day. "People came in and talked about all the handicaps," she explained. I asked her what a handicap is, and she said that it is something that makes it hard for someone to be like everybody else. I went on to ask her about one of our friends—a man who is our neighbor, my jogging partner, and a frequent visitor to our house, and who happens to be blind. "No Dr. M. is not handicapped," she replied indignantly, "he's just blind." Dr. M. is a mathematician who has amazed my daughter by answering all of her math questions and being able to do calculations in his head. My daughter also knows that his garden is the source of our supply of fresh summer tomatoes.

Although Dr. M. would be labeled "at risk" by many teachers because he is blind, my daughter sees him instead as a competent, capable individual who just can't see. She knows that blindness is not Dr. M's handicap, but one of his attributes, like his height, hair color, or skin color.

Why Children Are Considered to Be at Risk

Many children are at risk because society has labeled their attributes as problematic. Is Dr. M., who has a Ph.D. in mathematics and happens to be blind, an at-risk learner? If he is at risk, it is only because people in our society have decided that blind people are incapable of achieving intellectual goals.

As you read this book, you will see that at-risk children are just like other children. You will learn not to see the "at-risk" part, but to see a child who happens to have certain attributes that might or might not be problematic. In the case of Dr. M., his blindness is an obstacle only if people see him as limited and unable to perform like other people in society. Blindness is a physiological condition. In later chapters of this book we will discuss other risk conditions that have a physiological basis, such as chronic medical problems and attention deficit hyperactivity disorder.

Some children are labeled "at risk" because they are members of groups that many in our society feel are inferior. Paul, an African American student in my college class, talked to a group of future teachers about how it feels to be perceived as a problem by other people just because of one of his attributes, in this case his race. Paul said,

> When I walk down the street in a white neighborhood, white people will often cross the street rather than come near me. When I go into the local clothing store to browse, the clerks follow me around. They don't follow the white guys. When I get on an elevator with white women, they get all nervous and move away from me. Because my skin is black, they see me as a criminal. It's their problem, but I have to deal with it every day.

Until the 1954 Supreme Court decision in *Brown* v. *Board of Education,* African American children in many states were not permitted to go to school with white children. Even though our society has now made school segregation illegal, African American children still have to deal with discrimination from many in the larger society.

Racism is a social condition. This book will also explore other social conditions that put children at risk, such as having parents who are incarcerated, poor, or homeless, or being a member of a sexual or religious minority.

DEFINITION OF "AT RISK"

Just what does it mean to be at risk, and why is this concept important to teachers? Educational and psychological researchers have looked at children with certain identifiable traits, such as the ones noted above, and found that many of them had problems both at home and at school. Studies show that there is a correlation between certain living conditions or personal traits and certain behaviors at school. Educators have labeled conditions that are correlated with problems in school "risk conditions."

A correlation is a measure of relationship between two or more things—such as two or more sorts of conditions. When two traits are positively correlated, it means that when one event occurs the other occurs. For example, people in the auto insurance industry will tell you that males under age 25 tend to have more traffic accidents than people at other ages. They could say, in fact, that there is a positive correlation between males under 25 years of age and traffic accidents. That doesn't mean that age and male sex causes traffic accidents. Safety experts know that accidents are caused by going at an excessive speed, driving while intoxicated, and many other conditions. But nonetheless there is a relationship between young men and traffic accidents.

The label *at risk* confirms what most teachers know: Children do not play on a level playing field. Some children come to school with more things going for them than others. This book will help teachers use the label *at risk* as a shortcut to understanding the child and to meeting the child's needs appropriately in the classroom.

Many of the children with risk conditions qualify for special education services under the IDEA, a federal law that we will discuss in a later chapter. However, some children who are not eligible for special education services are in social situations that put them at risk.

DIFFERENTIAL EXPERIENCES

Not every child in the same risk situation will have the same kind of experience. Many factors affect how a child in a risk situation will fare. One factor is how other people perceive and react to the child's condition. Other factors include the child's age, developmental level, intelligence, personality, and individual resilience.

Children at risk must deal with special challenges. How people perceive the condition is an important variable in how the child will be treated. Let's return to the condition of blindness. Is it a risk condition? Dr. Kenneth Jernigan, former president of the National Federation of the Blind, often noted that if society treated people who are blind by giving them proper training and job opportunities, then blindness would be seen as being only a physical nuisance (Jernigan, 1992). Blindness is a risk condition only because many people feel that people who are blind cannot do work that in fact they are capable of performing.

Teachers can have preconceived notions of how someone with a particular condition will behave. Rosenthal and Jacobson (1968) found that teachers' expectations about student performance to some degree affects how students actually do perform. They called this phenomenon "self-fulfilling prophecy." If a teacher perceives a child as being unable to learn, the teacher will not teach the child and the child indeed will not learn. As teachers, we need to expect that all of the children in our class will learn regardless of the risk condition they are facing.

Children's age and developmental level, intelligence, personality, and resilience will also affect how they react to risk conditions. In future chapters we will discuss in detail how children at different levels respond to different conditions. Older children have much more sophisticated coping skills than younger children do, and they also have the power to take an active role in their world.

THE LABEL AT RISK

The label *at risk* can be either an asset or a liability to a child, depending upon how one uses it. It can be an asset if the label is used to meet the child's needs. It can be a liability if it is used to limit expectations for that child.

If you are told that a new student coming into your class is labeled "totally blind," you will know that you will have to make certain accommodations, such as making sure that her textbooks will be available in Braille. In this case the label is helpful. It enables you to make accommodations so the student will be able to work at her full capacity in the classroom.

On the other hand, if your principal says that you are getting a child who is aggressive, you have been told nothing helpful about the child. What does "aggressive" mean? Is being "aggressive" good or bad? One teacher might expect a 7-year-old version of Al Capone. This teacher might react by planning to be extremely repressive to make sure that the child doesn't get away with anything. Another teacher might interpret this news in a positive light and anticipate getting a youngster in the classroom who is full of energy and vigor. Think for a minute. If you were a high school teacher, how would you react if you were told that you were getting a really aggressive male student? How would you feel if you were an English teacher? the vice-principal? the football coach? the coach of the field hockey team?

At risk is a label that must be used with care. When a child has been labeled "at risk," it suggests that, all things considered, the child will experience the same challenges that other children in the same situation have experienced. Use the warning label *at risk* to help you understand the child and her life experiences, and use these insights to meet the child's needs in your classroom.

The label *at risk* will help you to prepare for the students in your classroom. Knowing the characteristics of the various risk conditions can help you to know when to step in and lend a hand, or when to suggest an alternative path to the goal. This knowledge will also help you to shape your teaching and behavior to best reach your children.

The label *at risk*

- Doesn't mean that a child is limited
- Doesn't mean that the child has a fatal flaw
- Does mean that the child might have difficulties in some areas at some point in time

Summary

The label *at risk* can be used or misused by teachers. You can use the information in this book about the risk conditions to help children be successful in your classroom.

RESEARCH IDEAS

Questions to Investigate

Is at risk a social or a biological condition?

If teachers viewed all children as unique learners would there be a need for an at-risk label?

Do all cultures identify children at risk the same way we do in the United States?

Resources to Explore

CHILDREN'S DEFENSE FUND (1992). *The state of America's children.* Washington, DC: Author. Southern Poverty Law Center's magazine *Teaching Tolerance* which is given free to teachers. (400 Washington Avenue, Montgomery, Alabama 36104).

References

BRITAIN, L. A., HOLMES, G. E., & HASSANEIN, R. S. (1995). High-risk children referred to an early-intervention developmental program. *Clinical Pediatrics, 34,* 635–641.

CULLEN, F. T., WRIGHT, J. P., BROWN, S., MOON, M. M., BLANKENSHIP, M. B., & APPLE-GATE, B. K. (1998). Public support for early intervention programs: Implications for a progressive policy agenda. *Crime and Delinquency, 44,* 187–204.

FOORMAN, B. R., FRANCIS, D. J., FLETCHER, J. M., SCHATSCHNEIDER, C., & MEHTA, P. (1998). The role of instruction in learning to read: Preventing reading failure in at-risk children. *Journal of Educational Psychology, 90,* 37–55.

HOVLAND, J., SMABY, M. H., & MADDUX, C. D. (1996). At-risk children: Problems and interventions. *Elementary School Guidance and Counseling, 31,* 43–51.

JERNIGAN, K. (Ed.). (1992). *What you should know about blindness, services for the blind, and the organized blind movement.* Baltimore: National Federation of the Blind.

MAHONEY, G., BOYCE, G., FEWELL, R. R., SPIKER, D., & WHEEDEN, C. A. (1998). The relationship of parent-child interaction to the effectiveness of early intervention services for at-risk children and children with disabilities. *Topics in Early Childhood Special Education, 18,* 5–17.

MCCLANAHAN, K. K., MCLAUGHLIN, R. J., LOOS, V. E., HOLCOMB, J. D., GIBBINS, A. D., & SMITH, Q. (1998). Training school counselors in substance abuse risk reduction techniques for use with children and adolescents. *Journal of Drug Education, 28,* 39–51.

MOORE, E., ARMSDEN, G., & GOGERTY, P. L. (1998). A twelve-year follow-up study of maltreated and at-risk children who received early therapeutic child care. *Child Maltreatment: Journal of the American Professional Society on the Abuse of Children, 3,* 3–16.

ROSENTHAL, R., & JACOBSON, L. (1968). *Pygmalion in the classroom: Teacher expectations and pupils' intellectual development.* New York: Holt, Rinehart & Winston.

SANACORE, J., & WILSUSEN, S. (1995). Success for young at-risk children: Treat them as we treat all children. *Reading and Writing Quarterly, 11,* 359–368.

VONBROCK-TREUTING, M., & ELLIOTT, S. N. (1997). Social behavior ratings of at-risk preschool children: Comparisons with typical preschool children by parents and teachers. *Canadian Journal of School Psychology, 13,* 68–84.

WERNER, E. E. (1996). Vulnerable but invincible: High risk children from birth to adulthood. *European Child and Adolescent Psychiatry, 5,* 47–51.

CHAPTER 2

Resilience and Stress

OBJECTIVE

After reading this chapter, you should be able to describe how children cope with a risk condition either by being resilient or by manifesting stress. You should also be able to explain how some children cope with stress by acting out and others cope by acting in.

CHAPTER OUTLINE

Resilient Children
    Attributes of Resilient Children
Dealing with Stress
    Acting In
    Acting Out
Promoting Resilience
    Role Models
    Helping Behavior
    Creating Positive Classrooms
    Teaching Problem Solving
Summary

RESILIENT CHILDREN

Some children seem able to cope with a risk condition and the stress that accompanies it. Educators call these children "resilient children." Other children seem to be bothered by the stress that accompanies a risk condition. They deal with this stress by either turning their feelings outward (acting out) or forcing them inward (acting in).

Most children can cope with life's difficulties. In most studies of stressful situations, researchers have found that the majority of children are able to survive the situation without serious difficulties. These children might experience discomfort, and might have to spend a significant amount of energy coping, but they will survive (Brodsky, 1999; Lowenthal, 1999; Werner, 1992; Werner, Bierman, & French, 1971; Werner & Smith, 1977, 1982, 1992).

Researchers have identified resilient children who adapt particularly well to life's events (Anthony, 1987; Luthar & Zigler, 1991). These resilient children seem better able to cope and manage things. They have the capacity to bend and stretch, but yet not break.

Attributes of Resilient Children

Rak and Patterson (1996) have looked at the strengths of children who have been exposed to risk factors in childhood and have identified some factors that they feel serve to buffer the harmful effects of the risk. These include personality characteristics of the child, the nature of her family, and relationships she has with other people in the community.

One factor is the personal characteristics of these children. Studies (Berg & Van Brockern, 1995; Burger, 1994; Garmezy, Masten, & Tellegen, 1984; Luthar & Zigler, 1991; Masten, 1982; Murphy & Moriarty, 1976; Rutter, 1983, 1985, 1986; Werner & Smith, 1982) have found that resilient children

- are problem solvers,
- can gain the positive attention of others,
- have an optimistic view of life,
- feel independent,
- seek novel experiences,
- approach life from a proactive perspective,
- feel that they can control their environment,
- have a sense of humor,
- are able to empathize with others,
- have effective problem-solving skills and coping strategies, and
- have an internal locus of control.

Resilient children share several family characteristics that help buffer the effects of stressful stations. Studies (Block, 1971; Garmezy, Masten, & Tellegen, 1984; Letourneau, 1997; Rutter, 1979, 1983, 1985, 1986; Werner & Smith, 1982) have indicated that these children have

- parents who are competent, loving, and patient,
- a good relationship with at least one parental figure,
- an array of alternative caretakers who step in when parents are absent,
- little separation from the primary caretaker during the first year of life, and
- a network of friends.

In addition, researchers have found that resilient children have a number of people who, although not family members, step up to provide mentoring and guidance. These people include teachers, school counselors, coaches, clergy, mental health workers, and neighbors (Beardslee & Podorefsky, 1988; Bolig & Weddle, 1988; Dugan & Coles, 1989; Garmezy, Masten, & Tellegen, 1984;). Haight (1998) looked at children who were connected to a church and found that spirituality serves as a protective factor in the lives of many African American children.

DEALING WITH STRESS

Risk conditions and stress often go together. The strain and work of dealing with a challenging situation often generates stress. We react to stress by either directing our feelings inward, which I call "acting in," or by directing our feelings outward, which is called "acting out."

Acting In

Some children react by turning their stress inward (acting in). This stress appears as depression and, in its most severe form, suicide. Not too many years ago, mental health professionals would have laughed at the suggestion that a 5-year-old child can be depressed, but no more. Now depression is taken seriously by mental health professionals.

Worries

Childhood is thought of as a time that is worry free. Yet some children begin to show that they are under stress by worrying more than the average child. Devin was a kindergartner who was worried about lots of things. She worried that she might get on the wrong bus at the end of the day. She worried that she would make her drawing on the wrong color paper. She worried that she would lose her crayons. Her teacher was concerned about Devin's pattern of worrying about too many things. This kind of behavior is often a precursor of more serious acting-in behavior.

Depression

Depression at any age can be viewed as an extreme way of turning stress inward. Mental health professionals use the *Diagnostic and Statistical Manual of Mental Disorders*, fourth edition, published by the American Psychiatric Association (1994), commonly called the *DSM-IV*, as the tool to define and label depression. For a more precise clinical discussion of depression, take a look at this reference source.

As teachers, we can watch for signs that a child might be depressed. If we see some of the following symptoms, we should be concerned about the child:

- Appearing tearful, talking about being sad, or being in an irritable mood
- Displaying little interest or pleasure in anything
- Being agitated or listless
- Showing signs of fatigue or lack of energy
- Talking about feeling worthless, or showing excessive inappropriate guilt
- Being unable to think or concentrate
- Having trouble sleeping
- Undergoing a dramatic change in body weight
- Talking or drawing about death

If you think that a child exhibits these symptoms, get that child professional help. Make careful observations of the child's behavior and document carefully what you observe. For example, a notation written by a concerned fifth-grade teacher about a boy in my therapy group said:

> On Tuesday morning during our writing activity, Jose was writing in his journal. He wrote that "Most of the time I think that everybody in the class hates me. I have no friends and my life is horrible."

Use your documented observations to advocate for special help for the child with your school's special education screening committee.

Some schools have counselors who are clinically trained and licensed to give the appropriate mental health therapy. Other schools have counselors who are not clinically trained but can help find appropriate community facilities to help depressed children.

Depression is an illness that is treated with talking therapy and/or medication. Talking therapy is given by licensed counselors, social workers, psychologists, or psychiatrists. (Licensing standards vary from state to state. To be licensed as a mental health professional, an individual usually must be trained in a program recognized by the accrediting agencies of professional organizations, agree to a code of ethics, pass a state licensing exam, and take continuing education credits). Medication can be given only by an M.D. (medical doctor). Psychiatrists are medical doctors who are especially trained to administer psychotropic medications, but other medical doctors often prescribe and monitor drugs for depression.

Suicide

One of the most extreme expressions of depression is suicide. Older children are more likely than younger ones to attempt suicide. Children often warn their teachers and friends that they are thinking about suicide or are about to attempt suicide; unfortunately, many times nobody picks up on the message and takes it seriously. If you are tuned into the warning signs, you will be better able to take action and intervene to try to prevent this drastic step.

Students will often communicate their feelings indirectly to teachers in conversations and through class writing assignments. These are some key signs to look for:

- Statements such as "The world would be better off without me."
- Comments such as "I have nothing to live for."
- A student who suddenly withdraws from all of his friends.
- A student who suddenly begins giving away all of her favorite things.
- A depressed student who suddenly appears calm and collected.
- A youngster who tells you, either in person or in their writing, that he is thinking about his own death.

What do you do as a teacher? How do you ask a child if they are thinking of suicide? If you go up to a child and ask them about suicide, do you risk giving them the idea? The answer is come right out and ask, "Are you thinking about hurting yourself?" If the student answers yes, you need to ask, "How are you going to do it?" If she replies with a thought-out, realistic plan, such as "I am going to go home and get my mother's sleeping pills, which she keeps in her dresser drawer, and I am going to lock myself in my room and take the whole bottle," then you need to take action immediately. A person with a plan is in immediate danger. Don't leave the student alone. Take her, by the hand if necessary, to the school counselor or principal for help. Make sure that she gets immediate help from a licensed professional. In an emergency, a school principal can always call an ambulance and have the child taken to the local hospital emergency room. You need to make sure that the child is safe, until a competent mental health person can determine whether the child is immediately at risk of hurting herself. This is an extreme measure for a teacher to take, but it might be necessary to save a life.

A child who has no specific suicide plan might not be in immediate danger, but this child still needs quick mental health intervention by a licensed professional.

A Success Story

Working with children and their families as a licensed social worker, I often see children who are unhappy. One of the most challenging children I ever worked with was Sam. Sam was extremely bright and extremely unhappy. He had a large vocabulary and was very gifted at insulting adults.

Sam was a second-grader who was brought to see me because he was miserable with himself and hostile both to his parents and to his teachers. He had no friends. Sam's parents asked me if I could make Sam "better." I told them that I couldn't guarantee anything, but that I would make a deal with them: I wouldn't quit if they wouldn't quit. I asked them to join me in having hope that things would get better if we worked at it. Although it took a long time and the help of other professionals, Sam did get better.

With the help of medication, family therapy, understanding teachers, and long hours of individual therapy, Sam learned to deal with his family situation, and he became a "normal" elementary school child.

In our last session, after Sam had begun appropriate medication to relieve his depression, we went for a walk. He said to me, "Look at the grass, isn't it green? Look at how blue the sky is, isn't it all beautiful? You know, I'm glad you guys didn't let me kill myself like I wanted to, life is so beautiful."

Acting Out

Other children deal with their stress by acting out their problems in the form of disruptive behavior. Ms. Arden, a third-grade teacher, talked to me about Billy.

> Billy is often disruptive. Sometimes he just pops off and will poke another kid in the class. Billy is having such a hard time at home. His parents are having problems and they often scream and yell at each other. He told me that he thinks his father, who he adores, is going to move this weekend. I feel so badly for Billy. I don't want to punish him. He has enough without me punishing him.

Acting out is a good way for a child to get help. Silent, depressed children can sit in the back of the room, not bothering anybody, and languish in their own misery, often without being noticed. Children who act out get attention. Acting-out behavior demands attention. It is a dramatic way to say, "Notice me! Help me! Do something!"

Children who are acting out need to get a threefold message from their teachers: I don't like your behavior; I will not permit it in my classroom; and I really like and value you. After our discussion, Ms. Arden said to Billy:

Billy, I know that you are having a really difficult time in your life. I really like you and want to help in any way I can. If you feel overwhelmed or angry and need to punch, just give me a "thumbs down" signal and I will let you leave the group to use the punching bag. But you hit Sara, and you know that you can't do that in this class. Our class is a safe place. You need to go to the time-out area.

Ms. Arden recognized that Billy needed to get out his anger, and she provided him with a way to do it—by requesting permission to hit the punching bag. "Play" materials are usually found only in kindergarten classrooms. But all teachers need to recognize that playthings are good outlets for children's emotions, and teachers should provide some age-appropriate play materials in every classroom to relieve stress.

PROMOTING RESILIENCE

Although we cannot change children's conditions and make their stress disappear, we can work to make them more resilient. There are several aspects to the teacher's role in promoting resilience in children. One is to serve as a role model. The other is to create conditions in the classroom that will foster children's growth and nurture their self-protective skills.

Role Models

When you teach, you are on display to your students. They notice what you wear, how you fix your hair, how you smell, and how you react when things don't go as planned. Every teacher has to deal with glitches—a computer that won't work during a demonstration, a wrong word on the board, a fire drill in the middle of an important test. An effective teacher copes with the daily glitches that happen during the school day.

The children will observe how you handle stress. Being a teacher is a great responsibility. You not only teach content such as reading and mathematics, but you also teach children how to live.

Your first task is to examine how you cope when things don't go as you would like. What do you do when things go wrong? How do you react when you hit bumps in your personal life? Your first objective should be to make sure that you are proud of your own behavior. If you are not, you might have to do some work on yourself.

Your next task is to remember that we teach by what we do. We can demonstrate to children the desirable ways to cope when things don't go according to plan. Mr. Brinson is an example. On a busy morning, he asked his class to quickly prepare for the music teacher. After the children put away their math materials, cleaned up the room, and cleared their desks, Shonte, one of his more secure students, pointed out that the music teacher was not scheduled to come until Friday. The class stared at Mr. Brinson to see his reaction. He laughed and said, "It seems that I really made a mistake! Oh well, lets go back to math. Maybe I will get it right tomorrow! Those things happen, and no harm was done."

In this case the teacher demonstrated a technique for solving problems. He made a mistake, owned up to it, and formulated a new plan of action. He demonstrated a healthy way to deal with adversity. Most of all, Mr. Brinson demonstrated that he is human and makes mistakes—and, better yet, that he accepts this in himself and doesn't beat himself up for making an error.

Helping Behavior

To promote resilience in children, teachers also need to know how to effectively help children. You must be able to establish a strong rapport with your students in order to influence their behavior. What kind of person must a teacher be, to earn the trust and confidence of students?

Carl Rogers (1958) looked at the characteristics of relationships that facilitate growth. Following are some of the things that, according to Rogers, you as a teacher must be able to do if you want your students to perceive you as someone who can help them:

- Be trustworthy, dependable, and consistent. Be yourself most of the time, even if you slip and are inconsistent once in a while.
- Be aware of your own feelings. Be aware that if you are annoyed by a child's behavior, your annoyance will color your communications unless you deal with the reasons why you are bothered.
- Have positive attitudes toward your students. Show them warmth, caring, liking, interest, and respect.
- Let your students become their own person. Give up any need you have for them to be dependent on you.
- Enter into your students' world and try and see life as they do.
- Accept all your students totally, just as they are—with their tatoos, their tasteless shirts, their questionable tastes in music, and all the rest they bring with them.

Ms. Johnson provides us with an example of one of the characteristics on Rogers's list: being aware of your own feelings. Ms. Johnson was a white student-teacher in a school with an African American student body. She cared deeply about her students, and she was hurt that when she tried to help Shikera, the young student charged that Ms. Johnson "was just like all the other white people and was no good and didn't care." Ms. Johnson immediately felt hurt by this. She felt that she worked very hard to help her African American students and that Shikera was off base. Then she realized that she was taking Shikera's remarks personally. Instead of becoming defensive about the level of her commitment to her students, she instead helped Shikera focus on why she was angry.

Rogers's work suggests that we must work hard to become people who are helpers. Our position as teachers does not guarantee that children will trust us and listen to us. We have to earn their trust through our behavior.

Creating Positive Classrooms

A third aspect of promoting resilience in children is to create a classroom atmosphere that fosters growth. The first priority is to show children that we have high expectations for them. If we expect children to learn, they will learn. If we expect them to be dumb and unmotivated, they will not disappoint us. It is essential that we let all children know that we will push them toward excellence. Our job is to have all children in our class working at their highest potential.

A second task to have a psychologically safe classroom where everyone works to support each other. Teachers need to create a supportive community of learners in the classroom, not a community of individuals working alone. This involves encouraging and rewarding children for helping each other. In group projects children learn to work together in a team, just as they learn to do in team sports and musical groups, and they learn that there are others who will come to their aid if they need help. In groups children learn how to seek help and how to give help to others.

The third task is to help children learn how to take the initiative in dealing with life. By having an active, hands-on approach to learning, you can help children learn how to take the initiative and solve problems. You need to ask questions that encourage the children to think critically, not just repeat the right answer. The experience of taking the initiative in school situations can generalize to other situations in children's personal lives. Design your classroom, whether at the kindergarten or the high school level, to help children learn to do things on their own.

Teaching Problem Solving

A final aspect of promoting resilience in children is to nurture and develop their ability to deal with life's problems by seeking positive solutions. Many of life's challenges present themselves as problems to be solved, and by teaching children a process for solving problems, we will enable them to extend the process they learn in school and apply it to their personal lives.

Problem solving is a learned skill. The first step in solving a problem is to have confidence that you can solve problems. Not all children have a good history of solving problems. Many parents impose solutions on their children instead of giving their children the opportunities to solve problems. The following interaction between Josh, a fourth-grader, and his teacher is an example of how to help children become problem solvers:

> Josh was having difficulty starting a creative writing project. He told his teacher, "I just don't think I can do it." Mrs. Martino helped Josh focus on a past victory when she asked him, "Josh, do you remember how you felt after you turned in your math homework yesterday and found out that you got them all right?" He replied, "Yea, I felt good." Mrs. Martino went on, "Josh, I want you to remember that feeling. Can you feel it now? Now keep that feeling. You were powerful when you did your math homework and you are powerful now."

In this case, Josh's teacher had him remember a former successful experience and bring it back to his awareness. With this "successful attitude" in mind, Josh was better equipped to solve the problem of getting started on his project.

The second step is to look at alternative solutions and note their advantages and disadvantages. Next, one would choose one alternative and try it. Reflecting on the outcome of this alternative, the learner would evaluate the choice to see if it is having the desirable effect. If the choice is not working as desired, one would then try another alternative.

Using Books

Children's literature also can help children develop self-protective skills. Children can be exposed to stressful situations that characters face in literature and can discuss what happened. In Maurice Sendak's tale for young children, *Where the Wild Things Are* (1963), Max has to deal with scary wild things. Children can read the story and discuss how Max coped and mastered the wild things. Many other children's stories feature conflicts where the characters must make choices.

Children can draw pictures or write stories of other ways Max could have dealt with the situation, or they can talk about how they would deal with the situation. Through literature, teachers can help children focus on the fact that situations have solutions.

Older children reading Anne Frank's diary might not be able to come up with a solution for the political situation in World War II, but they can speculate about how Ann coped with her world and discuss how they can cope with their world.

Storytelling

Many storytelling techniques are also useful for younger children. For example, the teacher can start the story and have the children make up the ending. They can be challenged to make up an ending where the child will be powerful and solve the situation. In Gardner's (1975) technique of mutual storytelling, the children make up a story and then the helping adult tells a similar story with the same characters but with a more productive ending. This technique can be helpful if the teacher has time to work one-on-one with a student.

Group Exercises

Older children can be given exercises that require them to solve a problem as a group. One teacher gave her urban seventh-grade class the assignment of deciding what equipment they would need in order to survive for a week in a rain forest. At first the students thought the problem was impossible to solve, but after doing some research about the rain forest environment, they were able to develop a survival plan. This hypothetical assignment helped the children realize that they were more resilient than they had thought they were.

Outward Bound–Type Experiences

Actual outdoor survival experiences quickly teach children to see how capable they are. Maria and several classmates spent a week in such a program, sailing on Chesapeake Bay in a small, primitive sailboat. At the conclusion of the experience, as dirty and tired as she was, Maria beamed with pride that she had mastered the elements and learned to sail a boat.

Summary

Although all children are resilient, some are more resilient than others. Some children can cope with a risk situation to which other children would respond by acting out or acting in. Teachers who know the attributes of resilient children can help children learn the skills they need to cope with stress. Teachers themselves can be role models of resilience, creating a helping relationship in the classroom, creating an environment that fosters growth and seeks to nurture and develop problem-solving skills in children.

RESEARCH IDEAS

Questions to Investigate

What role does genetics play in resilience?
Have some ethnic or racial groups learned how to be more resilient than others?
Can resiliency be taught, or is it an inherent personality trait?
What institutional changes could be made to promote resilience in children?

Resources to Explore

Center for Research on the Education of Students Placed At Risk
(CRESPAR)
http://scov.csos.jhu.edu/crespar/CReSPaR.html

Children, Youth, and Families At Risk (CYFAR)
http: www.reeusda.gov/new/4h/cyfar/cyfar.htm

International Resiliency Project
http://resilnet.uluc.edu

National Network for Family Resiliency
http://www/nnfr.org

Resilience Net
http://www.resilnet.uiuc.edu

References

AMERICAN PSYCHIATRIC ASSOCIATION. (1994). *Diagnostic and statistical manual of mental disorders* (4th ed.). Washington, DC: Author.

ANTHONY, E. J. (1987). Risk, vulnerability, and resilience: An overview. In E. J. Anthony & B. J. Cohler (Eds.), *The invulnerable child* (pp. 3–48). New York: Guilford Press.

BEARDSLEE, M. D., & PODOREFSKY, M. A. (1988). Resilient adolescents whose parents have serious affective and other psychiatric disorders: Importance of self-understanding and relationships. *American Journal of Psychiatry, 145,* 63–69.

BERG, D. V., & VAN BROCKERN, S. (1995). Building resilience through humor. *Journal of Emotional and Behavioral Problems, 4,* 26–29.

BLOCK, J. (1971). *Lives through time.* Berkeley, CA: Bancroft Books.

BOLIG, R., & WEDDLE, K. D. (1988). Resiliency and hospitalization of children. *Children's Health Care, 16,* 255–260.

BRODSKY, A. E. (1999). Making it: The components and process of resilience among urban, African-American, single mothers. *American Journal of Orthopsychiatry, 69,* 148–160.

BURGER, J. (1994). Keys to survival: Highlights in resilience research. *Journal of Emotional and Behavioral Problems, 3,* 6–10.

DUGAN, T., & COLES, R. (Eds.). (1989). *The child in our times: Studies in the development of resiliency.* New York: Brunner/Mazel.

GARDNER, R. A. (1975). *Psychotherapeutic approaches to the resistant child.* New York: Jason Aronson.

GARMEZY, N., MASTEN, A. S., & TELLEGEN, A. (1984). The study of stress and competence in children: A building block for developmental psychopathology. *Child Development, 55,* 97–111.

HAIGHT, W. L. (1998). Gathering the spirit at First Baptist Church: Spirituality as a protective factor in the lives of African-American children. *Social Work, 43,* 213–221.

LETOURNEAU, N. (1997). Fostering resiliency in infants and young children through parent-infant interaction. *Infants and Young Children, 9,* 36–45.

LOWENTHAL, B. (1999). Effects of maltreatment and ways to promote children's resiliency. *Childhood Education, 75,* 204–209.

LUTHAR, S. S., & ZIGLER, E. (1991). Vulnerability and competence: A review of research on resilience in childhood. *American Journal of Orthopsychiatry, 61,* 6–22.

MASTEN, A. (1982). *Humor and creative thinking in stress-resistent children.* Unpublished doctoral dissertation, University of Minnesota.

MURPHY, L. B., & MORIARTY, A. E. (1976). *Vulnerability, coping, and growth.* New Haven, CT: Yale University Press.

RAK, C. F., & PATTERSON, L. E. (1996). Promoting resilience in at-risk children. *Journal of Counseling and Development, 7,* 368–373.

ROGERS, C. A. (1958). The characteristics of a helping relationship. *Personnel and Guidance Journal, 37,* 6–16.

RUTTER, M. (1979). Protective factors in children's responses to stress and disadvantage. In M. W. Kent & J. E. Rolf (Eds.), *Primary prevention of psychopathology: Vol. 3. Social competence in children* (pp. 49–74), Hanover, NH: University Press in New England.

RUTTER, M. (1983). Stress, coping and development: Some issues and some questions. In N. Garmezy & M. Rutter (Eds.), *Stress, coping and development in children* (pp. 1–42). New York: McGraw-Hill.

RUTTER, M. (1985). Resilience in the face of adversity: Protective factors and resistance to psychiatric disorders. *British Journal of Psychiatry, 147,* 598–611.

RUTTER, M. (1986). Meyerian psychobiology, personality, development, and the role of life experiences. *American Journal of Psychiatry, 143,* 1077–1087.

SENDAK, M. (1963). *Where the wild things are.* New York: Harper & Row.

WERNER, E. E. (1992). The children of Kauai: Resiliency and recovery in adolescence and adulthood. *Journal of Adolescent Health, 13,* 262–268.

WERNER, E. E., BIERMAN, J. M., & FRENCH, F. E. (1971). *The children of Kauai: A longitudinal study from the prenatal period to age ten.* Honolulu: University of Hawaii Press.

WERNER, E. E., & SMITH, R. S. (1977). *Kuauai's children come of age.* Honolulu: University of Hawaii Press.

WERNER, E. E., & SMITH, R. S. (1982). *Vulnerable but invincible: A study of resilient children.* New York: McGraw-Hill.

WERNER, E. E., & SMITH, R. S. (1992). *Overcoming the odds: High risk children from birth to adulthood.* Ithaca, NY: Cornell University Press.

PART TWO

Psychological Conditions

CHAPTER 3

Children with Behavioral Problems

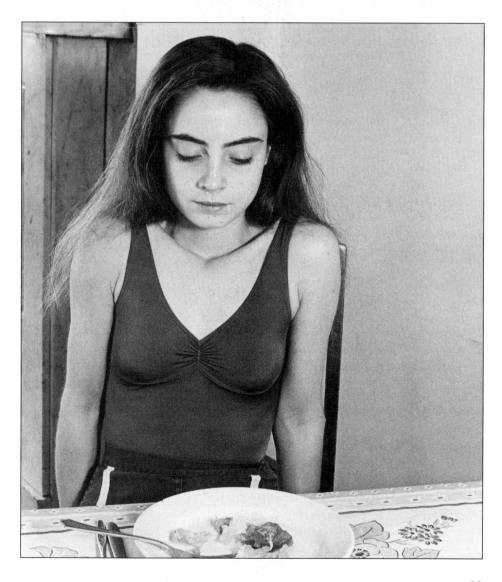

OBJECTIVE

After reading this chapter, you should be able to describe how to identify children with behavioral problems and how to get help for them by working with their parents and other professionals. You should also be able to discuss measures you can take in your classroom to deal with acting-out behaviors.

CHAPTER OUTLINE

Behavioral Problems
The Teacher's Role in Intervention
    Identifying Children in Need of Help
    Documenting Behavior
    Negotiating with Parents
    Referring Children for Help
The Teacher's Role in Treatment
    Service Providers
The Teacher's Role in the Classroom
    Preparing Parents for Future Involvement
    Proactive Measures
    Managing Acting-Out Behavior in the Classroom
    Changing Undesirable Classroom Behavior
Summary

BEHAVIORAL PROBLEMS

Teachers can play a role in identifying children with behavior problems, and they can work with mental health professionals to support therapeutic efforts to help these children. Both big and small problems can cause a child concern. One 3-year-old I saw in therapy feared that monsters resided under his bed at night. Timmy, a seventh-grader in a group for children coping with divorce, was concerned because his parents screamed and cursed at each other, threatening to walk out and leave the marriage. Nakisha, a tenth-grader in an adolescent group I co-led, was concerned about the loss of a girlfriend. All of these problems— imaginary monsters, parents fighting, the loss of a friend—were very big obstacles in the lives of these children, even though we as adults might see some of them as minor.

THE TEACHER'S ROLE IN INTERVENTION

Teachers can play an essential role in helping children with behavioral problems. Your task as a teacher has four steps:

1. Identify a child in need of help.
2. Document the child's behavior.

3. Negotiate with the child's parents.
4. Refer the child for help.

Identifying Children in Need of Help

Teachers are in the most ideal position to identify children with behavioral problems. Unlike parents, teachers are objective and not emotionally tied to the child. All children have problematic behavior at one time or another—sadness, fear, anger, withdrawal, and the like. Children in need of help express these normal emotions more often than other children, with a greater intensity, and often with little or no provocation. Your main role in helping children with behavioral problems is to identify those children with problems and channel them to a mental health specialist who can help.

Following is a list of behaviors that can indicate that a child is having problems. Remember that all children express some of these behaviors at one time or another. The key indicator in these behaviors is that in troubled children they occur with more force and persistence than for other children. Suspect that a child is in need of help if you observe any of these behaviors in the child:

- Frequently complains of being unhappy
- Frequently is tearful
- Frequently is anxious
- Frequently is frightened
- Behaves aggressively or destructively toward others, themselves, or property
- Has difficulty coping with the normal routines of school
- Has something interfering with their ability to learn
- Has something interfering with their ability to make friends
- Voices physical complaints that have no medical basis
- Acts immature

None of these behaviors guarantees that a child has problems. They are like warning lights on the car's dashboard. The lights indicate that something might be wrong and you need to check further.

Although young children can suffer from depression and be at risk for suicide, adolescents have greater means to carry out destructive behaviors. Adolescents often send out warning signals for life-threatening disorders. Teachers need to be aware of the behavior indicators of potential eating disorders, depression, and suicide when dealing with these older children.

Eating Disorders

The following two eating disorders are most often found in females:

- Anorexia nervosa—not eating enough to maintain a normal body weight
- Bulimia nervosa—repeated episodes of binge eating followed by self-induced vomiting, misuse of laxatives, fasting, or excessive exercise

Both types can be life threatening and might be difficult for a secondary teacher to recognize. These are some signs of eating disorders:

- A youngster who is extremely thin
- Indications in a student's writings or conversation that she perceives herself as being fat, even though she is very slim
- Use of inappropriate behaviors to prevent weight gain (e.g. vomiting after eating)
- Front teeth that become chipped and appear ragged due to permanent loss of dental enamel caused by excessive vomiting
- Binge eating
- Expressed fear of gaining weight
- Use of laxatives after eating

If you believe that one of your students has an eating disorder, consult with your school counselor to see how to best confront the child and her or his family with your concern. People with an eating disorder frequently lack the insight to see the problem, or have strong denial about their disorder.

Depression

Depression can have serious consequence for an adolescent. Unchecked depression sometimes leads to suicide. Not all children who appear to withdraw from their peers are depressed; some are just shy. (See chapter 2 for the behavioral symptoms of depression.) Often teachers will get indications of a child's feelings of hopelessness from conversations with the child or stories the child has written. Consult with your school mental health professionals if you see indications that a child is depressed.

Suicide

If an adolescent ever mentions suicide to you, either directly or in a veiled comment, you should always take it seriously. Warning signs for potential suicidal behavior are noted in chapter 2. If you see any of these problem behaviors, seek help for the student immediately. Take the student to the school counselor personally. Don't trust them to go on their own. Don't let them out of your sight until you get them to someone who can help them.

Documenting Behavior

The teacher's task is to document the child's behavior in an objective, nonjudgmental manner so that the child's parents and consulting professionals will have a clear view of how the child is behaving. Your goal is to report what you observe in a way that will make the reader of your written record feel that they witnessed the behavior firsthand. Prescott (1957, p. 154) suggests that teachers include the following information when making an anecdotal notation:

- Describe the setting (the situation in which the action occurred).
- Describe the actions of the child and the reactions of other people involved.
- Quote what the child said during the interaction.

- Supply mood cues—postures, gestures, voice qualities, and facial expressions—that give clues as to how the child felt.

With this objective record, you are ready to report your concerns to others.

Negotiating with Parents

To get help for a child who is a minor, you have to first deal with their parents or guardians. A complicating issue is that the parents' behavior might be an essential part of the child's problem (Haley, 1976; Minuchin 1974; Satir, 1967). In order for some parents to accept that their child has a problem, they first have to accept that they themselves have a problem—or at least that their behavior can be causing a problem for their child.

I saw Mark when he came to the local mental health clinic for help. Mark said he was depressed. He went on to describe his situation. He was a senior in high school, earning good grades. He had a job and was saving money for college. Mark's father adhered to the way things were done "in the old country" and would not let Mark date. Mark was becoming more and more isolated from his friends, and was frustrated that he couldn't date. He wanted to obey his father, but he was very unhappy. In this case Mark had the problem, but it was clearly caused by his father's inability to adjust to the way of life in his new country.

Confronting parents about their child's problem is a daunting task for many teachers. Teachers who are comfortable dealing with twenty-five or thirty children at a time are often terrified of talking to parents. Yet sometimes in order to help the child, you might have to deal with your fears and call in the parents for a conference.

As a teacher, you cannot diagnose a mental health condition, but you can share your concerns about the child's documented behavior, and suggest to the parents that their child needs help.

All teachers know that preparation is an important key to success in teaching. The same can be said for parent conferences. Before you ever have a conference with a parent, make sure that you know what resources are available to help the parents and child. Find out where the mental health services are in your community. Call or visit these centers and find out about their programs. Learn about their intake procedures, and how one makes an appointment. Also, find out about their fees and whether they accept insurance payments. Get cards from all of the services available in your school community and have them available. Now you are prepared for the conference.

Call the parents and ask them to come in and see you. Start the conference by describing positive things the child has done in your class. Communicate clearly that you like and value their child, and explain that you are concerned that the child is having a difficult time. Give the parents hope. Let them know that even though there are problems, professionals can help.

Frame your observations not as indictments, but as concerns. Give the parents hope that things can get better with help. Let them know that you will stick with them to get help for their child. We cannot guarantee that we can make things better, but we can guarantee that we will stick with parents and not quit.

Parent conferences can be scary for first-year teachers. Audrey is a recent graduate from our program, where she was an outstanding student, who just completed her first year as a licensed teacher. She described the first time she had to tell parents that she was concerned about their child:

> During the conference, the parents suddenly became very defensive and challenged me personally. You look very young, they said in a challenging tone. Do you have any children? How many years have you been teaching? Do you know what you are doing? I stayed calm and didn't get defensive and replied, I am licensed by the state to teach this grade. I am well trained and have graduated from a recognized teacher-training program. I want to help your child. I know this is hard, and I want to help your child by getting him help. We both want the same thing—to help your child be successful in school. Let's work together.

Notice that Audrey didn't become angry or defensive. She understood the parents' anxiety and turned their attention to the fact that she was qualified, competent, and on their side.

Referring Children for Help

When schools have a visible, full-time mental health counselor, children have more opportunity to get help for themselves. In some school districts, counselors are clinically trained and work as full-time faculty members, making themselves very visible to the children in the school. They can work on mental health issues in their classrooms, greet children as they get off the school bus, and be available to talk to on the playground (Frieman & Frieman, 1998).

Unfortunately, not all school districts have accessible mental health resources for children. Many school counselors work only part-time in a school or are tied up dealing with scheduling matters and college references. As teachers we still have an obligation to get the child help, even though we might not have the training or time to help a child with a serious problem on our own. We need to refer these children to trained mental health professionals who have the time and resources to help these children. This is often not easy. The line for treatment is long, and many treatment personnel work only part-time.

What can you do if the school personnel don't select your case as important enough for their services? Because most schools lack the resources to provide individual help for emotionally troubled young children, parents are often forced to seek counseling services from public and private clinics or independent practitioners. Most communities have mental health centers, and the child's parents will be one step ahead if you have on hand for them, when you first meet with them, information about local mental health centers—including their fees and intake procedures—and their business cards.

THE TEACHER'S ROLE IN TREATMENT

If a child is in treatment with a mental health professional, teachers can have a powerful role in the child's healing process. Once you are informed that the child is being treated, you can become an active partner in the therapeutic process. You can support the work of the therapist by effectively dealing with the child's acting-out behavior in class and by teaching the needy child ways to get the extra attention they need in a socially desirable way.

Service Providers

Usually treatment is given by social workers or psychologists—or by psychiatrists, who are medical doctors. All three of these professions are regulated by their respective professional organizations and state licensing laws.

All licensed providers can administer individual and group therapy, but each profession has a somewhat unique perspective. Social workers view children in the context of their general social settings; psychologists can administer various psychological tests; and psychiatrists, as physicians, can evaluate physiological conditions and prescribe medications. Therapists, regardless of profession, can have different theoretical orientations (behavioral, psychoanalytic, systems, Rogerian, Adlerian, etc.), which will be reflected in how they conceptualize the child's problem and how they deal with the child's classroom teachers.

All three categories of professional therapists are licensed by either state agencies or national professional organizations. Before becoming involved in a teacher-therapist partnership, verify the professional status of the child's therapist by inquiring about his or her licensing status. Teachers should be cautious in implementing the suggestions of an unlicensed therapist.

THE TEACHER'S ROLE IN THE CLASSROOM

Teachers play a key role in helping children with problem behaviors in their classrooms. These are your tasks:

- Prepare parents for future involvement.
- Use proactive measures to avoid classroom problems.
- Manage acting-out behavior.
- Work to change undesirable behavior.

Preparing Parents for Future Involvement

A major impediment faced by teachers attempting to deal with a troubled child is that they are not routinely informed when a child is in therapy. Many parents fear that teachers will make it worse, and not better, for their children if teachers know that these children are being counseled. Parents often fear that teachers will be less than professional in handling confidential information about their children and will either tell others about a sensitive family problem or pre-judge their child and treat him unfairly.

This attitude was apparent in a parent I saw in a mental health clinic. She expressed strong reservations when I asked her for permission to talk to her child's teacher so I could involve him in the mental health process. This parent told me:

> I don't want you to talk to Jane's teacher. Jane has a hard enough time in school getting along as it is. The last thing I want is for all the other children to think that she is crazy. If you talk to the teacher, all of the other kids in the class will know. I don't want him to think that Jane is crazy and treat Jane like she is weird.

This attitude is not helpful to the child because teachers often have an objective picture of the child's behavior and performance.

Proactive Measures

A teacher can be proactive in obtaining information about a child's therapy by encouraging the child's parents to see the teacher as part of the solution to the child's problems. Address concerns about confidentiality in a straightforward manner by assuring parents early in the school year that you adhere to an ethical code in regard to handling confidential information.

Such assurances can be made in several ways. In the initial parent-teacher group meeting, the teacher should inform parents about the reasons why they need to know what is going on in the child's home life, and about the ways in which they will safeguard the personal information. A note can also be sent to the home covering the same subject. Following is a sample note:

> Anything that happens in the life of your child this year—be it medical or in-volving things that are different in your family—will affect the way your child performs in school. I need to know what is happening in your child's life and within your family so that I can best help your child.
>
> I will be happy to work as a professional team member with any social worker, private physician, or psychologist in order to help your child. As a teacher I am bound by legal and ethical guidelines to keep confidential any in-formation you will share with me. I will talk to other professionals only if you give me written permission to do this. Information you share with me will be shared with other school professionals only if I feel that they need to know that information in order to help your child. They of course are bound by the same ethical and legal confidentiality requirements as am I.

Managing Acting-Out Behavior in the Classroom

Even when children are being treated by individual therapists, teachers still need to deal with acting-out behavior. Acting-out behavior can take many forms and usually involves behaviors in which the child calls attention to himself in a socially undesirable way—through crying, temper tantrums, hitting other children, and other behavior that disturbs the tranquility of the classroom.

Teachers must step in and stop this disruptive behavior. An important part of a teacher's response is to reassure the child that although she does not like the child's behavior, she still likes the child. That the classroom teacher should like the child is an essential feature to the therapeutic philosophy of Carl Rogers (1961). Rogers feels that the child must experience the positive approval of adults. Thus it is essential to make it clear to children that you approve of them as people even though you do not approve of what they are doing.

It is particularly important to reassure children that you still like them even though they are misbehaving. For example, a kindergarten teacher, when speaking to a child who hit a classmate, might say:

> Tony, I don't like it when you hit other children. If you have a problem with somebody, you are supposed to tell me and I will help you work out a solution. I will not tolerate hitting in this classroom. I still like you and still think that you are a good person, but because of your behavior you have to sit on the time-out chair for five minutes.

As illustrated here, teachers can be of great service to the child if they can couple disapproval for the disruptive behavior with a statement affirming the worth of the child.

Acting-out behavior can often be headed off by giving the child a means to receive the special attention she needs in a socially desirable manner. This is illustrated by my interactions with Melissa, who was dealing with the fact that her mother had moved out of the family home. When we were working together in therapy, 6-year-old Melissa became angry with me and hit me. I spoke to her when she calmed down and said:

> Melissa, I know that you feel bad inside when you think about your mother not being home anymore. Remember when we were playing on the playground and you fell down and bumped your foot? You told me that you had a "hurt" and I gave you a big hug. Sometimes we can have "inside hurts" when we think about things that worry us. If you have an "inside hurt," all you have to do is come and tell me and I will give you lots of hugs. I know that "inside hurts" hurt as badly as "outside hurts."

I gave Melissa a mechanism for receiving extra attention while behaving in a socially desirable way.

Another example of this phenomenon in the classroom is the case of Sherry. While observing her in her first-grade class, I noticed the following acting-out behavior: As the children were scurrying to go to the reading group, 6-year-old Marvin brushed against the arm of Sherry, a child who had earlier witnessed her father abusing her mother. Sherry screamed, "My arm is broken!" She began sobbing loudly, attracting the attention of the teacher and of all of the other children in the group.

It was apparent that Sherry was not reacting to being physically hurt but was using the situation to act out some deeper hurts. Her teacher, Ms. Manuel, reacted by telling Sherry that her arm was fine. Ms. Manuel also told Sherry that she knew that things were difficult at home and that Sherry might need special hugs to make her feel better. Sherry was told that all she had to do was to tell her teacher that she needed a hug and she would get it. Children who are dealing with difficult situations often need a great deal of extra reassurance and affection during the course of the day.

Older children need to be given the power to take care of themselves. Ben, a ninth-grader, had a problem controlling his rages. Sometimes things would set him off and he would "go ballistic" in class. In a calm moment, his teacher spoke to him and they made a deal. When Ben felt like he was losing it, he gave an agreed-upon sign to his teacher. Regardless of what was going on, the teacher nodded back and gave him permission to go to the men's room to collect himself and cool off. In this instance, Ben's behavior was ended before it had a chance to be a problem.

Adolescents need a safe, trusting teacher to talk to about problems. Remember that you just have to listen and show the child that you care and want to help him find a solution to his problem. One of Mr. Adamson's students talked to him about a pressing family problem. Mr. Adamson told the student that the school counselor would be able to help him deal with his parents. The youngster noted, "Look, Mr. A., I trust you, not him. I want you to help me. I don't want to talk to anyone else but you." Mr. Adamson replied:

> If you fell down and broke your arm, I would really care and want to help you. How could I do it? Should I treat your arm? Of course not. I am not trained as a physician. I would take you to the best doctor I could find and make sure that you got excellent care. I'm not trained to help with these kinds of problems, our school counselor is. I want you to get the best possible help. The counselor will help you, and I will be here for you as a support too.

What Mr. Adamson did was reassure Ben that he cared about him and wanted to help. He also let him know that he wanted to find an expert who had the skills to help him.

Changing Undesirable Classroom Behavior

Even though many therapists take a hard look at the causes of behavior, they still have to deal with the child's immediate disruptive classroom behavior. Techniques of behavioral therapists that focus on children's observable behavior, and not on "causes" of behavior, are helpful in this regard (Skinner, 1971).

An effective way to deal with undesirable classroom behavior is to use a behavior modification plan. The system involves three main steps:

1. Identify the behavior you want to change.
2. Pick an appropriate reinforcement.
3. Reinforce socially acceptable behavior.

The initial step in implementing a behavior modification scheme is to identify the behavior that you want to change. Perhaps you would want an elementary school child to stop roaming around the room during seatwork time. Or you might want a high school youngster to turn in her homework the day it is due.

The next step is to identify the reinforcement. Most children will not be motivated to work for fried liver and onions. An effective reinforcement is something that is of value to the child. The child can be consulted and asked what she would like to work to earn.

The teacher needs to be sure that the reinforcement is appropriate for the school situation and in the best interests of the child. For example, the use of candy as a reinforcement can be questioned on nutritional grounds. Often a good reinforcement for young children involves earning stars, stickers, or some other tangible object. Middle school children can work toward earning the right to have extra time on the computer.

The child might receive an actual token or coupon that can be redeemed for the reinforcement. In some cases, you might decide that the child needs to accrue a certain number of tokens in a school day in order to receive the reinforcement.

The final step is reinforcing the child when she is engaging in the desired behavior. In the first case, you would reinforce the child when you "caught" him working at his desk. In the other example, the youngster might be reinforced when she turned in her homework on time. Reinforcement is most effective when the child is reinforced on a random, variable basis. To keep the child on his toes, you want him to think that he might get a token any time he performs the desired behavior.

An issue when using reinforcement with one child is what to tell the other children. What if they also want stars for behaving? The best policy is to give the stars to all of the kids who want them. No cooperative child is going to be hurt by being recognized for good behavior.

Summary

Your job is to help identify children with problems and to make sure that they get the help they need. Your main task is to recognize behaviors that are possible indicators of underlying problems. In helping the child, you will have to communicate with the child's parents and with other professionals both inside and outside of your school. Working with other concerned professionals, you can help to facilitate the emotional healing of your students.

RESEARCH IDEAS

Questions to Investigate

Can you design community programs to help parents deal with their own issues? How can you make these programs affordable and available to most parents? Can a teacher reach all children?

Resources to Explore

American Academy of Pediatrics
http://www.aap.org

Behavioral Resources
  http://www.comfortconnection.org

ERIC Clearinghouse on Elementary and Early Childhood Education
  http://www.ericeece.org

Mental Health Net
  http://www.mentalhelp.net

The National Committee to Prevent Child Abuse
  http://www.childabuse.org

References

AZAR, B. (1996). Exercise fuels the brain's stress buffers. *APA Monitor* [Online]. Available: http://www.apa.org/monitor/jul96/neurala.htm.

BARAKAT, I. S., & CLARK, J. (1997). Challenges and choices: Stress management—The challenge of balance [Online]. Available: http://muextension.missouri.edu/xplor/hesguide/humanrel/gh6651.htm.

BOSS, P. (1992). Primacy of perception in family stress theory and measurement. *Journal of Family Psychology, 6,* 113–119.

FENLON, M. J., & MUFSON, S. A. (1994). Psychological first aid for children exposed to sexual violence. *School Counselor, 42,* 48–58.

FRIEMAN, M., & FRIEMAN, B. B. (1998). The elementary school counselor's special mail box. *Professional School Counseling, 1,* 58–59.

HALEY, J. (1976). *Problem solving therapy.* New York: Harper.

HYMES, J. L. (1955). *Behavior and misbehavior.* Englewood Cliffs, NJ: Prentice Hall.

JONES, H. A., & RAPPORT, M. J. (1997). Research to practice in inclusive early childhood education. *Teaching Exceptional Children, 30,* 57–61.

LANKTREE, C., & BRIERE, J. (1995). Outcome of therapy for abused children: A repeated measures study. *Child Abuse and Neglect, 19,* 1145–1155.

LESNIK-OBERSTEIN, M., KOERS, A., & COHEN, L. (1995). Parental hostility and its sources in psychologically abusive mothers: A test of the three-factor theory. *Child Abuse and Neglect, 19,* 33–49.

MARION, M. (1995). *Guidance of young children.* Upper Saddle River, NJ: Merrill/Prentice Hall.

MINUCHIN, S. (1974). *Families and family therapy.* Cambridge, MA: Harvard University Press.

PRESCOTT, D. A. (1957). *The child in the educative process.* New York: McGraw-Hill.

ROGERS, C. (1961). *On becoming a person.* Boston: Houghton Mifflin.

SATIR, V. (1967). *Conjoint family therapy.* Palo Alto, CA: Science and Behavior Books.

SKINNER, B. F. (1971). *Beyond freedom and dignity.* New York: Knopf.

STRAIN, P. S., & HEMMETER, M. L. (1997). Keys to being successful when confronted with challenging behaviors. *Young Exceptional Children, 1,* 2–8.

UMANSKY, W., & HOOPER, S. R. (1998). *Young children with special needs.* Columbus, OH: Merrill.

WALKER, J. E., & SHEA, T. M. (1999). *Behavior management: A practical approach for educators.* Upper Saddle River, NJ: Merrill/Prentice Hall.

CHAPTER 4

Children Who Are Alienated

—WITH MAURY FRIEMAN, M.S.W., Counselor, Pinehill Elementary School,
Dover-Sherborn Public Schools, Massachusetts

OBJECTIVE

After reading this chapter, you should be able to identify children who are alienated and help them if they are in your classroom.

CHAPTER OUTLINE

Who Are the Alienated Children?
Identifying Children Who Might Be Alienated
The Teacher's Role in Helping Alienated Children
    Getting Help
    Involving Parents in the Child's School Experience
    Involving Children with Mentors
    Teaming Up Adversaries
The Teacher's Role in Helping All Children
    Creating a Classroom Atmosphere of Acceptance
    Functioning as a Mediator
    Teaching Children How to Avoid Being Victims
Summary

WHO ARE THE ALIENATED CHILDREN?

Our nation is shocked when children with automatic weapons go on a shooting rampage at a school, terrorizing and killing fellow students. Many of the children who commit these antisocial acts have been described as alienated from mainstream American culture—as children who "do not fit in." Not all alienated children commit murderous acts, but many engage in criminal behavior. Amnesty International (1999) reports that in the United States 200,000 children per year are prosecuted in general criminal courts and over 11,000 children are currently being housed in prisons and other adult correctional facilities. Other alienated children are not criminals, but are estranged from their peers, suffering private emotional pain.

Children who are alienated can have problems in their homes and with their peers. Many of these children have no active parental influence in their daily lives. As Flannery, Williams, and Vazsonyi (1999) point out, growing demands on families and changing family structures have resulted in an increase in the number of latchkey children (children left to care for themselves after school on a regular basis). These children spend their after-school hours alone and unsupervised. These are the hours when many adolescents are at increased risk for victimization from violence, and when they have the opportunity to engage in delinquent behavior. Galambos and Maggs (1991) report that at least 2 million children under the age of 13 care for themselves after school. Even when they actually spend time with their parents, many alienated children describe the parents as not being emotionally there for them.

Many alienated children who have good parenting are rejected, or at least not readily accepted, by their peers. Children with learning disabilities and children who are socially awkward or very shy often are not accepted by higher-status peer groups. Children whose interests do not parallel those of their classmates, perhaps because they are very bright and interested in intellectual issues, are also often excluded from peer groups in schools. These children may be lonely and, as Bullock (1998) points out, often have poor peer relationships and feelings of sadness, malaise, boredom, and alienation.

As a result of feeling alienated, some children connect with antisocial peer groups, joining gangs perhaps in an attempt to have some active "family." Willwerth (1991), when investigating the gang world of southern California, described many of the gang members as armed and alienated children. Alienation from family members is one reason advanced by Hunter (1998) to explain why some adolescents are attracted to religious cults.

IDENTIFYING CHILDREN WHO MIGHT BE ALIENATED

Some behaviors are typical of alienated children. A child who exhibits any of the following behaviors should be referred to the school counselor for further evaluation and help:

- Abusing animals, even insects
- Picking on other children
- Bullying other children
- Withdrawing from classmates
- Constantly talking about violent themes
- Constantly drawing pictures with violent themes
- Constantly writing about violent themes
- Constantly playing violent video games
- Constantly reading violent comic books
- Strongly identifying with musical groups that focus on violent themes
- Isolating himself or herself from their peers

These children are also often the brunt of teasing by their classmates.

THE TEACHER'S ROLE IN HELPING THE ALIENATED CHILD

Getting Help

The most important thing that a teacher can do to help an alienated child is to make sure that the child gets professional psychological help. Alienation often has very deep roots in family dynamics and doesn't lend itself to a quick fix. The child might require long-term therapy by a trained professional to deal with this behavior. The steps to take to get help for a troubled youngster—documenting the child's behavior, negotiating with parents, and referring children for help—were spelled out in chapter 3.

Ask the child's parents to give you written permission to consult on an ongoing basis with the child's therapist. Most therapists ask parents to sign the necessary permission slips to allow therapist-teacher dialogue. These signed permission slips will be your legal permission to talk to someone who is outside of your school system. It is not necessary to get a permission slip to talk to another school employee. You must be careful as a teacher not to talk to anyone about the child's therapy unless you have the required written permission from the child's parents.

Once you are in contact with the child's therapist, you can discuss how to coordinate the therapy sessions with the school experience. For example, Leon drew pictures with violent themes. The therapist suggested that the teacher not allow Leon to draw violent cartoons in art class. Leon was allowed to draw the cartoons in therapy sessions where the counselor was there to help him process his violent feelings. Therapy is most effective when counselor and teacher work in concert.

Involving Parents in the Child's School Experience

Many alienated children are estranged from their parents. Teachers can try to promote interactions between children and their parents using various techniques. One technique that can be used with elementary school children is to create an assignment in which the child has to work with her parent. The things that many teachers have had success with are really simple assignments, such as these:

- Take a walk around your neighborhood with one of your parents. Pick out one thing in your neighborhood that you like. It can be a particular tree, a building, or anything that catches your eye. Tell your parent why you like the thing you picked. Have your parent do the same thing and tell you why he or she picked that thing. When you go home, write four sentences about what you both selected. Read your essay to your parents.
- Read one chapter of your independent reading book to one of your parents. Ask them what they liked the most about the chapter. Tell them what you liked the most.

You can give similar assignments to secondary school students. Here are some examples:

- Interview your parent about one thing they remember from their childhood. Write a four-paragraph essay reporting your results.
- Ask your parent to talk to you about what they liked to do when they were your age. Write an essay comparing what they liked to do with what you like to do. Read your completed essay to your parent.

Another technique is to write a newsletter. In the newsletter you can tell parents what their children have learned over the past few weeks. Suggest no-cost or low-cost things that they can do with their child in the local area.

Involving Children with Mentors

Although a mentor can never totally take the place of a parent, she or he can provide a positive force in the life of a child. A mentor is a teacher, an older child, or an adult from the community who can play the role of a wise counselor. As a teacher, you already serve as a mentor to the children you teach by giving them positive feedback and encouragement.

Teachers can train older children to mentor younger ones. Maury Frieman, in his work as a school counselor, set up a program in which elementary school children were mentored by students in a nearby middle school. He carefully selected mentors by screening out volunteers who were bossy and those who didn't really like younger children. The selected mentors received training in techniques to help children resolve conflicts. The training consisted of sessions in which the mentors learned how to do the following:

- Listen to what both sides are saying
- Make sure that each member of a disputing party can repeat the concern of her adversary
- Help children focus on points of agreement
- Help children define behaviors that are of concern to them
- Brainstorm alternative solutions to problems
- Conduct a group discussion

Once trained, each older student was assigned to one classroom where he or she met periodically with the class to discuss issues relating to getting along with others. The middle school peer counselors helped the younger children to focus on what it feels like to be harassed and bullied and to discuss how harassment has affected them personally and how it feels to be a victim.

Adult volunteers can also be used as mentors to help children resolve problems. Before any person is used as a mentor, they should be carefully screened and trained. As the teacher, you are responsible for any person who works in the classroom, and you need to be sure that they will be a positive force in the children's lives. Many school districts require police checks on all volunteers to verify that the candidate has not committed any crimes involving children.

In secondary schools, children have the opportunity to participate in many extracurricular activities that are run by faculty members. These activities include clubs, music groups, and sports. Many coaches not only teach children about their particular sport, but also provide lessons in teamwork and sportsmanship that teach life skills.

Teaming Up Adversaries

Another way to help these alienated children is to involve them in cooperative projects with classmates. Some classic research suggests that tension between hostile groups can be reduced by having them work together on mutually beneficial projects (Sherif et al., 1961). Using this model, you can have two children who have been feuding work together on a project in which they both can contribute equally and both can gain something that they want.

THE TEACHER'S ROLE IN HELPING ALL CHILDREN

Teachers can take actions in the classroom that will provide a healthy climate of acceptance, and teach children how to deal with those who would attempt to bully them. These actions include

- creating a classroom atmosphere of acceptance,
- functioning as a mediator, and
- teaching children how to avoid being victims.

Create a Classroom Atmosphere of Acceptance

Teachers can create a classroom atmosphere of acceptance by having zero tolerance for teasing. Teachers need to stop all teasing no matter how "innocent" and not just draw the line when teasing becomes nasty and hurtful. (The concept of zero tolerance is discussed in greater detail in later chapters.) Children have made teasing into an art form. "Doing the dozens" is a game that adolescents play to insult each other. Although this seems to be in fun, it is unproductive because it encourages children to look at their differences instead of their similarities and encourages an atmosphere of condemnation rather than acceptance.

Teachers can attempt to sensitize their students to how the targets of a racist, sexist, or ethnic "joke" might feel if they heard it. One way to sensitize students is to place them in the position of the one being teased and have them reflect on how they feel when they are teased. I used this exercise in my university class when we were discussing how ethnic humor makes people feel. I told the class about a football game I had just watched on television. The Washington Redskins had scored a touchdown, and their "mascot," a man dressed in a Native American costume, rode around the stadium on a horse to the cheers of the fans. The label *redskin* is considered offensive by Native Americans. To help my students understand how Native Americans might feel about a "redskin" mascot, I had them reflect on this scenario: The football team is called the Papists, in honor of the many Catholics who live in the area. After every touchdown, a man dressed as the pope parades around the stadium on a throne carried by priests. The cheerleaders are dressed as nuns.

My students, many of whom were Catholic, were rightly horrified. They pointed out that this would be extremely disrespectful to the large Catholic population in our state. Using this technique, my students could understand how the Native American people felt when they watched the "Redskin" ride around the stadium. Somehow ethnic jokes don't seem as funny when people are laughing at you. By having students reflect on situations where they can identify themselves as the victimized person, teachers can create opportunities for students to learn how it feels to be the brunt of jokes.

The same strategy can be used for jokes in which the target is a group. We have all heard our share of "dumb blond" or "Polish" jokes. It would be ideal if all people would stop making fun of groups. However, children are going to make fun of other people, and I think that it is preferable for them to learn a way to do it without offending anyone.

A way to deal with group "jokes" is to follow the lead of Isaac Bashevis Singer (1953), a winner of the Nobel Prize for Literature. The people who lived in his fictional town Chelm were the brunt of many jokes that, instead of being based on contempt for others, simply reflected the human propensity to do dumb things. However, these people are not real. We can encourage children to make up a group of imaginary people who can become the brunt of jokes. In this way, you can allow your students to have fun, but teach them how to do it in a way that will not hurt anybody.

Functioning as a Mediator

To help children learn to solve problems, adopt a "resolution strategy" when they bring you their complaints about their peers:

1. Listen to both sides of the dispute.
2. Resist the temptation to resolve the problem using a "teacher ruling."
3. Help the children identify things that they agree upon (for example, neither person wants the other to say bad things about their mother).
4. Help the children reach their own compromise.

Using these techniques, you can serve as a mediator instead of a decision maker. Hopefully, you can help the children to see that they are not "tattling" by coming to the teacher, but instead helping to solve their own problems by themselves.

Teaching Children How to Avoid Being Victims

Teachers must intervene to prevent physical bullying, but students often have to deal with psychological bullying on their own. Many have a strong belief that children should not inform or tattle on a classmate to the teacher. You need to be aware of this value and not expect children in your classroom to bring to your attention all problems involving bulling. Instead you need to keep your ears and eyes open, focusing on the children who might be vulnerable to teasing, and look for these behaviors yourself.

To help a child deal with psychological harassment, teachers need to equip the child to understand the bully and have a strategy to deal with the harassment. The first step in this process is to create a classroom in which respect rather than disrespect is the norm. As teachers we have a great deal of power and are in a position to be tyrants. You have to make sure that you never bully students. Your goal is to model how to deal with people in a respectful way.

The second step is to help the "target" of the bullying realize that he is a valuable person who is worthy of respect. We do this as teachers by treating children with respect and pointing out all of the things that they do well. You should try to shower all students with praise when you observe them doing something well, whether it is getting an A on a paper or concentrating and not disrupting any other students during class.

The final step is to teach the student how to react to being bullied. Children can be taught to ignore the bully or outsmart the bully. Bullies are like actors, in that they perform for the rest of the class. If the target of the abuse fails to respond, the bully will get bored and move on to try another person. One can be taught to outsmart the bully by not taking the bully's comments seriously. Often a child can laugh or smile at the bully's comment, indicating to others that he is not bothered by the remarks. You can best teach these lessons in a private conversation with the target of the abuse.

Teachers can help children learn how to avoid becoming victims. Students often must deal with class bullies who like to control them by intimidation. If we teach children how to deal with bullies, we will empower them to act before they become an alienated member of the class.

Summary

Teachers can learn how to identify potentially alienated children and see that they get professional help. You can help prevent alienation by helping to involve parents in their child's school experience and providing mentors to work with selected children. By creating a classroom of acceptance and teaching children how to deal with psychological harassment, you can help children learn how to avoid being victims.

RESEARCH IDEAS

Questions to Investigate

1. Are there aspects of inherited personality that make people more prone to be alienated?
2. Is the current health-care system responsive to the needs of troubled children and their families?
3. Why do people tell ethnic or racial jokes?

Resources to Explore

American Orthopsychiatric Association
http://www.amerortho.org

American Psychiatric Association
http://www.psych.org

American Psychological Association
http://www.apa.org

Legal Information Institute
http://www.law.cornell.edu

References

Amnesty International. (1999). Amnesty International report: Too many children incarcerated in America [Online]. Available: http://www.walrus.com/~resist/resist_this/112498chilprison.htm.

BULLOCK, J. R. (1998). *Loneliness in young children* (ERIC Digest). Champaign, IL: ERIC Clearinghouse on Elementary and Early Childhood Education. (ERIC Document Reproductive Service No. ED 419 624).

FLANNERY, D. J., WILLIAMS, L. L., & VAZSONYI, A. T. (1999). Who are they with and what are they doing? Delinquent behavior, substance use, and early adolescents' after school time. *American Journal of Orthopsychiatry, 69,* 247–253.

GALAMBOS, N. L., & MAGGS, J. L. (1991). Children in self-care: Figures, facts, and fiction. In J. V. Lerner & N. L. Galambos (Eds.), *Maternal employment and adolescents* (pp. 131–157). New York: Garland.

HUNTER, E. (1998). Adolescent attraction to cults. *Adolescence, 33,* 709–714.

SHERIF, M., HARVEY, O. J., WHITE, B. J., HOOD, W. R., & SHERIF, C. W. (1961). *Intergroup conflict and cooperation: The robber's cave experiment.* Norman: University of Oklahoma Press.

SINGER, I. B. (1953). *Gimble the fool.* New York: Fawcett Crest Books.

WILLWERTH, J. (1991, November 18). From killing fields to mean streets. *Time,* pp. 103–106.

CHAPTER 5

Children Whose Fathers Are Absent

OBJECTIVE

After reading this chapter, you should be able to discuss the effects of father absence on children and suggest steps that you can take as a teacher to keep fathers involved in the lives of their children.

CHAPTER OUTLINE

A FATHER'S PHYSICAL AND EMOTIONAL ABSENCE

Some children have fathers who are both physically and emotionally present in their lives; others must learn to deal with situations that are less than ideal. A father who is physically present in a child's life can be a great asset in the child's emotional development only if that father is also emotionally present.

Fathers can be physically absent from the home for reasons like divorce, military service, incarceration, or work that requires travel. Though these fathers are not present all of the time, they can still maintain emotional ties to their children. Mark, an 8-year-old in my group for children dealing with parental divorce, was upset when his father, a soldier in the U.S. Army, was temporarily given an assignment in a dangerous area of the world where his children could not visit. Mark described himself as being "close" to his father. His father told him that even though he would be away, he would still think about him and still be able to "talk" to him every day. He bought Mark a computer and signed him up for e-mail service. Before he deployed, he taught his son how to use e-mail on his new computer. During his father's absence, Mark talked to him via e-mail every day and still felt that his father was a part of his life. Thousands of miles did not weaken the emotional bond between father and son.

Some fathers are emotionally absent from their children. This includes the father who lives in the same home as his children but never emotionally connects with them. This type of father might provide money and gifts, but not himself, to his children.

Other men choose to be both physically and emotionally absent from their children. They choose to procreate and then take no interest in the process of fathering. These are the men or boys who intend to have children but who never intend to live with the child's mother and their child as a family. They might occasionally visit their children or provide them with money, but they don't take part in the process of fathering. They are fathers in title only.

Psychologically absent fathers are not always poor and uneducated. They come from all socioeconomic classes.

Extent of Father Involvement in Child Rearing

The "American dream" is for children to be raised in homes where mother and father work as a team. Two parents are able to provide a measure of financial security that one parent alone often cannot. Two parents can share the parenting responsibilities and workload of maintaining the home. Yet there are many single-parent families in the United States. Researchers at the National Fatherhood Initiative point out that in 1996 almost 27 percent of American families were headed by a single parent, usually a woman ("Research Confirms the Risks," 1996).

In reality, fathers as a group are the least reliable of the parenting partners. Many fathers never assume the roles and responsibilities of fathering. Blankenhorn (1996) feels that the United States is increasingly becoming a fatherless society and that we are losing our idea of fatherhood. Many men are having sex with women and conceiving children without having any interest in fathering those children. It is a challenge for educators to involve these men in the lives of their children.

Many advocacy groups, such as the American Coalition for Fathers and Children, report data from the U.S. Bureau of Census, the Centers for Disease Control and Prevention, and other organizations that paint a grim picture of children who have absent fathers. According to data compiled by the American Coalition for Fathers and Children (1999), compared to children whose fathers are present, children from fatherless homes are

- 20 times more likely to have behavioral disorders,
- 9 times more likely to drop out of high school,
- 10 times more likely to abuse chemical substances, and
- 20 times more likely to end up in prison.

It is important to remember that all of the data they report is correlational and does not prove that father absence causes these conditions.

WHY DO FATHERS LEAVE THEIR CHILDREN?

Fathers leave their children for a variety of reasons, and the reason the father is absent can play a large role in how the child copes with having no father available. Some fathers are absent due to military service. These men have elected a military career of service to their country and live with the reality of temporary absences from their children.

Children whose fathers are absent due to military service in a conflict zone have to deal with a mother under stress. She has the sudden strain of having to take over the family at a time when she might be anxious about a husband who is in combat or some other dangerous situation.

Other fathers are absent due to divorce. A divorce does not necessarily mean that the father will have to give up being a full-time parent. Although custody of the children is usually awarded to the mother, the courts are free to award custody to the father if he is the best parent for the child. Even when the mother is the custodial parent, judges are increasingly awarding joint custody to parents regarding major decisions involving their children, such as decisions about schooling and medical care.

Divorced noncustodial fathers can still be full-time fathers emotionally— just as they can also choose instead to be part-time uninvolved fathers or totally uninvolved fathers. Depending upon how their father chooses to deal with divorce, the child can feel an array of emotions, from personal abandonment to anxiety about their dad if he is now living alone.

However, some divorced fathers choose to disengage from the parenting role because they feel that it will make the separation from their ex-wife easier. Arendell (1992) looked at postdivorce parental absence and found that father absence after divorce is often an intentional strategy. The objective of this action is to avoid situations involving conflict, tension, and emotion. This is an example of fathers placing their own comfort and welfare ahead of the needs of their children.

Some fathers are involuntarily separated from their children and families due to incarceration. These fathers might have been involved or noninvolved fathers before their jail sentence. Children whose fathers are incarcerated face different issues than other children with absent fathers. As Gabel (1992) points out, in these children behavioral or emotional disorders probably are related more to factors associated with parent incarceration, such as the meaning of the incarceration to the child, the remaining caretaker's psychological characteristics and psychopathology, the parenting relationship between the caretaker and the child, and the resources of the family, than to the separation itself.

Some children lose their father because he dies. The age of the child at the father's death will determine how the child reacts. The permanent loss of a father due to death often leaves the child with a surviving mother who is herself deeply wounded and grieving. Often grieving parents are temporarily so tied up in their own mourning that they have little energy left to parent their children. In these cases, the child will feel abandoned by both parents.

EFFECTS OF FATHER ABSENCE ON CHILDREN

As McLanahan (1999) points out, growing up with a single parent usually means that the family has

- fewer financial resources to devote to upbringing and education,
- less time and energy to nurture and supervise children, and
- reduced access to community resources to supplement the parent's efforts.

An active father plays an important role in the emotional development of his child. Beaty (1995) found that father-absent boys evidenced a poorer sense of masculinity as well as poorer interpersonal relationships than did father-present boys. Golombok, Tasker, and Murray (1997) found that children raised in fatherless families from infancy experienced greater warmth and interaction with their mother, and were more securely attached to her, although they perceived themselves to be less cognitively and physically competent than their peers from father-present families.

A completely absent father can generate different feelings than one who is occasionally present. Younger children can have unique feelings about the absence of their fathers. Rose (1992) studied 6-year-old children who had "ghost fathers" whom they had never met or knew little about. These children had positive feelings and fantasies about their absent fathers, whereas children who had a small amount of contact with their fathers felt that their fathers viewed them negatively. These children felt rejected and blamed themselves for their father's absence.

Regular contact with a father is even significant during the undergraduate college years. Shook and Jurich (1992) studied college undergraduates whose parents were divorced. They found that contact with the nonresidential father had a significant impact on the self-esteem of daughters.

THE TEACHER'S ROLE WITH CHILDREN WHO HAVE ABSENT FATHERS

The following are some actions teachers can take to help children with absent fathers:

- Involve males to serve as role models in the classroom.
- Arrange for services for physically absent or noncustodial fathers.
- Alter the curriculum to make it male friendly.

Male Role Models

Only about one-fourth of our nation's teachers are males (Bowler, 1999). Particularly in elementary schools, most public school teachers are women. The stereotype that men are not competent nurturers of young children is dying, but very slowly. As a consequence, father-absent children are more likely to have a female teacher than a male teacher who could serve as a surrogate role model.

Female teachers, aware that children need men in their lives, can make strides to incorporate "surrogate fathers" in the classroom lives of their father-absent students. However before a teacher thinks of bringing any non-school-system adults into the classroom, she must be sensitive to safety and security issues. School system personnel must certify that all volunteers coming into the school are not a threat to children. Some states require criminal background checks done by local or state police departments on all people who work with children. Although it might make you uncomfortable to ask a person who is willing to volunteer and help a child to undergo a police check, such checks are necessary. No volunteer should be offended. They only need be told something like this: "If your child were in this school, you would want us to make sure that no people would be in the school if they had the potential to do harm. It is our obligation to protect all of the children." A teacher should never let a person volunteer in the classroom and have access to her students unless she has been prudent and done all that she could to make sure that this person will do no harm. Of course all parents should be informed that the school has a volunteer program.

Once sure that male volunteers are safe, teachers can train them to work with children. Volunteers need to be instructed or refreshed in how to relate to children in a developmentally appropriate manner. Teachers need to help volunteers establish the appropriate limits to their relationships with children. Volunteers need to be taught to be "teacher-like" and not "peer-like" to the children. Appropriate acceptable behaviors of children need to be spelled out, so the volunteer will know the rules of the classroom and follow them.

With these precautions, teachers can bring community men into the classroom to serve as surrogate role models to fatherless children. Teachers need to think about where there are large groups of men willing to help. A neighborhood factory or business might be persuaded to form a partnership with a school in which its male employees will spend some time in the classroom linking one-on-one with fatherless children. With the proper training, these men can tutor fatherless children academically, read to younger children, or give career or vocational guidance to older children. The goal of the interaction is to provide the young child with a male to look up to, someone who can answer the child's questions and give the feedback that a father would normally give.

Older men in the community are a great source for male role models. Retired men, living in retirement communities and nursing homes, often have the time and energy to share with younger children.

Men's service organizations or church, mosque, or synagogue brotherhood groups are another source of available men. Religious groups often have many retired male members who are interested in doing service projects. Of course, in public schools religious groups have to agree to keep religion out of their relationship with children.

Female teachers need to scour the neighborhoods of their schools to locate potential sources of "surrogate fathers." With a little detective work, you can locate many potential male volunteers.

Services to Fathers

Teachers can reach out to noncustodial fathers or unmarried fathers and still involve them in the classroom activities of their children. In the beginning of the year you can make sure that both parents are listed on emergency data cards. A letter can be sent home to all parents noting that your classroom policy is to involve both parents in the education of their child. You can note that all evidence suggests that their children will do better in school if they have the support of both parents, whether they are living together or not.

You would also want to ask mothers if there are any legal reasons they would not want the father of their child contacted. In some cases of abuse, judges might issue a court order forbidding a father to see his child. Mothers in this situation will usually take the initiative and present a court order to the school without being asked.

Report cards can routinely be sent home to two homes. The report going to the father should be mailed. This is an additional expense for a school, but the potential benefits of having the father involved balance out the expense of postage. Sending correspondence by mail relieves the child of the pressure of being the messenger. Anything that can be done to keep the child out of the middle of any disputes between his parents is helpful.

One can also mail to the father all regular school correspondence, including classroom newsletter, announcements of long-range projects, the high school football schedule, and lists of required school supplies.

Teachers can arrange to call absent fathers monthly to keep contact. The call should be a positive one. Ms. Levy made a list of all of the father-absent children in her class and called one of them each week. A teacher might start such a phone conversation like this: "Mr. Jones, I am Johnny's second-grade teacher. I want you to know that your son did particularly well on his math this week. All of his homework was done and he worked hard in class."

All of these activities on the part of teachers will help to keep fathers connected to their children. Children will benefit from a teacher's extra effort.

Father-Friendly Curriculum

Boys who do not learn fathering skills by observing an active father might be able to learn these important skills in school. The following example from a kindergarten class suggests how teachers can help young boys learn fathering skills. A teacher watched some of her children playing in the housekeeping corner, where the girls were pretending to cook dinner for the boys. She realized that one of the boys had an absent father and might never have seen a man cook. She approached this boy and asked him, "Can fathers cook for children too?" The boy looked puzzled and didn't reply. This young boy didn't know that men could be nurturing and take care of children. By discussing topics like this with the boy, and engaging him and other boys in nurturing activities, the teacher can help the boys learn skills they will need to have in order to one day be good fathers.

In kindergarten we often let children explore occupations through play and discussion. Why not let them also explore the job of father? Teachers will bring police officers into the classrooms to talk about their jobs, or take children to a fire station where they can see what a fire fighter does. Why not invite fathers into the classrooms to talk about what they do as fathers?

Teaching about fathering can also be facilitated by children's books and stories that present fathering in a positive light. A large variety of books present positive images of men and confront issues involving absent fathers. Here are some good examples (*Men in Children's Lives Booklist*, 1999):

Martha Hickman, *When Andy's Father Went to Prison*

Jeanne Lindsay, *Do I Have a Daddy?*

Kathy Stinson, *Mom and Dad Don't Live Together Anymore*

Jane Thomas, *Daddy Doesn't Have to Be a Giant Anymore*

Judith Vigna, *I Live with Daddy*

Sharon Dennis Wyeth & Raoul Colon, *Always My Dad*

Charlotte Zolotow, *A Father Like That*

When their students are making holiday presents or writing invitations to school events, teachers need to remember that not all children have a person to call "Father." Instead of asking children to write a letter home inviting their fathers to come to the winter concert, or asking them to make holiday cards for their fathers, teachers should suggest to children that they can make the invitation or card to their father or any other important male person in their life. This way the child with an absent biological father but with an adult male in his life will not feel deprived.

Some children must deal with their mother being absent. Mother absence is usually due to maternal drug use or incarceration.

Summary

Fathers can be absent from the home for a variety of reasons. The effects of the absence on their children will be significant. Although teachers cannot make fathers become involved parents, we can make sure that they are invited to participate in the child's school life.

RESEARCH IDEAS

Questions to Investigate

1. What can be done to help young men take the responsibility of fathering seriously?
2. At what age should "father education" start?
3. What traits are shared by men who take fathering seriously?

Resources to Explore

American Coalition for Fathers and Children
   http://www.acfc.org

American Psychological Association
   http://www.apa.org

Father Net
   http://www.cyfc.umn.edu/FatherNet/FatherNet.htm

National Center on Fathers and Families
   http://www.ncoff.gse.upenn.edu

References

AMERICAN COALITION FOR FATHERS AND CHILDREN. (1999). The cost of father absence [Online]. Available: http://www.acfc.org/fpage/absence.htm.

ARENDELL, T. (1992). After divorce: Investigations into father absence. *Gender & Society, 6,* 562–586.

BEATY, L. A. (1995). Effects of paternal absence on male adolescents' peer relations and self-image. *Adolescence, 30,* 873–880.

BLANKENHORN, D. (1996). *Fatherless America: Confronting our most urgent social problem.* New York: Harper Perennial.

BOWLER, M. (1999, March 24). Missing in class: Male teachers. *Baltimore Sun.*

GABEL, S. (1992). Behavioral problems in sons of incarcerated or otherwise absent fathers: The issue of separation. *Family Process, 31,* 303–314.

GOLOMBOK, S., TASKER, F., & MURRAY, C. (1997). Children raised in fatherless families from infancy: Family relationships and the socioemotional development of children of lesbian and single heterosexual mothers. *Journal of Child Psychology & Psychiatry and Allied Disciplines, 38,* 783–791.

MCLANAHAN, S. S. (1999). Father absence and the welfare of children. In Hetherington, E. M. (Ed.) *Coping with divorce, single parenting, and remarriage: A risk and resiliency perspective.* Mahwah, NJ: Lawrence Erlbaum Associates, 117–145.

MEN IN CHILDREN'S LIVES BOOKLIST. (1999, March 29). [Online]. Available: http://www.kcls.org/webkids/men.html.

Research confirms the risks associated with growing up in a fatherless home. (1996, August). *American Psychological Association Monitor,* p. 6.

ROSE, M. K. (1992). Elective single mothers and their children: The missing fathers. *Child and Adolescent Social Work Journal, 9,* 21–33.

SHOOK, N. J., & JURICH, J. (1992). Correlates of self-esteem among college offspring from divorced families: A study of gender-based differences. *Journal of Divorce and Remarriage, 18,* 157–176.

CHAPTER 6

Children with Disabilities

OBJECTIVE

After reading this chapter you should be able to see that children with disabilities are at risk because they are vulnerable to being teased by peers, and have difficulties achieving in school, both of which can have an adverse effect on how they feel about themselves. You should also be able to discuss ways to help your students see children with disabilities in a favorable light and to discuss how to modify your classroom to accommodate children with disabilities.

CHAPTER OUTLINE

Who Are Children with Disabilities?
    The Label *Child with a Disability*
    Disability: Handicap or Characteristic?
Children with Disabilities and the Classroom
    Federal Law Concerning Disabilities
    Advantages of Inclusion for Children with Disabilities
    Benefits of Inclusion for Children Without Disabilities
Parents of Children with Disabilities
    Initial Reactions
    Reactions During Child Rearing
    Stress
Learning Skills and Appropriate Child-Rearing Techniques
Feelings of Children with Learning Disabilities
The Teacher's Role in Including Children with Disabilities
    Team Member
    Modifying Teaching Strategies for Selected Conditions
Summary

WHO ARE CHILDREN WITH DISABILITIES?

In the Individuals with Disabilities Education Act (IDEA) of 1990, Congress spelled out what conditions children must have in order to be labeled "disabled." The IDEA notes that the term *children with disabilities* means children with

- mental retardation,
- hearing impairments including deafness,
- speech or language impairments,
- visual impairments including blindness,

- serious emotional disturbances,
- orthopedic impairments,
- autism, traumatic brain injury, other health impairments, or
- specific learning disabilities,

who, by reason thereof, need special education and related services. The term *children with specific learning disabilities* is further defined as

> those children who have a disorder in one or more of the basic psychological processes involved in understanding or in using language, spoken or written, which disorder may manifest itself in imperfect ability to listen, think, speak, read, write, spell, or do mathematical calculations.

This term does not include children who have learning problems that are primarily the result of environmental, cultural, or economic disadvantage (IDEA, 1990).

The Label "Child with a Disability"

To receive services under the IDEA, children must be labeled as having one of the listed conditions. Many parents and professionals have problems about labeling children. A label is just a tool that can be used in a positive way or in a negative way.

For example, Ms. Anderson, a second-grade teacher, was told that Tonya was highly allergic to bee stings. If stung while on the playground or a field trip, Tonya would need to get medication immediately or her health would be in danger.

Seeing the label *allergic to bee stings* on Tonya's emergency data card, Ms. Anderson could make plans to meet her needs even before she entered her class. In this case, she consulted with school health officials and they trained Ms. Anderson in the appropriate procedures for dealing with this emergency. Ms. Anderson made sure that the school always had an emergency plan to help Tonya in case she was stung. She also knew that in case of bee sting, she would have to get Tonya help immediately.

This example illustrates how labels can be helpful. The appropriate label, be it for a medical condition or a learning disability, can help a teacher to plan to meet the exact educational needs of a child.

On the other hand, labels can be and have been used to hurt children. In the early 1900s, many of the Italian and Jewish immigrants coming into the United States were given an intelligence test. The test was given in English. These immigrants did not speak English, and based on their performance on the test they were labeled "retarded." When the children got to school, many of their teachers did not expect them to learn because they accepted the claim that the children were "retarded," and they did not put much energy into teaching them. Fortunately, even in the early 1900s many other teachers were skeptical of labels and taught the children anyway.

Disability: Handicap or Characteristic?

The way we use language in describing children is important. The IDEA made an important change in its predecessor Public Law 94-142: The IDEA used the term *children with disabilities* instead of the previous term, *disabled children.* The older term focuses on the disability; we tend to think of "disabled children" in terms of what they cannot do instead of in terms of what they can do. The newer term puts our focus on the children, who happen to have a disability.

Kenneth Jernigan, a giant in fighting for the rights of people who happen to be blind, liked to describe blindness as a characteristic rather than as a handicap or disability. Dr. Jernigan pointed out that many people have characteristics that are limitations. The limitation is a handicap only if it gets in the way of the task to be performed. For example, if you need to hire a teacher of American colonial history, and your candidates are a sighted person who is an excellent auto mechanic but knows no history, and a blind person who is an expert in American colonial history, which candidate is limited?

People with limits learn alternative techniques to do the things they need to do. People who are blind learn to navigate with other means, such as a cane. People who have a math learning disability learn how to use calculators. It is important that teachers see children with disabilities as children who need to learn alternative techniques to achieve their goals, not as disabled or handicapped individuals.

CHILDREN WITH DISABILITIES AND THE CLASSROOM

Federal Law Concerning Disabilities

The U.S. Congress has addressed the rights of children with disabilities with several major pieces of legislation. The Education for All Handicapped Children Act (Public Law 94-142) was the landmark piece of legislation addressing the rights of children with disabilities. Other legislation amended Public Law 94-142, and finally the Individuals with Disabilities Education Act (IDEA, or Public Law 101-476), passed by Congress in 1990, reauthorized the original law and changed its name.

There are several major provisions of laws dealing with children who have disabilities. First, the law provides a *free appropriate public education* to all children with disabilities. "Free" means that the education has to be furnished without cost to parents and that related services such as transportation, speech therapy, and other such services must be covered. An "appropriate" education might include a placement in an out-of-district school.

A second provision of the law is that an *individual educational plan (IEP)* must be prepared for each child with a disability. The IEP is a written document that details the educational goals for the student and the services that will be provided to the student. The plan is developed in a meeting in which all of the relevant school specialists and teachers and the child's parents participate. As a classroom teacher you will be part of the team implementing the IEP.

Providing the education for the child in the *least restrictive environment* is another major provision of the law. Students who have disabilities are to be educated to the greatest extent possible with students who do not have disabilities. This provision of the law has provided the basis for *inclusion*. The goal of inclusion is to educate as many children with disabilities as appropriate with regular children in the regular classroom.

Inclusion is the term used to describe including children with disabilities in settings designed for children without disabilities. These children are included in regular classrooms for either the whole school day or parts of the school day. The amount of time children with disabilities spend in the regular classroom depends upon their needs as judged by school professionals and agreed upon by the child's parents.

An example of a child who would appropriately be included in a regular classroom is Ming, a bright 6-year-old girl who has cerebral palsy. She needs a wheelchair to get around, and she has problems with small muscle control that make handwriting difficult. Ming has appropriately been placed in a regular first-grade classroom, with all of the other students, and she receives in-room support from a special education teacher who is teaching her how to use a computer to write.

Not all children with disabilities are included or "mainstreamed" in a regular classroom. Because of the nature and severity of their disabilities, some children with disabilities are best served in special classrooms and special schools. As a classroom teacher you can expect to see only those children with disabilities who have the potential to prosper and learn in your regular classroom setting.

Greg, a 6-year-old, highly autistic boy, is an example of a child who should not be included in a regular class. He cannot stand to be touched. If he must be in a room with more than two other people, he panics and usually sits in a corner or under a table and rocks back and forth chanting an unrecognizable word to himself. The appropriate placement for Greg is in a special school where he can receive one-to-one instruction from a highly trained special educator. It would be cruel to put Greg in a regular classroom because of the intense anxiety he would feel there.

Advantages of Inclusion for Children with Disabilities

Being included in a regular classroom provides many advantages for children with disabilities. The classroom is the normal setting for a child. By being in a regular classroom, children with disabilities can experience what their other peers experience. When children with disabilities grow up, they will have to live in the world with people who do not have disabilities. Children with disabilities who are included in classrooms with children who do not have disabilities have the opportunity to socialize with and make friends with all kinds of people. Inclusion provides these children with skills and experiences that will enable them to live successfully in the wider world as adults.

Benefits of Inclusion for Children Without Disabilities

Including children with disabilities in the regular classroom gives the other children many benefits as well. By having the chance to know children with disabilities as people, children who do not have disabilities learn to see beyond the disability to the child (Diamond et al., 1997; Peltier, 1997). Jennifer, my third-grade daughter, came home from school at the beginning of the year bursting with news about her new friend, Ebony. "We sat together at lunch and were in the same math group," she told me. The whole week was filled with stories about things that she did with Ebony. During the middle of the second week, Jennifer reported that they ran a mile for a physical fitness test, and she came in first. I asked, "Did Ebony run with you?" Jennifer replied, "Dad, she can't run. She uses a wheelchair." Jennifer had found the fact that her friend was in a wheelchair not important enough to report it to her parents. She saw Ebony as a person, and not as a "disability." Jennifer was able to form a bond with Ebony based on their mutual interests, to which Ebony's wheelchair was not important.

By being exposed to some of the unique skills of children with disabilities, such as the ability to read Braille or use American Sign Language, other children can learn that these skills are positive rather than negative. After having taught sighted children to understand and write in Braille, Frieman and Manecki (1995) found that the sighted children had a positive perception of the abilities of blind people. The experience of having children with disabilities as classmates helps children without disabilities see the child and not the disability.

PARENTS OF CHILDREN WITH DISABILITIES

Parents of children with disabilities have a much different experience than do parents of children without disabilities. The presence of a child with disabilities in a family affects every member of the family.

Initial Reactions

When the diagnosis of the special condition is first made, many parents react in a similar pattern. Elisabeth Kübler-Ross (1969) identified this pattern first when she studied people who discover that they are dying. The first reaction is denial—"No, this is not happening to us." Next one would expect anger. The anger can generalize to other people, such as the physicians who delivered the child, or to God. The third stage is bargaining: "If my child were only regular, I would. . . ." Often the bargaining is with God. The fourth stage is depression: "Yes this is really happening, and I am mourning the loss of a normal child." Finally the family moves to the final stage, acceptance, where they come to grips with the condition and are ready to go on and deal with the situation.

Reactions During Child Rearing

During child rearing, parents of children with disabilities experience stress from dealing with their child's disability. They also must learn new skills, and how to treat their child like any other child.

Stress

In comparing parents of children with developmental disabilities with parents of children who do not have disabilities, Dyson (1997) found that the parents of the children with disabilities experienced more parental stress than did the other parents. Parents that I have counseled have talked about their stress. Mr. Jones noted his feelings about dealing with his son, who was diagnosed with cerebral palsy:

> It is a constant struggle. Tyrone has so many needs and we are stretched thin trying to meet all of them. Trips to doctors and trips to therapists alone would be a full-time job, but I have to work to pay for all of this stuff too. Sometimes it seems like I am going to have to give up sleeping in order to get everything done.

Mr. Jones obviously feels overwhelmed by all that he has to do. Many parents of children who do not have disabilities feel overwhelmed, and they have less to do than parents with children with disabilities.

Mrs. Scott, mother of Alan, a 7-year-old with severe learning disabilities, talked of feeling isolated and alone:

> Alan's behavior has been so problematic for so long that other kids don't want to play with him. I was never able to join playgroups because Alan would cause turmoil, and I would end up leaving feeling embarrassed. Sometimes I think that I have nobody in my life who really understands. I have to keep it all to myself.

Although support groups exist to help parents like Mrs. Scott, parents do not always seek them out. Many parents are too embarrassed to discuss their situation with others and pass up joining groups.

LEARNING SKILLS AND APPROPRIATE CHILD-REARING TECHNIQUES

Many parents who have a child with a disability have to learn new skills. Some of these skills are necessary to manage their child's life—such as learning to manage treatments necessary for certain medical conditions. Other skills might be needed to communicate with their children, as in the case of parents of deaf children who have to learn American Sign Language.

Imagine what would happen if a typical American family adopted a child who spoke only Russian. If everyone else in the family spoke only English, none of them would be able to communicate effectively with their new family member. Hearing parents who have a deaf child are in a similar position. Unless the parents and other hearing family members learn American Sign Language, they will be unable to help the child learn to communicate and will be unable to communicate with the child when she learns sign in school.

Parents also must learn child-rearing skills that are appropriate for their child's disability. They must try to understand the world from their child's point of view and at the same time guard against their own tendency to want to overprotect their child.

Some parents of children with disabilities can be overprotective. It is understandable that parents want to protect their child, but sometimes this protective behavior gets in the way of the child's development. Blind children need to go out into the world and earn their scrapes and bruises just as other children do, but sometimes their parents are afraid to let them face the normal trials of life. With encouragement and support, the parents can be helped to see that they need to let their blind youngsters have the same experiences as sighted children, even though the experiences might sometimes have some risk and danger.

Parents can find it hard to really understand how their child experiences the world. Mr. Harold thought his 12-year-old son, Eric, was just unwilling to follow his rules:

> I'm a single parent and Eric has to pitch in. I don't ask much. When he comes home, I have a small list of chores for him to do. He has to walk the dog, take out the trash, straighten up the living room, and make himself a snack and clean up any mess he makes in the kitchen. He just refuses to do everything. I ask him and he says he forgot. How can he forget? There aren't that many things to do.

Eric had learning disabilities and had trouble following directions in sequence. Because his father did not share his perceptual difficulty, Mr. Harold had a hard time understanding that Eric was not a bad child—he just thought differently. I explained the nature of the learning disability to Mr. Harold and suggested that he devise a written checklist for his son to follow when he comes home from school. After that, every day when Eric came home from school, he checked off the tasks on his list as he did them. It can be hard for parents to really know how their child perceives the world if they have never perceived the world that way.

It is important for teachers to understand how parents perceive their child's abilities and limitations. Knowing the problems parents perceive, teachers can help parents to understand the need to treat their children as normally as possible. You can do this by pointing out to parents how competent their child is in the classroom and helping parents find resources that will give them the skills necessary to better understand their children. For example, a teacher might help a parent find a course in American Sign Language, or help a parent with a child who has a learning disability find a parent support group.

FEELINGS OF CHILDREN WITH DISABILITIES

Children's feelings are shaped by the nature of their disability. The way they are treated is a sign of how other people perceive their disability. These children have to deal with issues of self-esteem, isolation, and being teased and patronized by others.

Having a disability can affect the child's self-esteem in a negative way. In the case of Eric, the child with a learning disability who was helped by being given a checklist for his tasks, not only didn't his father understand the nature of his learning disability, but Eric didn't understand it either.

> Sure, everybody tells me I'm smart. I don't believe them. I try and try, but I still can't get it sometimes. The other kids learn it easily, but not me. I don't care what they say, I think I am stupid. If I was smart, I wouldn't struggle so much.

Children can learn to have positive feelings about themselves by having successful experiences. Often children with disabilities are kept out of positions where they can be successful, and they have few chances to have positive experiences. If one never lets a blind child travel around outside in the neighborhood, that child will not get the positive feelings of mastery that sighted children get from being free to move around outdoors.

With the help of a therapy group, Eric began to understand that his learning disability reflected how he learned and not his intelligence. After accepting the fact that he had a learning disability, Eric concentrated on ways he could compensate for his weaknesses.

Isolation can be a part of the experience of children with disabilities. Children who are deaf might not be able to communicate with their classmates or their regular teacher. Children who require hospitalization often have to miss school and feel isolated from their peers. Children whose behavior makes them different can scare off other kids and may end up having few friends in school. This is particularly true of children with emotional problems that cause them to act out in ways that alienate and scare their classmates.

Children can be cruel. Children commonly tease each other, including children who are different. Because they sometimes appear "not to get it," children with learning disabilities are easy victims for teasing. Vulnerable children with emotional problems are also ripe targets for class teasing.

Some children with disabilities are not given access to the full school experience. I am writing this book on a computer, but I write down my phone messages and notes with a pen and paper. Many children who are blind or have limited vision are not taught Braille. They are thus deprived of the ability to write notes or take down a friend's phone number.

THE TEACHER'S ROLE IN INCLUDING CHILDREN WITH DISABILITIES

The classroom teacher plays a critical role in ensuring that any child with a disability in the classroom will have a good educational experience. The teacher's role in ensuring the success of the inclusion experience for all children involves both working with other professionals as well as making alterations in teaching strategies in the classroom. Two of the things a teacher can do to include children with disabilities are these:

- Create a support team
- Modify instruction

Team Member

Designing a teaching strategy to facilitate the learning of a child with disabilities is not the sole responsibility of the classroom teacher. Classroom teachers are just one member of the school team that reviews the individual educational plans (IEPs) of children with disabilities who are included in their classrooms. This team consists of the classroom teacher and other specialists in the school such as the psychologist, social worker, speech therapist, counselor, principal, reading teacher, and resource teacher.

Working together, members of the team combine their expertise to devise a plan to meet the needs of the child. In many ways the classroom teacher is the most important part of the team, in that he or she generally knows the child best.

It is often the classroom teacher who contributes a sense of practicality to the educational plan. Your job as teacher is to make sure that all of the ideas contributed by the specialists will actually work in the classroom. You have to determine whether you have the time and opportunity to implement the various ideas while still being responsible for all children in the class. You also have to consider the impact of the proposed plan on the other children.

Ms. Phillips was asked to consider an idea proposed by the school psychologist to help manage the behavior of Colleen, a child with an emotional problem. The psychologist worked up a behavior management scheme that called for the classroom teacher to give Colleen a chocolate candy, her favorite, whenever she was "caught" behaving as she should. Ms. Phillips was quick to point out the consequences of giving one child in the class a chocolate candy while not doing the same thing for all of the other children. She correctly vetoed the idea.

Once the IEP is set, you will work with all concerned to implement it. There has to be careful coordination to make sure that everyone is consistent and following the plan to the letter. If it is decided that Sally, a blind child, will be given the usual pass and allowed to go to the bathroom alone just like a sighted child, that policy must be followed regardless of who her teacher is at the time. If one member of the team chooses to "freelance," the success of the IEP is jeopardized.

Modifying Teaching Strategies for Selected Conditions

Teachers will have to modify their teaching strategies to adapt them to the child's particular disability. In some cases the modifications will be very minor, and in others they might be more extensive.

A Child Who Is Blind

To meet the needs of a child who is blind, teachers need to make some minimal adjustments. The child will have a special teacher who teaches the child Braille and mobility skills. The classroom teacher will have to make several adjustments. All material that one usually puts in print will have to also be put into Braille. If bulletin boards are labeled in print, they should also be labeled in Braille. In classrooms for younger children, one must make sure to have on hand children's books in Braille.

Braille. Braille is a system of making letters and words from arrangements of dots to be read with the fingertips. Computer equipment is available that can convert text to Braille relatively simply. A school system might have a Braille printer available in a central location. Teachers do have to prepare in advance so there is time to have the material Brailled. All classroom handouts can be Brailled. Braille can also be written by using a pointed stylus to punch dots through heavy paper using a Braille slate as a guide. This method of writing compares to writing notes with a pen and paper.

Most states have libraries for the blind that stock and lend Braille books and tapes. Braille books are quite large, but to facilitate their circulation Congress has passed a law making it possible for books to be mailed to blind people free of charge. Not all books are produced in a Braille edition, and this often leads to problems. Advocate organizations do lobby the Library of Congress to include specific books, and blind people can use audio books on tape that are marketed for sighted people.

Recorded books on tape have become quite popular, and many public libraries have large collections of them. Unfortunately, many of these recordings are abridgments.

Older children who are blind will also need textbooks in Braille. With a little lead time, the special teacher in the district can provide the books. Children who are blind can use computers to write stories just as sighted children can. In our modern world, keyboard skills are important for everyone to learn.

Children who are blind will be taught mobility skills by a special teacher. The child will be taught how to use a white cane, moving it back and forth in front of the body, tapping the cane to get information about the environment.

If you have a child who is blind in your class, you will of course have to initially orient the child to the classroom. If you later move any major pieces of furniture or equipment, you should tell the child so she or he can become oriented to the new positions of things.

A Child with Hearing Loss

Classroom teachers need to make a few adjustments to meet the needs of children with hearing losses. One must remember to look at the youngster when speaking. Many classroom teachers write on the board and talk at the same time. This of course doesn't work for a child with a hearing problem. She needs to see you when you talk. Often, seating a child with a hearing problem in the front row helps her see the teacher better.

Other children in the class can also be reminded to look at this youngster when they speak to her. As the child with a hearing problem learns in the regular classroom, she could also share her skills in American Sign Language and teach it to her classmates. This will help the hearing children understand how she is communicating and appreciate the skill level needed to use American Sign Language.

A Child with a Medical Condition

Before a child with a medical condition joins your classroom, you should demand that the school district teach you how to meet this child's routine needs and emergency needs. For example, one can be taught how to correctly help someone who uses a wheelchair.

If a child has a life-threatening condition, teachers need to be trained how to react in an emergency. Most schools do have nurses and others who are trained to do emergency medical procedures, but teachers are usually the ones there first. If the child is in your class, you need to be prepared to help him immediately.

The other children also need to be taught how best to help their classmate. Usually the child can tell the other kids what kind of help he needs and when he needs it. Other students can learn to ask the child with the disability whether he needs help or not.

Children who have chronic conditions that require hospitalization often must be absent for periods of time. Working with the hospital teacher, the classroom teacher can plan work and assignments to keep the child up-to-date while in the hospital. If the hospital has an e-mail connection, teachers can ask the school to loan the child a computer so he can keep in touch with his classmates via e-mail. If this is not possible, teachers can arrange times when the hospitalized child can call the school and talk to classmates, or even join in the class by way of a conference call.

A Child with a Learning Disability

Working with a special resource teacher, you will be given help in meeting the cognitive needs of a child with a learning disability. Often this involves altering your techniques somewhat in order to teach the child through the channel in which she learns best. Sometimes your expectations need to be modified. A child with a learning disability in the area of spelling, for example, might never be able to pass the regular spelling test. Care should be taken not to put the child in a position, such as having a class spelling bee, where she will obviously fail and look stupid to the other children.

If the child has a disability in writing, teachers can let him dictate stories into a tape recorder. If a child has a disability in learning multiplication facts, teachers can allow the child to use a calculator. And how will the other children react to these exceptions? Will they want to do the same thing? Probably, but your job is to explain to the children that you will meet all special needs of all children: If a student without disabilities needs extra help in math or reading, you will give that student special help too.

A Child with an Emotional Problem

To best deal with a child with an emotional problem, particularly if the problem involves acting out in the classroom, teachers need to have a plan in advance. The school team has to have a strategy that spells out exactly what a teacher will do in a particular circumstance. Linda, a third-grade child I saw in therapy, was subject to fits of rage. Knowing her background, one would understand why this happened. The teacher knew how to handle the outbursts. When Linda lost control, the teacher would ask her if she needed time to collect herself. If caught early, Linda could go to the counselor by herself; if not, the counselor would respond to a prearranged signal and come right to the classroom to get Linda. When Linda cooled off, the counselor would take her back to her regular classroom. In this case there was a plan, and the teacher and counselor knew their roles and played them well.

A youngster's acting-out behavior can scare the other children in the class. When this happens, teachers need to reassure the other children that they are in no danger and that the teacher is in total control of what is happening in the classroom.

At other times the behavior of children with emotional problems can make them the brunt of teasing or jokes from the other children. Teachers need to head this off by explaining to the other children that some children have problems that they are working on and that we need to understand and support them with kindness.

Teachers need to help children see these kids not as problem children but as children who are working on improving a problem. All children can relate to some situation in which they had a problem and needed help. The empathy that every child can learn in this situation can be a great learning experience.

A Child with Mental Retardation

Children with mental retardation who are included with younger children are usually easily accepted. Many children treat them like younger siblings and know how to deal with their behavior. As a teacher, you might have to use a discipline technique with these children that is more typically used with younger children. Of course, the key to meeting this special child's needs is to get information from the team on the functional level of the child and relate to her accordingly. You would gear your discipline strategy to the child's functional age rather than to her chronological age.

Summary

The IDEA spells out how public schools should serve children with disabilities. Your goal is to see the child who happens to have a disability just as you see the other children, and help the other students in the class do the same. Teachers also need to be sensitive to the needs of parents of children with disabilities. By making small changes in your classroom routine, you will be able to modify your teaching to meet the needs of children with disabilities who are members of your class.

RESEARCH IDEAS

Questions to Investigate

1. Should all children be educated in regular schools?
2. Do teachers and other professionals use labels correctly?
3. Who should be responsible for helping the parents of children with special needs?

Resources to Explore

American Speech-Language Hearing Association
http://www.asha.org

Association for Retarded Citizens
http://www.thearc.org

Center for the Study of Autism
http://www.autism.org

Council of Exceptional Children
http://www.cec.sped.org

Education of Individuals with Disabilities Act
http://www/rp.com/ed/idea_old.htm

National Association for the Mentally Ill
http://www.nami.org

National Association of Developmental Disabilities Councils
http://www.igc.ape.org

National Federation of the Blind
http://www.nfb.org

Office of Special Education Rehabilitative Services
http://www.ed.gov/offices/OSERS/index.html

United Cerebral Palsy Association
http://www.ucpa.org

References

DIAMOND, K. E., HESTENES, L. L., CARPENTER, E. S., & INNES, F. K. (1997). Relationships between enrollment in an inclusive class and preschool children's ideas about people with disabilities. *Topics in Early Childhood Special Education, 17,* 520–536.

DYSON, L. (1997). Fathers and mothers of school-age children with developmental disabilities: Parental stress, family functioning, and social support. *American Journal of Mental Retardation, 102,* 267–279.

EDUCATION OF INDIVIDUALS WITH DISABILITIES ACT. (1990). Pub. L. No. 101-476, 20 U.S.C. Chapter 33. [Online]. Available: http://www.lrp.com/ed/idea_old.htm.

FRIEMAN, B. B., & MANECKI, S. (1995). Teaching children with sight about Braille. *Childhood Education, 71,* 137–140.

KÜBLER-ROSS, E. (1969). *On death and dying.* New York: Macmillan.

PELTIER, G. L. (1997). The effect of inclusion on non-disabled children: A review of the research. *Contemporary Education, 68,* 234–238.

CHAPTER 7

Children Who Are Gifted

OBJECTIVE

After reading this chapter, you should be able to explain that children who are gifted are otherwise normal children with age-appropriate social skills, but happen to be exceptionally bright. You should also be able to discuss strategies you can use in your classroom to meet the needs of these children.

CHAPTER OUTLINE

CHILDREN WHO ARE GIFTED

It might seem strange to you to include children who are gifted in a discussion of children at risk. One tends to think of these children as having it made. They are smart. They can do well in school. So why are they at risk? They are at risk because they are different.

These children are often not identified as gifted, and their behavior is easily misinterpreted by teachers. Often a teacher doesn't know how to respond when a child tells her that the work is too easy. For example, Ms. Johnson at first didn't know how to take Keisha when she complained that the math assignments were too easy. After all, the other children in the fourth grade were struggling to master the material. At first Ms. Johnson thought that Keisha was just posturing to look good, but then she realized that Keisha really was incredibly skilled in math and was bored with the work. Teachers need to learn that some bright children are bored unless their schoolwork is challenging.

Children who are gifted have unique attributes. Although many of these characteristics make teaching easier, others can make it more difficult. If you understand how gifted children think, you can make appropriate adjustments in the instructional and social climate of your classroom (Cole & Frieman, 1998).

Children who are gifted have special needs that have to be met in order for them to be successful academically and emotionally in your classroom. If these needs are not met appropriately, these children can be at risk for developing social and emotional problems (Moon & Hall, 1998). Kwan (1992) notes that some gifted students, particularly girls, are highly susceptible to crises of self-esteem, alienation, anxiety, and locus of control. Thus, although these children are gifted academically, they are susceptible to emotional problems.

WHO ARE GIFTED CHILDREN?

Davis and Rimm (1998) point out that there is no one definition of "gifted" or "talented" that is universally accepted. As a practical measure, you will be bound by the definition adopted by the school district in which you teach. This definition will determine who will get the special services available for gifted children.

School-smart children who have the intellect and personality to do well and the ethic and drive to work are seen by teachers to be gifted. Such "traditionally gifted" children often have the backing of supportive parents and the skills to do well in your classroom.

This definition could discriminate against many populations of students who, although bright, lack the skills necessary to do well in school. This group includes the poor, minority groups, non-native speakers of English, underachievers, and females. Runco (1997) cautions that programs for the gifted that require that the student produce something might exclude children who do not have the expressive skills to communicate their insights.

Teachers need to expand their view of giftedness to include children who are intelligent in areas other than the traditional areas measured by school intelligence tests. Gardner (1983, 1993) expanded the definition of intelligence to include eight kinds:

1. Verbal/linguistic intelligence is related to words and language, both spoken and written. This type of intelligence would be found in a student who does well on written essays and can speak well in response to questions.
2. Logical/mathematical intelligence deals with deductive thinking and reasoning, numbers, and the recognition of abstract patterns. Students who do well in mathematics and physics would have this type of intelligence.
3. Visual/spatial intelligence deals with the ability to visualize objects and create mental images or pictures. These are the skills that are used by architects, sculptors, and artists and would be found in students who have exceptional art skills.
4. Musical intelligence is related to the ability to recognize tonal patterns and to be able to hear, perform, and compose music. Students who are exceptionally skilled in singing or playing instruments would have this ability.
5. Bodily-kinesthetic intelligence deals with the ability to use all or part of one's body to perform in either an artistic dance arena or an athletic contest.
6. Intrapersonal intelligence relates to one's understanding of oneself—one's own strengths, weaknesses, feeling, emotions, and thinking styles—and using that understanding to plan and carry out activities. Students with this ability might be future poets or philosophers.
7. Interpersonal intelligence includes the ability to understand the actions and motivations of other people and to use that information to deal with people.

Students who are exceptionally skilled at negotiating with others or are exceptional in aspects of student government organizations display this ability.

8. Naturalistic intelligence can be seen in the way one relates to one's surroundings. Students who are sensitive to changes in weather patterns or are adept at distinguishing nuances between large numbers of similar objects display this ability.

Verbal/linguistic and logical/mathematical are the two kinds of intelligences traditionally measured on standardized intelligence tests and most readily recognizable by schools.

After a few years in the classroom, you will quickly be able to identify children who are especially gifted in one of these areas. Your job is to use the broadest possible concept of giftedness to meet their needs in your classroom.

Characteristics of Gifted Children

After studying many groups of children who are gifted, researchers have noticed certain traits that they seem to have in common. In the intellectual area, teachers will find that these children are

- intrinsically motivated across all subject areas and in school in general (Gottfried & Gottfried, 1996),
- developmentally advanced in language and thought, and
- early literates, having begun to read and write at an early age.

In the area dealing with the emotions, one will find that these children have

- sensitivity and intensity (Tucker & Hafenstein, 1997),
- spiritual sensitivity, which is an understanding of the universality of spiritual concepts such as forgiveness of others, and the development of a philosophy of life (Lovecky, 1998),
- feelings of isolation from their peers (Robinson, 1996), and
- the emotional strengths of resilient persons—task commitment, reflectiveness, ability to dream, maturity, internal locus of control, and self understanding (Bland, Sowa, & Callahan 1994).

By looking for these traits, you will better be able to meet the needs of the gifted children in your classroom.

THE TEACHER'S ROLE WITH GIFTED CHILDREN

Teachers can be successful with gifted children if they keep in mind that these children are

- normal children who happen to be smart,
- not better than others because they are smarter,
- driven to learn,
- holistic learners, and
- productive when given assignments that are the same as, but different from, the assignments given to other students.

Normal Children Who Happen to Be Smart

Although children who are gifted often think like adults, their social behavior is still age-appropriate. It is tempting to look at a child with an advanced intellect and sophisticated verbal skills as an adult, but one should remember that she is still a child. Young children who are gifted will be silly and playful like all other children and in most social situations will behave like children and not adults.

Even though these children behave in an age-appropriate manner, their intellect often leads to many problematic situations. In the following instance, the student's concern about the feelings of others became problematic to her teacher: During a discussion of the news in a fourth-grade classroom, one student, Carlos, mentioned that he had seen a crying child on an evening news report about refugees. Carlos was concerned about this child and began bombarding Mr. Billings, his teacher, with questions. Later in the day, the class was celebrating during a holiday party by eating homemade candy. Carlos was still focused on the injustice that forced that child to be a refugee. He felt that the class should not eat the candy because the little girl seen on television was suffering. Mr. Billings was pleased with Carlos's display of compassion and sense of justice, but was a bit frustrated that his constant focus on the refugee child was putting a damper on the holiday celebration. The intellect of children who are gifted operates without the balance of the sophisticated social skills that develop in adulthood. An adult would be sympathetic to the refugee child, perhaps even do something to help the situation, but still not feel guilty about eating the candy at the party. Carlos's strong sense of justice got in the way of his social interactions with his classmates.

Another example of a child's feelings about an important issue getting in the way of her social interactions is what happened to Rekeya. Officer Friendly was a police officer invited to speak to the class. Rekeya questioned him about his use of the term *policeman* when women too could be police officers. Officer Friendly agreed and went on with his presentation. Rekeya wouldn't let the issue slide and kept raising her hand to argue with the officer about why he used the term *policeman* instead of *police officer*. Fortunately, her teacher understood that Rekeya was not intending to be rude, but was just following her strong feelings about gender equity. Her teacher told Rekeya that she understood and shared her concern for the equal treatment of women. Because she was a child, Rekeya didn't have the sophisticated social skills an adult would have to handle the situation more tactfully.

Smarter Children Are Not Better Children

Just because some children are academically gifted doesn't make them better or more important than any other child in the class. As a teacher you want children to feel good about their talents, but not superior to other children.

You can help gifted children learn a sense of pride and appreciation for their intellect while still recognizing the worth and abilities of others. It is important to tell gifted children that they are smart, but they also need to be praised when they are kind, nice, good class members, and display other traits that make them valued by their peers.

Sometimes you have to teach gifted children tact. Mrs. Hayes overheard Charissa, one of the seventh-graders in her math class, complaining to Mike, a struggling student sitting next to her, that the math test was too easy. After class Mrs. Hayes took Charissa aside and privately told her that indeed the test was easy for her because she was bright in math, but that when she bragged about her ability to Mike it made him feel bad. Mrs. Hayes pointed out that Mike was kind to Charissa and that she really liked him as a friend. Charissaa understood the message.

When you acknowledge the intellect of a child who is gifted, you help these children develop a strong positive self-concept. By teaching these children to be sensitive to others' feelings and respect them, teachers can facilitate these children's acceptance into the social network of the class.

Driven to Learn

Children who are gifted have an inner drive to learn. Although their parents might put them in stimulating situations, children who are gifted have their own motivation to learn. Teachers can accommodate these children's curiosity by giving them freedom to explore their interests in the classroom. Mrs. Berkeley handled that situation with Kelly. Kelly blasted into her kindergarten classroom and cornered Mrs. Berkeley to tell her about the volcano she had seen in the newspaper. Mrs. Berkeley had planned to read *Fox in Sox* to the class, but knew from past experience that Kelly would be distracted and would be asking millions of questions about volcanos. Mrs. Berkeley acknowledged Kelly's interest in the topic by saying, "You really seem to be excited about volcanos. You can use the computer to research this topic while I am reading a story to the class. Then you can take *Fox in Sox* home and read it to your parents tonight." Mrs. Berkeley accommodated Kelly's intellectual interest, while still having her read the same story as the rest of the class. A discipline problem was also avoided by anticipating that Kelly would not be focused on the story and would sidetrack the conversation to volcanos.

Holistic Learners

Many children who are gifted seem to learn things intuitively. For example, although intellectually gifted children can read with a high level of comprehension and solve mathematical problems, they might not be able to explain the meanings of all the words they read or explain how they solve their math problems.

These children are holistic learners and often use strategies different from the conventional ones that most children use to solve problems. If these children are evaluated in a conventional manner, they might fail to demonstrate knowledge of the discrete skills.

Evaluate children who are gifted on the basis of what they know and not how they got to that knowledge. These children often do not follow the conventional path to the answer. An example of this approach can be seen in the behavior of Ms. Wheeler, a sixth-grade teacher. Mrs. Wheeler noted that Jack seemed to get all of the answers correct on his long division problems but didn't show his work. His teacher quickly realized that he could solve the problems correctly without going through the usual steps. Ms. Wheeler realized through questioning that Jack was solving problems with his own strategy. Rather than frustrating Jack by making him show the steps he used in solving the problems, Ms. Wheeler gave him other, more challenging math problems to do.

It is not important if children who are gifted get to the end point of a skill or concept in a conventional manner. If teachers evaluate the end-point learning, while being open to alternative, correct strategies rather than focusing on documenting all the conventional steps for solving the problem, they will be able to accommodate the individual differences of children who are gifted.

Same Assignments, but Different

Children who are gifted come to school with a storehouse of knowledge about a variety of topics. Having them study something they already know will only bore them. Bored children can easily become discipline problems.

Teachers don't want to give children assignments that are too easy, but it would be a lot of work for a classroom teacher to create an entirely new curriculum for just one child. Instead, you only need to create differentiated assignments for children who are gifted. For example, all of the children might be studying about space by drawing a picture of the solar system. To differentiate the assignment for a gifted child who already knows about the location of the planets, the teacher might let this child select her own topic regarding space and do extensive research in the library and on the Internet to produce a report on it. In this case the teacher builds on what gifted child knows and allows her to investigate the subject under discussion on a deeper level, and produce a more sophisticated product that demonstrates what she has learned. In this manner, children who are gifted can study the same things as other children in the class, but at an academic level that is more appropriate for them.

Another example illustrating the same point with a younger child comes from a kindergarten where the children were studying farm animals. The children in the class were given the task of finding information about one animal of their choice. Ms. Fletcher, the teacher, anticipating that Sara Lynn would already know about farm animals and even mammals in general, assigned her the task of discovering mammals that do not live on land. Sara Lynn dove into this task with enthusiasm.

It is unrealistic to think that you will be able to prepare different assignments for all children in your class. By using differentiated assignments, you can challenge gifted children without having to prepare a separate curriculum.

Summary

Children who are gifted are normal children with age-appropriate social skills who happen to be exceptionally bright. By using some of the strategies discussed in this chapter, you can ensure that they perform up to their maximum potential in your classroom.

RESEARCH IDEAS

Questions to Investigate

1. What would happen in the classroom if the teacher treated all students as if they were gifted?
2. How should we educate the most gifted of the gifted?
3. Should gifted children skip grades in school?

Resources to Explore

ERIC Clearinghouse on Disabilities and Gifted Education, Council for Exceptional Children
http://www.cec.sped.org

Hollingworth Center for the Study and Education of the Gifted, Teacher's College, Columbia University
http://www.tc.columbia.edu

Institute for the Academic Advancement of Youth, Johns Hopkins University
http://www.jhu.edu

References

BLAND, L. C., SOWA, C. J., & CALLAHAN, C. M. (1994). An overview of resilience in gifted children. *Roper Review, 17,* 77–80.

COLE, L., & FRIEMAN, B. B. (1998, March). Parenting questions and answers. *Parenting for High Potential,* pp. 12–14.

DAVIS, G. A., & RIMM, S. B. (1998). *Education of the gifted and talented* (4th ed.). Boston: Allyn and Bacon.

GARDNER, H. (1983). *Frames of mind: The theory of multiple intelligences.* New York: Basic Books.

GARDNER, H. (1993). *Multiple intelligences.* New York: Basic Books.

GOTTFRIED, A. E., & GOTTFRIED, A. W. (1996). A longitudinal study of academic intrinsic motivation in intellectually gifted children: Childhood through early adolescence. *Gifted Child Quarterly, 40,* 179–183.

KWAN, P. C. F. (1992). On a pedestal: Effects of intellectual giftedness and some implications for program planning. *Educational Psychology: An International Journal of Experimental Educational Psychology, 12,* 37–62.

LOVECKY, D. V. (1998). Spiritual sensitivity in gifted children. *Roeper Review, 20,* 178–183.

MOON, S. M., & HALL, A. S. (1998). Family therapy with intellectually and creatively gifted children. *Journal of Marital and Family Therapy, 24,* 59–80.

ROBINSON, N. M. (1996). Counseling agenda for gifted young people: A commentary. *Journal for the Education of the Gifted, 20,* 128–137.

RUNCO, M. A. (1997). Is every child gifted? *Roeper Review, 19,* 220–224.

TUCKER, B., & HAFENSTEIN, N. L. (1997). Psychological intensities in young gifted children. *Gifted Child Quarterly, 41,* 66–75.

CHAPTER 8

Children with Incarcerated Parents

OBJECTIVE

After reading this chapter, you should be able to discuss how you can help children and their surrogate parents cope with the experience of their parents being incarcerated.

CHAPTER OUTLINE

WHO HAS INCARCERATED PARENTS?

An estimated 200,000 children in the United States have an imprisoned mother, and more than 1.6 million have an imprisoned father (Seymour, 1998). These children have to deal with the consequences of their parents' behavior.

The parental behavior that led to the prison sentence often causes serious family situations. Children who are raised in these situations face a whole array of problems. Parents' criminal behavior, particularly drug use, does not make for quality parenting. In addition, parents who commit crimes frequently have a great many problems before they are caught and sent to jail. Often, they are living in poverty and have to deal with its repercussions.

Fathers engaged in criminal behavior often do not live with their children. They are also not likely to be a part of the child's day-to-day care. On the other hand, 70 to 80 percent of convicted women are mothers (Hooper & McCence, 1983). When these mothers commit their crimes, they are far more likely than fathers to be the day-to-day caretakers of small children (Kiser, 1991).

EFFECTS OF A PARENT'S INCARCERATION ON CHILDREN

Many variables affect the impact that having an incarcerated parent will have on a child. The variables include these:

- Age of child
- Coping ability of the child
- Quality of the parenting before the incarceration
- Whether one parent is still free to care for the child
- Length of the parent's jail term
- Ability to regularly visit their parent
- Quality of the child's care in the parent's absence

As with many other life events, some children will be able to deal with the situation better than others.

From a research point of view, it is difficult to isolate a single variable related to the parent's incarceration as being the one responsible for the child's behavior. This is due to the fact that the child probably was in a less-than-ideal situation before the parent was sentenced to jail. Are we seeing the results of the child's experience before the parent was jailed or after the parent was jailed? Nonetheless, we can anticipate that the child of an incarcerated parent will experience one or more of the following problems (Gabel, 1992a, 1992b):

- School difficulties
- Antisocial behaviors
- Anxiety
- Depression

Children with jailed parents have to cope with several difficult issues. The first is separation. The incarceration causes a disruption in the family bonds. The separation issue can be particularly acute if the jailed parent is the one who was the primary caretaker of the child. Young children will have a very difficult time understanding why and for how long their parent will be away, because their understanding of time is primitive. They often have trouble understanding the difference between yesterday, today, and tomorrow, and therefore they will not be able to understand how long their parent will be in jail. From their point of view, it might seem that their parent will never come back. Older children must deal with the same issues, but they have a greater understanding of what is going on in the family. The impact of losing a parent to incarceration is still a very severe blow to any child.

The separation can mean that the child moves to a new place to live, with new people, new routines, and new parenting expectations. This can be very traumatic. Separation is further complicated if the caregivers deceive the children as to why their parent has left. Telling the child that the parent had to take work in a different town, although done with good intentions, might trigger greater feelings of abandonment and resentment than if the child knew that the parent has been jailed and is away against his or her will.

Some groups see jail as a rite of passage for young men and do not look down on someone who has been incarcerated. Behavior problems of children who grow up in these groups are likely to arise from already existing family discord and dysfunction. Other groups attach a strong stigma to the person who has been jailed. Children who come from a group that has a negative view of people who have been incarcerated might have to deal with feelings of shame for having a parent in jail.

WHO TAKES CARE OF THE CHILD WHEN THE PARENT IS JAILED?

When a parent is jailed, several kinds of arrangements can be made to take care of the child. The parenting arrangement can depend upon several factors, including these:

- The availability of the remaining biological parent
- The willingness of the remaining biological parent to take over
- The length of the parent's incarceration
- The age of the child
- Support from the extended family

These factors will help determine what type of parenting situation will be best for a child whose parent is incarcerated.

The Remaining Parent

One alternative is to have the child remain in the care of the remaining, nonjailed parent. This arrangement of course requires no legal action. In most cases, it is the father who is jailed and the mother remains as caretaker. If the parents had been living together and sharing parenting, the mother will be suddenly faced with becoming a single parent, quite often with poverty and its consequences. If the father has been absent from the family and is jailed, the mother will face no real changes in her day-to-day obligations.

If the mother of the family is jailed, an active father can step in and care for his children. He too will face the challenges of being a single parent. An absent father might choose to take no responsibility for the care of his children.

Kinship Families

If no parent is available or willing to care for the child, family members often step in to become the surrogate parent. Grandparents or other relatives who step in to assume care of the child face several unique challenges. They must deal with

- helping the child cope or grieve for the jailed parent,
- their own anger and disappointment with their jailed relative, and
- taking the child for parental visits at the jail, which might be distant.

Kin who take over the responsibility for a child are faced with the decision of how permanent to make this relationship. If the parent is being jailed for a long time and the child is young, the kinship caregiver faces two choices—adoption or guardianship. For the caregiver to adopt the child, the court will have to terminate the parental rights of the biological parent. This is often hard for members of the family, as it often makes them feel disloyal to the incarcerated parent.

Another option is for the relative to become the legal guardian of the child. In this case, rights and responsibilities are assigned to the caregiver, while still preserving the jailed parent's rights.

Foster Care by Nonfamily Persons

If family members or relatives do not step in to take care of the children, the children might be placed in foster care. This care might be provided by friends who know the child or by people who are complete strangers to the child. The trauma of being uprooted from one's parent and being sent to a new home with a stranger is obvious. In addition, the foster parents might not do much to maintain the child's contact with the jailed parent. Because of their own fear of prisons, the foster parents might be reluctant to take the children to visit. Beckerman (1989) points out that maintaining mother-child contact during the period of incarceration is one step in minimizing the negative consequences of incarceration subsequent to release. Yet the child is dependent upon the foster caregiver to enable this contact to occur.

Foster care by its nature is temporary. At some point a difficult decision has to be made by those legally responsible for the child. In many cases the decision is made by people in state agencies. How long is too long to wait? Is the child too young to wait 10 years for their parent to be released from prison? This difficult decision should be made in the best interests of the child and not in the interests of the jailed parent.

THE INCARCERATED PARENT

The incarcerated parent who hopes to reunify with his or her children after the jail term is served will need to maintain meaningful contact with his or her children when serving the jail sentence. This is not always easy. Often prisons are far from where their children live, and public transportation, if existent, can be expensive, and travel can be time-consuming. Prison security requirements often complicate the visit between a parent and a child. In some visiting situations, parents and children are separated by a glass security barrier and cannot touch each other.

THE TEACHER'S ROLE WITH CHILDREN WHOSE PARENTS ARE INCARCERATED

As a teacher, you will face many challenges in dealing with children who have an incarcerated parent. One challenge is to establish a helping rapport with the youngster. Most probably, the child has been growing up with less-than-ideal parenting.

The incarceration of the parent will be another stressor in the child's life. In teaching a child with an incarcerated parent, make every effort to do the following:

- Establish trust with the child.
- Create a discipline plan to deal with acting-out behavior.
- Know your school resources.
- Give the child role models.
- Hold the child responsible for his or her classroom behavior.
- Do not permit classmates to tease the child.
- Work with both the old and the new parents.

Establishing Trust

Your first goal is to establish a sense of trust with the child. You need to acknowledge that you know that the child's parent has been jailed. Why pretend? Word gets out in a community and everybody knows what has happened. Pretending that it didn't occur just suggests that there is something for which the child should be ashamed (Weissman & LaRue, 1998).

Assure your student that they are not responsible for their parent's behavior. They will face rough times and you can acknowledge that and tell them that you will be there if they need help.

Acting-Out Behavior

You need to have a plan to deal with the child if he acts out in your classroom. Frequently a child's behavior will change drastically after a traumatic event. All of the anxiety that the child is dealing with often explodes and is vented in inappropriate ways. We call this behavior "acting out."

This disturbing behavior can involve crying, temper tantrums, hitting other children, oppositional behavior, and other behavior that disrupts the tranquility of the classroom. While working in a classroom helping Mary, a first-grader whose mother had been just incarcerated, I saw another student accidentally brush her arm. Mary screamed, "My arm is broken!" She began sobbing loudly, attracting the attention of the teacher as well as of all the other children in the class. It was apparent that Mary was not reacting to being physically hurt but was using the situation to act out or express some deeper pain.

You can help children like Mary deal with their pain by giving them a socially acceptable way to get the attention and comfort that they need. I said to Mary privately:

> Mary, I know you feel bad inside when you think of your mother not being home anymore. Remember when you fell down on the playground and cut your foot? You came over to me and told me that you had a "hurt" and I gave you a big hug. Sometimes we can have "inside hurts" when we think about things that worry us. If you have an "inside hurt" when you think about your mother, all you have to do is come and tell me and I will give you lots of hugs. I know that an "inside hurt" sometimes hurts more than an "outside hurt."

In this way, I gave Mary a mechanism for receiving extra attention while behaving in a socially desirable way. Children who are dealing with difficult situations in their lives often need a great deal of extra reassurance and affection during the course of the day.

Older children might be too embarrassed to ask their teacher for a hug. Recognizing that they sometimes feel bad and don't want to be seen by classmates, a teacher can give them the option of leaving the room to "go to the lavatory" if they need some time to collect themselves. You might suggest to a child that when they start having sad thoughts about their absent mother, they go to the lavatory, wash their face, take a few deep breaths, and then come back to class. This arrangement can be set up in a conversation that acknowledges that the child is dealing with a tough situation.

You might have to deal with acting-out behavior that needs to be controlled. Even if a child is suffering inside, you cannot let him disrupt the learning taking place in class, and you cannot let him take his anger out on another student. An important part of your response should be to reassure the child that although you do not like his behavior and will not tolerate it, you still like and value the child. In effect you are saying, "I don't like what you do, but I still like you."

School Resources

Knowing that children of incarcerated parents will have issues to deal with, your first task is to explore school or community resources to make sure that the youngster has professional counseling. You need to consult with your school counselors and lobby them to provide their services to the child or else to link the child up with appropriate community resources (Chaney, Linkenhoker, & Horne, 1977). As the classroom teacher, you will have neither the time nor the expertise to give the child extensive individual help in dealing with this difficult situation.

Role Models

Children who have parents who engage in illegal behaviors do not have positive parental role models. You can help these children by exposing them to positive role models. You, of course, are an important role model. A child often needs role models of their same sex. If you are female and the child is a male, you might try to find a male faculty member, or member of the school community, who can serve as a mentor and role model for the youngster. Male teachers can do the same for female students.

The child can also be assigned an older student as a "buddy." This young role model should be an older child who can spend time with their buddy, perhaps helping them with reading homework. Schools have been successful in using older children from adjoining high schools to work with younger children. For example, Larry was a brash middle school child who was in a therapy group. Tae, the peer counselor, was a high school student who was a member of the football team, and looked up to by the middle school boys. Larry talked about how he thought it was "cool" to push around the smaller boys in his class.

Tae piped up that if he did that in high school the other boys would think that he was a jerk. Larry, who admired Tae, suddenly saw his own behavior in another light, and said he didn't want to do anything that would make the high school boys think he was a jerk. In this case, a positive peer role model was able to have an impact.

Responsible Class Behavior

All children, especially children who have no rules or limits imposed at home, need to learn to be responsible for their own actions. It is natural to feel sorry for a child because she is dealing with a difficult situation, but we still need to help these children learn how to be responsible for their own behavior.

One way to do this is to encourage them to be involved in school activities that call for them to practice responsible behaviors. Sport is one such activity. One can learn through participation in sports to be a responsible member of a team. A good coach can help a youngster understand that her behavior can affect her fellow team members in a positive way, and that for the team to be successful all of its members must work hard.

The same skills can be learned in a musical group or a theater group. School councils and organizations can also give children an arena in which to practice and observe the importance of being a responsible member of society.

Class Activities

Teachers need to be sensitive when dealing with class activities that involve parents. On Valentine's Day or Mother's Day, children might be encouraged to make cards for all of the significant people who care for them. Cards for incarcerated parents can be mailed by the teacher.

If teachers get wind of children teasing the child who has a parent in jail, they must take action immediately to end the behavior. We need to have a zero tolerance for teasing in the classroom. Classmates can be confronted with the fact that children are not responsible for their parent's behavior, and that teasing can make someone feel bad. Most important will be your posture not to accept any classroom behavior that can hurt another class member. Your classroom must be a psychologically safe place for all of your children.

Old and New Parents

You can be dealing with both biological parents and new parents when you have a child whose parent is incarcerated. Most of your attention will be focused on the child's custodial parent. If this parent is new, your first step is to establish a rapport with them. By acknowledging an understanding of the surrogate parent's situation and being supportive and helpful, you will take the first step in developing a positive relationship with the new parent.

Your second goal will be to provide them with information that will enable them to help the new child in their house to be successful in school. Take some time and give the new parent the normal beginning school talk. Explain the school rules, policies, and procedures, and your expectations for homework and school behavior.

And finally, let the new parents know that you understand their situation and are willing to listen to their concerns. If they are interested in having a more permanent relationship with the child, these new parents might be concerned about having the jailed parent remain in contact with the youngster. They might occasionally vent their frustrations about dealing with a child in a difficult situation. Although you cannot solve these problems, you can listen and help them vent. You can reply to their frustrations by saying things such as these:

It's hard, isn't it?

How does that make you feel?

Is there anything I can do to help you?

Your goal with biological parents is to send them information. You can mail them copies of progress reports, school bulletins, and other newsletters so they can be informed about the progress of their children and still feel a part of their lives. This is a very important way to keep a link between parent and child so that the parent, when released from jail, might still feel a part of the child's life. Many fathers who are in prison still care about their children. For example, Hairston (1989) reported that fathers who were long-term prisoners were still interested in improving their parenting skills.

Summary

By understanding what children and their new and old parents are experiencing, you can help both children and their surrogate parents cope with the experience of a parent being incarcerated. You will face many challenges—from dealing with an emotionally hurt child to dealing with several sets of "parents." With an understanding of the experience, you will be able to help a child cope with a difficult situation.

RESEARCH IDEAS

Questions to Investigate

1. How do you deal with a culture that makes going to jail a rite of passage for men?
2. Can you teach incarcerated parents how to improve their parenting skills?
3. Should parents who are incarcerated for a long period of time still retain some rights as parents?

Resources to Explore

Aid to Incarcerated Mothers
   http://www.atim.qpg.com

Child Welfare League of America
   http://www.igc.apc.org

Family Resources Coalition of America
   http://www.frca.org

References

BECKERMAN, A. (1989). Incarcerated mothers and their children in foster care: The dilemma of visitation. *Child and Youth Services Review, 11,* 175–183.

CHANEY, R., LINKENHOKER, D., & HORNE, A. M. (1977). The counselor and children of imprisoned parents. *Elementary School Guidance and Counseling, 11,* 177–184.

GABEL, S. (1992a). Behavioral problems in sons of incarcerated or otherwise absent fathers: The issue of separation. *Family Process, 31,* 303–314.

GABEL, S. (1992b). Children of incarcerated and criminal parents: Adjustment, behavior, and prognosis. *Bulletin of the American Academy of Psychiatry and the Law, 20,* 33–45.

HAIRSTON, C. F. (1989). Men in prison: Family characteristics and parenting views. *Journal of Offender Counseling, Services, and Rehabilitation, 14,* 23–30.

HOOPER, C. B., & MCCENCE, K. (1983). *The forgotten sufferers: Children of inmates.* Cited in LeFlore, L., & Holston, M. A. (1989). Perceived importance of parenting behaviors as reported by inmate mothers: An exploratory study. *Journal of Offender Counseling, Services and Rehabilitation, 41,* 5–21.

KISER, G. C. (1991). Female inmates and their families. *Federal Probation, 55,* 56–63.

SEYMOUR, C. (1998). Children with parents in prison: Child welfare policy, program, and practical issues. *Child Welfare, 77,* 469–493.

WEISSMAN, M., & LARUE, C. M. (1998). Earning trust from youths with none to spare. *Child Welfare, 77,* 579–594.

CHAPTER 9

Children Dealing with Death

OBJECTIVE

After reading this chapter, you should be able to discuss how children's understanding of death is dependent on their developmental level. You should also be able to discuss how you can help children deal with the death of a family member, parent, friend, or classmate.

CHAPTER OUTLINE

Who Is Dealing with Death?
Effects of Deaths of Others on Children
    Preschool-Age Children
    Children in the Elementary School Years
    Immediate Reactions
    Death of a Classmate
    Dealing with Death
The Teacher's Role in Helping Children Deal with Death
    Dealing with Your Own Feelings
    Role Model
    Helping Behaviors
    Death of a Family Member
    Helping Classmates Cope
    Death of a Classmate
Summary

WHO IS DEALING WITH DEATH?

Many of the children in your classrooms will have to deal with the death of a parent, family member, friend, neighbor, or classmate. If teachers and other school professionals deal with this issue properly, they can help ease a child's suffering during this emotional life event. Consider the following (Maryland State Teachers' Association, 1999):

- One out of every 750 children of high school age dies each year.
- One child in 20 will have a parent die before she or he graduates from high school.
- One percent of U.S. children live with a widowed parent.

Death and the resulting grieving are part of the lives of the children in your class. While talking to a group of urban kindergarten teachers, I was taken aback when one reported to me that over half of the children in her class had seen someone die. Most of the deaths they had witnessed were on the streets and the results of drug disputes. Unfortunately, gunfire and death are no strangers to many of the youngest children in our schools. Children need help in dealing with the powerful feelings they will have in response to a death, and classroom teachers can help provide that support.

EFFECTS OF DEATHS OF OTHERS ON CHILDREN

Several factors affect how a child will react to a death. Of primary importance is the child's age and developmental level, because this will affect how the child understands death. Another variable is the personality of the child; as we noted in chapter 2, some children are more resilient than others. A third factor is the nature of the relationship between the deceased and the child. The death of a parent will have a different impact than the death of a distant neighbor. A final factor is the loss history of the child (Hatter, 1996; Schumacher, 1984).

Preschool-Age Children

A child's understanding of death and her reaction to it is dependent upon her cognitive developmental level. Preschool children view death differently than do older children. They see death as a temporary and reversible state. They often see cartoon characters on television be flattened, run over, or shot full of holes and then pop up again, full of life.

These young children have trouble grasping the fact that death is permanent. Their concerns are of an immediate nature. In a classic study, Nagy (1948) discovered that children this young had a great curiosity about what happens to a person after he dies. They wanted to know where the person continued to live. Death is disturbing to young children because it separates people from each other and because life in the grave seems dull and unpleasant (Pettle & Britten, 1995).

Children in this age bracket often take things very literally. When dealing with preschool children, one must choose one's words carefully. In one case, an act of kindness confused a 5-year-old child I was working with in a mental health clinic. Molly's grandfather died after a long illness. At the funeral, the family minister explained to Molly that "God loved your grandfather very much and wants him to be near." Several weeks later the minister came by Molly's house to check on the family. In the course of his visit, he told Molly, "Remember, God loves you very much." The next day Molly's parents noticed strange behavior. Molly was very calmly giving all of her toys away to her friends in the neighborhood telling them that she wouldn't need them anymore. When her father asked her about this, Molly said, "The minister told me that God loved me. He told me that God loved grandfather and that's why he took him home. God loves me so I am going to die like grandfather." When helping a young child deal with death, we have to choose our words very carefully because young children will take what we say very literally.

Children in the Elementary School Years

Children 5 to 10 years old gradually absorb the concept of the irreversible nature of death, but they will still relate to death in terms of its concrete rituals, such as viewings and funerals. According to Nagy (1948), children at this age tend to personify death. They see death as final, a reduced form of life. But the child has a protective feature—personal death can be avoided; a child can trick the "death man" and not die.

An example of this kind of thinking is the origin of a traditional children's game:

> Ring-around the rosy
> Pockets full of poseys
> Achoo achoo [or "ashes ashes," depending upon the region]
> All fall down.

Kastenbaum (1973) explains the origin and meaning of the chant. He notes:

> Medieval society was almost totally helpless against bubonic plague—Black Death. If adults could not ward off death, what could children do? They could join hands, forming a circle of life. They could chant ritualistically and move along in a reassuring rhythm of unity. Simultaneously acknowledging and mocking the peril that endangered each of them individually, the children predicted and participated in their own sudden demise: "all fall down!" The children beat death and arose to play again.

By the age of 9 or 10, children have a more adult view of death. However, children don't believe that it will happen to them or anybody else they know. During the preadolescent and adolescent years, many children tend to think of themselves as invulnerable.

Immediate Reactions

Death is a powerful emotional experience, and you should anticipate that children will react to it often with some force. Examples from the children I worked with in a mental health center illustrate the point. Every child might react differently, depending upon their personality, but you could expect to see some of the following behaviors:

- *Nightmares.* Six months after her grandfather died, Hannah started waking up with the same nightmare. In her dream she saw her grandfather walking around in the bathroom calling to her. She woke up each time terrified and subsequently was afraid to go into the bathroom alone. (After several weeks of psychotherapy she learned how to deal with the death in a healthier manner and the nightmares stopped.)
- *Blaming themselves.* Twelve-year-old Gabe's father was killed in a car accident on the way to the grocery store. Gabe blamed himself. "If I just didn't tell him I wanted ice cream, he wouldn't have died."

- *Anger.* Carl was angry at everybody after his mother died. He would fight with his fifth-grade classmates at the drop of a hat and was alienating all of his friends.
- *Regression.* Before her mother died, 4-year-old Selma dressed herself. After her mother's death, Selma reverted to a more childlike state, in which she claimed that she needed someone to dress her.
- *Withdrawal.* After his father died, 16-year-old Bart pulled back from all of his sport activities. He quit the baseball team and didn't want to hang around with his friends.
- *Fear.* After his father died, Joon was no longer his normally independent self. He was afraid to let his mother out of his sight. He didn't want to go to school because he was worried that something might happen to his mother.

All of these examples are extreme, but real. Not all children will react so strongly, but many will display some of these behaviors in some degree. All of the examples cited were children who were successfully helped in a community mental health center.

Death of a Classmate

Of immediate concern to teachers is helping children deal with the death of classmates. Many schools recognize the need for teacher support in the case of natural disasters, accidents, or violent attacks on schools, and send in crisis teams, composed of trained counselors, to help. As the teacher, you will have to deal with your own feelings. To do this, you need to seek the support of your colleagues and professionals. Your class will be looking to you for a model of how to handle the situation. You can let them see that it is permissible to grieve and mourn the loss of someone.

Children will not all react the same way to the death of a peer. Wharton, Levine, and Jellenik (1993) point out that children are most likely to experience intense grieving when they

- were best friends or enemies of the deceased child,
- were present at the time of death,
- have little social support,
- are experiencing a concurrent crisis, or
- are predisposed to depression.

As teachers, we know who these children are and can make sure that they are top priority for getting help.

Dealing with Death

Children need to deal with their feelings when a death occurs. Children should be encouraged to talk about the deceased and their feelings about the death. In this way you will have a window into how the children are thinking and can intervene appropriately to help them cope. These are some of the things children need when they are dealing with a death (Christian, 1997; Worden, 1996):

- Adequate information
- To have their fears addressed
- Reassurance that they are not to blame
- Careful listening
- Validation of their feelings
- Involvement in rituals after the death
- Someone to model how to handle grief and remember the deceased
- Teachers and other adults who are willing to focus on the children during the time of grief

THE TEACHER'S ROLE IN HELPING CHILDREN DEAL WITH DEATH

The teacher plays a key role in helping children deal with death. You will be able to help the children by doing the following:

- Dealing with your own feelings
- Being a role model
- Practicing helping behaviors
- Helping children deal with a death in their family
- Helping children in the class respond to the grieving child
- Helping your students deal with the death of a classmate

Dealing with Your Own Feelings

Your first task is to deal with your own feelings about death. According to a pioneer in helping people deal with death, Dr. Elisabeth Kübler-Ross (1969), we can come to an understanding and acceptance of death as a part of the life cycle. This task requires a great deal of self-reflection and thinking and often calls for examining our religious or moral views about death.

Role Model

Once you have dealt with your own feelings, you are capable of becoming a role model for your children. Children need to be taught how to grieve, and you can help show them. You can demonstrate that tears at the appropriate time can be soothing. In your actions they will see how one can express sympathy and support to the survivors.

Helping Behaviors

As teachers, we get to know our students well over a long period of time. We have the time and opportunity to build up a trusting relationship and make ourselves accessible to their needs. Here are several guidelines for helping children deal with death:

- Keep an open line of communication.
- Be aware of the child's age and respond in a developmentally appropriate manner.
- Answer all questions truthfully.
- Answer only what is being asked.
- Be aware that your religious views might differ from those of the child's family and direct all questions involving religious views to the child's family members or clergy.
- Encourage the child to express their feelings using words, art, music, or any other vehicle.
- Accept their feelings as real.

Death of a Family Member

When a member of the child's family dies, you can support the child and the family, and also mobilize the class to be supportive. On a personal level, you can be supportive and allow the child to talk to you. You can even encourage the child to write stories or draw pictures about how they are feeling.

As teachers, we can be patient, kind, and supportive, and allow the child time to grieve and deal with the death. By allowing the child to talk to you about the loss, you provide a valuable, immediate vent for their feelings. But what do you say? There are no words that can "make it better." You can only listen and validate the child's feelings that things are hard. You need not think that you must say something profound. Actively listening, validating the child's feelings, and caring are the strong commodities that teachers have to offer.

When the child returns to school after the death, you might see a change in behavior. As we noted earlier, you might have to deal with aggression, anxiety, distraction from classwork, and somatic complaints. You still have to limit behavior as you did before the death. You can't allow a grieving child to hurt another child. If this happens, you might take the child aside and say, as did a teacher I observed: "I know things are really hard for you now and you are feeling bad about your mother, but you still can't hit anyone else in the class. Go to the bathroom and wash your face, then get a drink of water and come back into the class." You can offer support to the family by keeping them informed about the progress of their child.

Most teachers are not trained to deal with death. Remember that you can use the school counselor as a valuable resource for help. When the child returns to school, the school counselor should be notified so that she can see the child individually on a regular basis to help the child work through the death.

Helping Classmates Cope

Children who have not experienced death often don't know how to respond to their grieving classmates. They might visit their bereaved classmate at a funeral home or attend religious services associated with the death. You can help by explaining the meanings and expected behaviors at these life events. Local clergy might also help explain religious rituals (Grollman, 1995; McLaughlin, 1995). If the classmates know what is going to happen, they will be less apprehensive and fearful.

Often children (like many adults) will not know what to say to someone who has experienced a loss, so instead they avoid them and say nothing. You need to give the classmates of the grieving youngster a model of what they can say and encourage them to stay involved with their friend.

Before the child returns to school you can give the children some suggestions of what they can say to their classmate. Suggest some statements like these:

I was thinking of you.

I'm glad you are back.

I am your friend.

If you want to talk about things, I will listen.

Death of a Classmate

When a classmate dies, you should seek the help of the school counselor or other school mental health people. The whole class, including yourself, will be grieving. A significant amount of class time needs to be spent processing feelings, and other work needs to take a back seat.

The class members can decide how best to bring closure to this loss. They might elect to plant a tree in honor of the child, or mark the child's life in some other tangible manner. The children need to be supported and encouraged to find some way to remember the child and register their loss.

Summary

Children's understanding of death is dependent upon their developmental level. You may be called upon to deal with the death of a child's parent or loved one, or the death of a student in your class or school. Death is hard for anyone to deal with—adult or child. As teachers we have a great opportunity to help teach children how to cope with this inevitable life event.

RESEARCH IDEAS

Questions to Investigate

1. How should a teacher discuss death with children who come from different religious backgrounds?
2. How do you deal with the religious issues of death in a public school classroom?
3. Does the death of a loved one have a permanent adverse effect on a child?

Resources to Explore

American Association for Retired People
http://www.aarp.com

Association for Death Education and Counseling
http://www.adec.org

Hospice Foundation of America
http://www.hospicefoundation.org

National Hospice Organization
http://www.nho.org

References

CHRISTIAN, L. G. (1997). Children and death. *Young Children, 52,* 76–80.

GROLLMAN, E. A. (1995). Explaining death to children from Jewish perspectives. In E. A. Grollman (Ed.), *Bereaved children and teens: A support guide for parents and professionals* (pp. 141–157). Boston: Beacon Press.

HATTER, B. S. (1996). Children and the death of a parent or grandparent. In C. E. Coor & D. M. Corr (Eds.), *Handbook of childhood death and bereavement* (pp. 131–148). New York: Springer.

KASTENBAUM, R. (1973). The kingdom where nobody dies. *Saturday Review Science, 60,* 33–38.

KÜBLER-ROSS, E. (1969). *On death and dying.* New York: Macmillan.

MARYLAND STATE TEACHERS' ASSOCIATION. (1999, April). Action line: Helping your grieving student. Action line [Online]. Available: http://www.msta.nea.org/a1994_grief.html.

MCLAUGHLIN, M. A. (1995). Life, death, and the Catholic child. In E. A. Grollman (Ed.), *Bereaved children and teens: A support guide for parents and professionals* (pp. 129–140). Boston: Beacon Press.

NAGY, M. (1948). The child's theories concerning death. *Journal of Genetic Psychology, 73,* 27.

PETTLE, S. A., & BRITTEN, C. M. (1995). Talking with children about death and dying. *Child: Care Health and Development 21,* 395–404.

SCHUMACHER, J. D. (1984). Helping children cope with a sibling's death. *Family Therapy Collections, 8,* 82–94.

WHARTON, R. H., LEVINE, K., & JELLENIK, M. S. (1993). Pediatrician's role after hospital-based death and permanent disability in school-aged children. *Clinical Pediatrics, 32,* 675–680.

WORDEN, W. (1996). *Children and grief: When a parent dies.* New York: Guilford Press.

PART THREE

Physiological Conditions

CHAPTER 10

Chronic Medical Problems

WITH DR. JOANNE SETTEL, PH.D., PROFESSOR OF BIOLOGY,
BALTIMORE CITY COMMUNITY COLLEGE

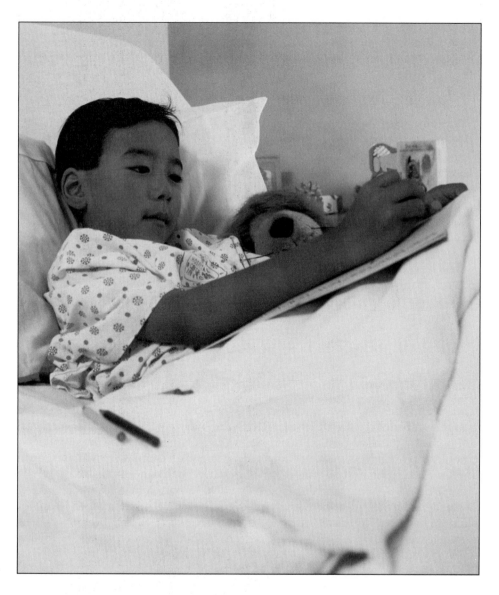

OBJECTIVE

After reading this chapter, you should be able to describe how chronic illness affects children. You should also know how a knowledge of common illnesses will help prepare you to meet the specific needs of children with medical problems and their healthy peers.

CHAPTER OUTLINE

WHO HAS CHRONIC MEDICAL PROBLEMS?

Chronic illnesses such as asthma, diabetes, epilepsy, and sickle-cell anemia afflict a large number of children in the United States. A chronic illness is a medical condition that requires continued treatment. Various estimates place the numbers of chronically ill children in the millions. According to an estimate by Hobbs, Perrin, and Irey (1985), 7.5 million children in the United States under the age of 18 have chronic illnesses. More recently, Goldberg (1990) reported that 1 million children in the United States are afflicted with severe chronic illness and another 10 million children have less significant chronic disorders. Newacheck and Taylor (1992) additionally report that, nationwide, 31 percent of children under the age of 18 have chronic conditions.

EFFECTS OF ILLNESS ON CHILDREN

Children with chronic medical conditions bring additional baggage to the classroom. Not only are they dealing with trying to learn their school subjects, but they are also dealing with learning to cope with their chronic medical condition. The impact of the illness on the child's school experience will depend largely on the child's age and developmental level.

Young Children

Illness of younger children is usually managed by their parents. It is the parent who has to make sure that the child takes the proper medication at the proper time. Parents control the diets of younger children. The following situation in a kindergarten illustrates the point that younger children often don't mind having a special diet: Ashley proudly announced to her kindergarten class members that her father would be bringing in cupcakes for a snack in honor of her birthday. She also noted that she would have a special cupcake because she was allergic and couldn't eat "the regular stuff." When the cupcakes were served, Alice asked Ashley if she could taste her cupcake. Alice announced to the other children, "It tastes good."

Adolescents

Adolescents want to blend in and be the same as their peers. To an adolescent it is a big deal to stand out as different. A physician reported the following story to me:

> I was having a particularly difficult time in getting 16-year-old Martha to manage her diabetes. Martha knew why she had to eat a controlled diet, but rebelled at having to stand out and be different. All of her friends went out after school and feasted on doughnuts, candy, and soda, and she wanted to be a member of the group and do the same. Regardless of the medical consequences, Martha did not want to stand out and not eat what everybody else was eating.

The drive to conform is so strong that many adolescents like Martha will face life-threatening consequences in order not to stand out from their peers.

THE TEACHER'S ROLE WITH CHILDREN WITH CHRONIC MEDICAL PROBLEMS

As a teacher with a student who has a chronic illness, you need to do the following:

- Work with the student's parents.
- Have a knowledge of the illness and its process and what action to take in an emergency.
- Know how to include the child in the classroom.

With the large number of chronically ill children in the population, there is a high probability that most teachers will, at some point, work with one or more of these children in the classroom. A survey of North Carolina public school teachers conducted by Johnson, Lubker, and Fowler (1988) found that 78 percent of respondents had taught children with chronic health conditions at some time during their career. Although most teachers encounter these children, studies indicate that teachers do not feel that they have adequate information about chronic illnesses (Johnson, Lubker, & Fowler, 1988; Lynch, Lewis, & Murphy, 1993).

To more effectively meet the needs of the chronically ill child, teachers need to be well informed in several important areas, including the best ways of working with parents, the basic elements of the disease process and relevant aspects of medical management, and the best approach to including the child in the classroom.

Working with Parents of Younger Children

An important aspect of working with the parents of a child with a chronic illness is the formation of a partnership between the teacher and the parent. In developing this relationship, the teacher needs to understand that the chronic illness of a child is a stressor affecting the entire family (Cherry, 1989; Eiser, 1990; Hauenstein, 1990; Kazak, 1989; Koch-Hattem, 1987; Patterson, 1991; Patterson & Gerber, 1991; Pless & Nolan, 1991). Families must deal with the pain of watching a loved one suffer, as well as worries about the child's health, medical crisis periods, nights in hospitals, scared siblings, and bills for medical care. Teachers need to understand the stresses parents are facing, and to form a partnership with the parents of children who have chronic illnesses.

Parents are usually the best people to provide information about a disease and how their child copes with it, but some parents fear that teachers will be insensitive in handling confidential information about their children. Often parents are afraid that their child will be teased if, for example, the other children find out that he has to take drugs for his epilepsy.

In a written note sent to the home, as well as in the initial parent-teacher group meeting, you should inform parents about the reasons why you need to know what is going on in the child's life, and about the ways in which you will safeguard any personal information (Frieman, 1993). A teacher might send a note like the following home to parents at the beginning of each year:

> Anything that happens in the life of your child this year—be it medical, psychological, or changes in your family—will affect the way your child performs in school. I need to know what is happening in your child's life and within your family so that I can best help your child.
>
> As a teacher I am bound by legal and ethical guidelines in dealing with any confidential information you will share with me. Information you share with me will be shared with other school professionals only if I feel that they need to know that information in order to help your child. They, of course, are bound by the same ethical and legal restrictions as I am.

Working with Parents of Adolescents

Parents still play an important role in helping the teacher understand older children with medical problems. These parents are still the "experts" in understanding their child's illness and how she copes with it. As a teacher, you need to incorporate them into the learning partnership, but with an eye to making sure that the child does not lose status with her peers. While talking in a support group, Jara's parents volunteered the following story:

> When asked about American Education Week, Jara, an eighth-grader, announced to her parents that "nobody" was visiting the school. Her parents insisted that they would indeed visit the school. Jara laid down the law. If they did visit her classroom, they would have to obey several rules. They could not tell anybody whose parents they were. They could not talk to her. They could not even look at her. They could talk to no other children, because if they did she would be "humiliated."

Interactions with parents of adolescents is essential, but it must be done discretely to avoid embarrassing the child. It might be better to have conversations over the phone so the parent can avoid a visit to the school.

With older children, both teachers and parents have to work in concert to empower the adolescent to take control over her medical condition. Teachers can often help youngsters with strategies for dealing with their peers. For example, Martha needs a strategy for covering up her diabetic diet. She might not want to tell her friends that she cannot eat doughnuts because she is diabetic, but she might be willing to tell them that she won't eat that stuff because it is fattening.

Obviously, the goal is for a person to be able to routinely mention their physical condition without any embarrassment or concern about how others will react. Hopefully most individuals will adopt this mature position after adolescence. Of course, some children are strong enough to deal with their medical conditions, but teachers should not expect to find this attitude in all children with a chronic illness.

Knowledge of the Disease Process

Another important element in the process of effectively meeting the needs of a chronically ill child is for the teacher to have a basic knowledge of the process of the child's disease and relevant aspects of medical management. With this information, the teacher not only will be able to teach the other children in the class about the disease, but also will be prepared to meet the child's medical needs within the classroom.

Teachers also need to be prepared to answer questions that other children might have about the various medical conditions. Some conditions look scary to a child, and they generate irrational fears, giving rise to questions like these:

Can you catch diabetes?

Will that happen to me?

Will Johnny die?

What do I do if Sara has a seizure?

Imagine what a seizure would look like to a young child who had no idea what was happening. It might be terrifying.

You can help the child with the medical problem by talking about the condition with the entire class. One can deal with the issue of the child's privacy by asking the child for permission to talk to the class about various medical conditions. A discussion of diabetes at an appropriate developmental level can take the mystery out of the condition and reduce the fears of children who are healthy and worry about getting the disease.

Trained school professionals can administer medications to children if they have a prescription with exact instructions from the child's physician. Many schools have trained nurses who can respond to any medical emergency.

Teachers, however, need to be prepared to take action in certain circumstances. Teachers should demand that they get emergency instructions from trained medical personnel before a child with a chronic medical condition is placed in their classroom. For example, if you have an epileptic child in your classroom, you need to be trained in how to react if the child has a seizure. Every school should have professional medical personnel ready as backup for the teacher who must handle a medical emergency, but it is always better if teachers feel comfortable dealing with emergency situations themselves.

COMMON MEDICAL CONDITIONS

We will discuss four of the most common medical conditions in schoolchildren. If you as the teacher understand the facts of the medical condition, you will be better prepared to help the children in your class.

Asthma

Asthma afflicts roughly 12 million Americans, approximately 5 percent of the U.S. population. A majority of asthma cases are diagnosed in children between the ages of 2 and 17. Asthma is the leading cause of disease and disability in this age group (Daniele, 1988).

The Disease Process

Asthma is a condition in which the person experiences difficulty breathing as a result of a narrowing of small airways in the lungs. These airways, known as bronchi and bronchioles, form a complex network of tubes that transport air to the deep tissues of the lungs. During normal breathing, the bronchi and bronchioles are opened and air passes easily through them. During an asthmatic attack, these airways become blocked, causing shortness of breath, chest tightness, wheezing, and coughing.

Several factors contribute to the problems that lead to asthmatic attacks. Most asthmatics have some persistent inflammation of the tissues that line the bronchi and bronchioles. As the linings of these airways swell, their openings narrow. The swollen airways become highly sensitive to a variety of environmental irritants. Irritants can trigger one or more reactions, leading to increased blockage of already narrowed passageways. These reactions include increased inflammation, spasmodic contractions of smooth muscles that surround the airways, and excess mucus production. The following factors can trigger asthmatic attacks (National Jewish Center for Immunology and Respiratory Medicine, 1992):

- Allergic reactions to pollens, mold spores, animal dander, certain chemicals, and other allergens
- Nonallergic sensitivities to aspirin and food additives
- Respiratory tract infections
- Exercise
- Irritants such as cigarette smoke, aerosol sprays, and strong odors

Classroom Medical Management

A teacher with an asthmatic student should be alert to signs of an asthma attack. These can include wheezing, shortness of breath, and excessive coughing after exercise. If an asthmatic child seems to be having trouble breathing, the teacher should calmly take the child aside and have him sit, relax, and catch his breath. The youngster should be encouraged to focus and breathe deeply. The teacher could model deep breathing and encourage the child to follow along. It can also be helpful to have the child sip warm water. When these techniques are not effective, the teacher should seek help (National Jewish Center for Immunology and Respiratory Medicine, 1992).

Diabetes Mellitus

According to the Centers for Disease Control and Prevention, approximately 7.2 million people in the United States have diabetes. Of those, 5 to 10 percent have Type I diabetes, the kind most common in children (Centers for Disease Control, 1991).

The Disease Process

Diabetes mellitus is a disease that impairs the body's ability to use glucose to obtain energy. Glucose, a form of sugar, is the preferred energy source for the body's cells. It is formed during the digestion of starches and sugars. It can also be manufactured by the liver from breakdown products of fats and proteins.

For cells to adequately take in glucose, the hormone insulin must be present. Insulin is produced by the pancreas, a flat organ located just under the stomach. In children with Type I (insulin-dependent, or juvenile) diabetes, the pancreas produces little or no insulin. Without insulin, glucose levels build in the blood and urine. At the same time, because it can't use sugar for energy, the body burns stored fats for energy. The breakdown of fats results in the release of acidic chemicals called ketones. These can become poisonous when they build up in the blood. Without proper treatment, a diabetic can fall into a coma and require hospitalization (Tortora & Grabowski, 1993; Olefsky, 1988).

The Daily Routine for Type I Diabetics

A child with Type I diabetes must take steps to ensure that glucose blood levels are kept close to normal. To do this, the child must control food, insulin, and exercise. The diabetic child will need to take one or more injections of insulin a day. The child might also require a midmorning and/or a midafternoon snack. It is important that snacks and meals be eaten at a regularly scheduled time, to ensure that insulin and glucose levels are kept in balance. A diabetic child might also need to test her blood sugar, using a finger prick method, at several times during the day.

Classroom Medical Management

A teacher of a diabetic child should keep an emergency supply of sugar cubes, fruit juice, or lifesavers on hand. The teacher should also be aware of two important facts:

- Food makes glucose levels rise.
- Exercise and insulin make glucose levels fall.

If the child has eaten too little food, exercised vigorously without eating, or taken too much insulin, she might experience a drop in glucose levels known as hypoglycemia. These are the symptoms of hypoglycemia:

- Confusion, inattention, inappropriate responses, crankiness
- Drowsiness
- Pale complexion, perspiration
- Headache
- Lack of coordination, dizziness
- Trembling
- Sudden hunger

Teacher's should consult with the child's physician and develop a plan to help the child if he experiences hypoglycemia. Most physicians will suggest that the teacher provide sugar immediately. The sugar can be in the form of

2 large sugar cubes, or

½ cup of fruit juice, or

regular soda, or

6 or 7 candy mints.

If the child does not improve in 10 to 15 minutes, the teacher should continue to provide sugar and call the parent or physician.

Thus, the teacher needs to help the child monitor her intake of food and insulin during the day. Diabetic children should be given advance notice before exercise, so that they can make the appropriate adjustments. An emergency supply of appropriate sugar products or snacks could be provided by the parent for the teacher to keep in reserve.

Epilepsy

Approximately 1 out of every 100 people have some form of epilepsy. Epileptic disorders can result from either inherited genetic factors or head injuries and infections that cause injury to the brain. In many cases, epilepsy can be adequately controlled with medications that prevent seizures. However, depending on the individual, teachers still might encounter children who have seizures in the classroom (Engle, 1988; Epilepsy Foundation of America, 1989a, 1989b).

The Disease Process

Epilepsy is the common name for more than twenty types of seizure disorder. Individuals with epilepsy experience recurrent seizures, involving temporary overactivity in the electrical discharges in some or all of the brain. Seizures tend to be brief, lasting only seconds or minutes. They might involve obvious symptoms such as convulsions and loss of consciousness, or more subtle changes such as dazed behavior and altered sensory experience. Once a seizure is over, the individual returns to normal functioning.

Classroom Medical Management

Because seizures can take a wide variety of forms, and behavior during a seizure often resembles normal classroom behavior, it is important that teachers recognize these signs of a seizure in young children:

- Short periods of inattentive, unresponsive, or dazed behavior
- Sudden unexplained falls
- Unusual sleepiness, and irritability when wakened from sleep
- Rapid blinking, head nodding or eyes rolling upward
- Repeated complaints that things look, smell, feel, or taste odd
- Repeated unnatural movements of the mouth or face
- Involuntary jerking of an arm or leg

Teachers should be aware of the fact that a single occurrence of one of these symptoms in a child does not necessarily indicate that the child has a seizure disorder. However, if the teacher observes repeated occurrences of these symptoms in a child not known to have epilepsy, it is important that the teacher submit a follow-up report to both school authorities and parents.

General Guidelines for Responding to a Seizure

The response to the seizure will depend upon what type of seizure the child is having. In general, once a seizure has begun, there is nothing that can be done to stop it. The teacher, however, can do a number of things to keep the child from injuring herself and to maintain calm in the classroom.

Generalized Tonic Clonic Seizures

Generalized tonic clonic seizures are convulsions involving massive jerking movements and unconsciousness. The teacher will need to let the seizure run its course and protect the child from injury. The child should not be restrained, and it is vital that the teacher *not* force the child's mouth open, hold the tongue, or place anything in the mouth. The teacher can turn the child gently onto his side to allow fluid to drain from his mouth. Something soft should be placed under the child's head, and any hard, sharp objects should be moved out of the way.

When the seizure ends, the child should rest until he is fully awake. At this time, the teacher might offer the child a drink of water.

If a seizure lasts beyond 5 minutes, or if the child seems to pass from one seizure to another without regaining consciousness, the teacher should call for medical assistance immediately.

Partial Seizures

Partial seizures involve a variety of aimless, unresponsive, or automatic behaviors lasting 1 to 2 minutes. If the child is moving around the room, the teacher should respond by taking the child's arm gently and calmly guiding her to a quiet spot in the classroom where she can sit down. If the child is seated, the teacher should allow the seizure to take its course, while ensuring that the child is not in danger of injury. Following the seizure, the child might be confused, and it might be necessary to re-orient her to her environment (Epilepsy Foundation of America, 1992).

Sickle-Cell Anemia

In the United States, sickle-cell anemia occurs most commonly in African Americans and Hispanics of Caribbean ancestry. Individuals with sickle-cell disease have inherited two genes for sickle cell, one from each parent. Individuals who carry only one gene for sickle cell have sickle-cell trait.

It is estimated that about 1 in 12 African American adults has sickle-cell trait. These carriers have normal health but can pass the sickle-cell gene on to their children. Sickle-cell disease occurs in roughly 1 in every 400 African Americans (National Institutes of Health, 1990).

The Disease Process

Sickle-cell anemia is an inherited disorder of the red blood cells involving painful episodes of reduced blood flow to vital organs. The disease results from an abnormality in a chemical found in red blood cells called hemoglobin. Hemoglobin molecules pick up oxygen from the lungs and release it in other parts of the body. All tissues of the body must have this oxygen to stay alive.

In individuals with sickle-cell disease, the abnormal hemoglobin molecules tend to change their form when they release large amounts of oxygen. The altered hemoglobin molecules stick together, creating long, rigid rods inside the red blood cells. These rods make the red blood cells change from their natural round shape, to a curved or sickle shape.

There are several problems with sickled red blood cells. Unlike normal red blood cells, which have a life span of 120 days, the delicate sickle cells last in the blood for only 10 to 20 days. The red blood cells are lost more rapidly than the bone marrow can replace them, and the individual develops anemia. A child with anemia may be pale, easily fatigued, and short of breath.

A second problem with sickle cells is that they are stiff, no longer flexible enough to squeeze through tiny blood vessels. Occasionally these cells will clump together, clogging the small blood vessels and blocking the transport of oxygen to the tissues of a particular organ or joint. This produces episodes of pain and damages the oxygen-starved tissues (Forget, 1988).

A sickle-cell episode can last for hours or days and is sometimes serious enough to require hospitalization. Individuals with sickle-cell disease vary greatly in the number of episodes they experience. Some have very infrequent episodes; others have as many as twenty a year.

Classroom Medical Management

The teacher should understand that a sickle-cell crisis can occur without warning, causing a child to experience sudden excruciating pain in the back, chest, or extremities. Exercise can sometimes lead to a crisis, but often there is no obvious external trigger (Forget, 1988).

If a crisis occurs in the classroom, the teacher should offer the child water or juice and keep the child comfortable and calm until his parents can pick him up.

CLASSROOM INCLUSION

The chronically ill child is a normal child and not a disease. You need to expect the same standards of acceptable behavior from the chronically ill child as you do from any other child. The child should be praised when praise is appropriate and disciplined when necessary. Even with a child who has a serious illness, you must set appropriate limits for behavior.

There are, however, several areas where the teacher needs to make accommodations for the chronically ill child. The classroom environment must be compatible with the medical restrictions of the child. For example, the dietary restrictions of the diabetic child need to be considered before cooking experiences are planned. Classroom teachers must also anticipate the sensitivity of some asthmatic children to animal dander and strong odors. High school science teachers might have to be particularly sensitive to this issue. When this is a problem, the teacher can advise the cleaning staff of the child's condition so that they can avoid using powerful cleaning materials in the classroom.

A teacher can also help a child deal with the fact that she does not have control over her condition by being sensitive to the child's special needs. For example, children with some conditions will need a warning before engaging in strenuous physical activities so they can adjust their food intake or medications. A diabetic child might have to make some adjustment in their diet or insulin input before physical activity, and some asthmatic children might need to premedicate themselves before physical exertion. When a child has to miss school for periods of time, the teacher needs to keep him connected with his peers. This can be done in a number of ways. For example, the children might write a daily classroom message to the child or use a portable phone to call the child directly from the classroom to discuss their daily activities.

An Emergency Medical Plan

Teachers should have an emergency medical plan written out for each chronically ill child in their classroom. The plan should be prepared by parents, in consultation with their child's physician. Teachers need to memorize each child's emergency plan so that when a child has a crisis, the teacher will be able to re-act quickly and confidently. All school personnel should be informed of the medical plan, including the janitors.

Teaching the Other Children

All children in the classroom could benefit from understanding chronic ill-nesses. In the past it was common to ignore any reference to a child's illness and pretend that it didn't exist. This strategy is like having an elephant in the class-room but never talking about it. It is there, all the children know it, and by not talking about the obvious the teacher gives the message that there is something wrong. The illness should be discussed as naturally as one would discuss any other biological issue.

Teachers can help break down stereotypes about chronic illness by teaching children the facts about the disease as part of a science unit focusing on the hu-man body. Diseases can be springboards for interesting science lessons on such topics as how we breathe (asthma), how the brain works (epilepsy), how blood carries oxygen (sickle-cell disease), and how our bodies use food (diabetes).

One can teach children that the proper response to a child with a medical problem is compassion and not teasing. Children can also be informed that chronic illness is not communicable. By explaining why the chronically ill child has the particular disease, the teacher can alleviate the fears of the other children who might worry that they too will come down with the disease.

Informed children will not be as frightened when there is a medical crisis in the classroom. If and when a medical emergency does arise, the children who have been prepared will respond in a helpful and supportive manner. When children understand what a seizure is, for example, they will not be horrified when one of their classmates has one. Instead they will be able to respond with concern, support, and understanding.

HOSPITALIZATION

It is possible that a child with a chronic illness will be hospitalized during the school year. If a child is hospitalized, your job is to help her keep current with her schoolwork and keep in contact with her classmates.

Keeping up with schoolwork gives the child a chance to be in touch with her normal life, and gives her the message that she will be returning to school. Al-though many hospitals have special teachers on staff, your input is important. With a few key assignments you can keep the youngster connected to her nor-mal class.

The telephone is a lifeline to connect the child who is hospitalized with her school friends. You can arrange a time when classmates are allowed to call. Classmates can call during the day from a school phone. The Internet is another channel of communication if the hospital has a phone line and the sick child has a computer.

Before the child returns to school, you need to prepare the class for her reentry. If the child will have a change in appearance, you can discuss that with the class and help them figure out how they will approach their returning classmate.

When the child who was hospitalized returns, give her the option of talking to the class about her experience. Younger children usually enjoy being in the spotlight, but older children might not want to talk about their experience, and their feelings should be respected.

Summary

By understanding how chronic illness affects children you will be better able to deal with the children in your classroom. A knowledge of common illnesses will prepare you to meet the specific needs of children with medical problems and their healthy peers. Parents and other professionals are valuable allies in helping you meet the needs of children in your classroom with chronic medical problems.

RESEARCH IDEAS

Questions to Investigate

1. Will telling children about a disease make them afraid?
2. Should a student's disease be discussed openly, or is the student entitled to privacy?
3. How involved should parents be in the medical treatment of their adolescents?

Resources to Explore

American Academy of Pediatrics
http://www.aap.org

American Psychological Association
http://www.apa.org

National Institutes of Health
http://www.nih.gov

References

CENTERS FOR DISEASE CONTROL. (1991). *National health interview survey.* Washington, DC: U.S. Government Printing Office.
CHERRY, D. B. (1989). Stress and coping in families with ill or disabled children: Application of a model to pediatric therapy. *Physical and Occupational Therapy in Pediatrics, 9,* 11–32.
DANIELE, R. P. (1988). Asthma. In J. B. Wyngaarden & L. H. Smith, Jr. (Eds.), *Cecil textbook of medicine: Part 7. Respiratory diseases.* Philadelphia: W. B. Saunders.
EISER, C. (1990). Psychological effects of chronic disease. *Journal of Child Psychology and Psychiatry and Allied Disciplines, 31,* 85–98.
ENGLE, J., JR. (1988). The epilepsies. In J. B. Wyngaarden & L. H. Smith, Jr. (Eds.), *Cecil textbook of medicine: Part 22. Neurologic and behavioral diseases* (pp. 2217–2228). Philadelphia: W. B. Saunders.

EPILEPSY FOUNDATION OF AMERICA. (1989a). *Recognizing the signs of childhood seizures.* Landover, MD: Author.

EPILEPSY FOUNDATION OF AMERICA. (1989b). *Seizure recognition and first aid.* Landover, MD: Author.

EPILEPSY FOUNDATION OF AMERICA. (1992). *The teacher's role.* Landover, MD: Author.

FORGET, B. G. (1988). Sickle-cell anemia and associated hemoglobinopathies. In J. B. Wyngaarden & L. H. Smith, Jr. (Eds.), *Cecil textbook of medicine: Part 12. Hematologic diseases* (pp. 936–941). Philadelphia: W. B. Saunders.

FRIEMAN, B. B. (1993). What early childhood teachers need to know about troubled children in therapy. *Dimensions of Early Childhood, 21,* 21–24.

GOLDBERG, B. (1990). Children, sports, and chronic disease. *Physician and Sportsmedicine, 18,* 44–50, 53–54, 56.

HAUENSTEIN, E. J. (1990). The experience of distress in parents of chronically ill children: Potential or likely outcome? *Journal of Clinical Child Psychology, 19,* 356–364.

HOBBS, N., PERRIN, J. M., & IREYS, H. J. (1985). *Chronically ill children and their families.* San Francisco: Jossey-Bass.

JOHNSON, M. P., LUBKER, B. B., & FOWLER, M. G. (1988). Teacher needs assessment for the educational management of children with chronic illness. *Journal of School Health, 58,* 232–235.

KAZAK, A. E. (1989). Families of chronically ill children: A system and social-ecological model of adaptation and challenge. *Journal of Consulting and Clinical Psychology, 57,* 25–30.

KOCH-HATTEM, A. (1987). Families and chronic illness. *Family Therapy Collections, 22,* 33–50.

LYNCH, E. W., LEWIS, R. B., & MURPHY, D. S. (1993). Educational services for children with chronic illnesses: Perspectives of educators and families. *Exceptional Children, 59,* 210–220.

NATIONAL INSTITUTES OF HEALTH. (1990). *Sickle-cell anemia* (NIH Publication No. 90-3058). Washington, DC: U.S. Government Printing Office.

NATIONAL JEWISH CENTER FOR IMMUNOLOGY AND RESPIRATORY MEDICINE. (1992). *Understanding asthma.* Colorado: Author.

NEWACHECK, P. W., & TAYLOR, W. R. (1992). Childhood illness: Prevalence, severity, and impact. *American Journal of Public Health, 82,* 364–371.

OLEFSKY, J. M., (1988). Diabetes mellitus. In J. B. Wyngaarden & L. H. Smith, Jr. (Eds.), *Cecil textbook of medicine: Part 16. Endocrine and reproductive diseases* (pp. 1360–1380). Philadelphia: W. B. Saunders.

PATTERSON, J. M. (1991). A family systems perspective for working with youth with disability. *Pediatrician, 18,* 129–141.

PATTERSON, J. M., & GERBER, G. (1991). Preventing mental health problems in children with chronic illness or disability. *Children's Health Care, 20,* 150–161.

PLESS, I. B., & NOLAN, T. (1991). Revision, replication and neglect: Research on maladjustment in chronic illness. *Journal of Child Psychology and Psychiatry and Allied Disciplines, 32,* 347–365.

TORTORA, G., & GRABOWSKI, S. R. (1993). *Principles of anatomy and physiology.* New York: HarperCollins.

CHAPTER 11

Children with Attention Deficit Hyperactivity Disorder

OBJECTIVE

After reading this chapter, you should be able to describe the biological condition ADHD. You should also be able to discuss the role teachers can play in helping children with ADHD.

CHAPTER OUTLINE

THROUGH THE EYES OF A CHILD

William, one of the boys in my therapy group, looked like all the other sixth-grade boys in his middle school. From his haircut to his baggy jeans, he fit right in with his classmates. He was a bright guy who could have an intelligent conversation with you about what was going on in the world, yet he did things that dramatically set him apart and made him an easy target for his peers' jokes.

In history class, two of his classmates whispered to William to make noises like a pig. William didn't wait until the teacher's back was turned, nor did he try to disguise where the noise was coming from. He stood up while the history teacher was talking and preceded to oink. The other students in the class laughed, but the teacher was not amused and gave him detention.

When I asked him why he did it, he replied, "Because they told me to." I asked, "Did you think about what the teacher might do when you oinked." "No", he replied. "I just did it."

Ethan, another one of the middle school group members, also did impulsive things. He was standing in the lunch line and for no reason punched the guy standing in front of him. As it turned out, this boy was the biggest, toughest, meanest boy in the middle school. He responded by punching Ethan so hard that he was knocked to the floor. Ethan was noticed by the teacher in charge and received after-school detention for himself and the guy who punched him back.

After the incident, I asked Ethan, "Why did you choose to punch him?" "I don't know," he replied. I asked, "Did you think about what this kid would do to you if you punched him?" Ethan told me, "The thought never crossed my mind at the time. I just did it. I didn't think."

A tendency to perform impulsive acts sets William and Ethan apart from their peers. Both have a horrible time with peers, seem to be the brunt of all the jokes, and are always picked on by the other boys in the class. As a result, both of them have very low self-esteem, and both think of themselves as "losers."

IDENTIFYING CHILDREN WITH ADHD

Ethan and William have been diagnosed as having attention deficit hyperactivity disorder (ADHD). The essential feature of ADHD is a persistent pattern of inattention and/or hyperactivity-impulsivity that is more frequent and severe than is typically observed in individuals at a similar level of development (American Psychiatric Association, 1994, p. 78.)

The diagnostic criteria for ADHD are spelled out in the *Diagnostic and Statistical Manual of Mental Disorders,* 4th edition, published by the American Psychiatric Association (1994). This book, referred to as the *DSM-IV,* gives the following diagnostic criteria for attention deficit hyperactivity disorder:

> The person will have six or more of the following symptoms of either inattention or impulsivity, which have persisted for at least six months, to a degree that is maladaptive and inconsistent with developmental level:
>
> Inattention
>
> 1. often fails to give close attention to details or makes careless mistakes in schoolwork, work, or other activities
> 2. often has difficulty sustaining attention in tasks or play activities
> 3. often does not seem to listen when spoken to directly
> 4. often does not follow through on instructions and fails to finish schoolwork
> 5. often has difficulty organizing tasks and activities
> 6. often avoids, or is reluctant to engage in, tasks like homework which require sustained mental effort
> 7. often loses things necessary for school assignments such as pencils, papers, and books
> 8. is easily distracted in the classroom by extraneous stimuli
> 9. is often forgetful in daily activities
>
> OR
>
> Hyperactivity-Impulsivity
> Hyperactivity
>
> 1. often fidgets with hands or feet or squirms in seat
> 2. often leaves seat in classroom or in other situations in which remaining seated is expected

3. often runs about or climbs excessively in situations in which it is inappropriate (an adolescent may have feelings of restlessness)
4. often has difficulty playing quietly
5. is often "on the go" or acts as if "driven by a motor"
6. often talks excessively

Impulsivity

7. often blurts out answers before questions have been completed
8. often has difficulty awaiting a turn
9. often interrupts or intrudes on others [e.g., intrudes into conversations or games]

A diagnosis of ADHD requires that some of these symptoms have been present since before 7 years of age. Impairment from the symptoms has to be present in two or more settings, such as school and home. There must be clear evidence of clinically significant impairment in social and academic functioning. Finally, other, more serious mental disorders must be ruled out as causes of this condition.

THE ORGANIC NATURE OF ADHD

Rhee and others (1999) point out that approximately 5 percent of children are affected by ADHD, and more boys are affected than girls. Searight and McLaren (1998) point out that during the past decade there has been an increase in the diagnosis and treatment of ADHD. They feel that the reasons for the increased ADHD prevalence include changes in diagnostic standards and the rapid effects of stimulant medication on cognitive functioning. They further note that social, cultural, and economic factors can also contribute to increased diagnosis.

All of the evidence suggests that ADHD is an organic condition. Faraone and Biederman (1998) note that family, twin, adoption, and molecular genetic studies show that ADHD has a substantial genetic component.

The workings of the brains of some children with ADHD seem to be different from the norm. These children have behaviors over which they have little or no control. They just act and don't think about the consequences of their action. It is often hard for parents and others to understand why children with ADHD behave as they do. If you are not impulsive and you think about what you do before you do it, you might have a difficult time understanding why a child with ADHD doesn't exert self-control. Many kids describe it as "like being controlled by an alien force over which you have no control."

Many children with ADHD also have learning disabilities, and many are quite bright. This suggests that they have the intellectual ability to do well in school if they can learn to deal with their ADHD.

Bussing and others (1998) looked at special education students to see how many of them who qualified for the diagnosis of ADHD were actually receiving care for the condition. They found that girls were more than three times as likely as boys to have unmet service needs. Minority status, low income, and health maintenance organization coverage also emerged as possible risk factors for unmet service needs.

EFFECTS OF ADHD

The consequences of the child's impulsive behavior, inattention, and hyperactivity affect him at home with his parents and in school with his teachers and peers. As a side effect of these difficulties, the child's self-concept suffers.

Impulsive Behavior

Impulsive behavior can affect a child with his family. William's mother discusses how her son's impulsive behavior affected him at home:

> I love my son. He is a great kid, with a wonderful heart. Sometimes he will just come over to me and give me a hug and tell me that he loves me. He really wants to do the right thing, but often really causes havoc in the house. He blurts out just the wrong thing at the wrong time and sets his father off, and does something inappropriate to anger his big brother. I know he is really a great kid, but he is hard to raise.

As a consequence of William's impulsiveness, his parents are often frustrated at home and complain of being burned out from the stress generated by their child's behavior. Worst of all, they say, is their feeling of helplessness because they are unable to make things better for their child.

The behavior of the child with ADHD frequently spills over and affects other members of the family. The target of impulsive behavior is often a sibling, who has to deal with living with an impulsive person every day. This has caused Kendall (1998) to suggest that there is a need for increased social and mental health services for all members of the family of children who have ADHD.

Impulsiveness also has a consequence in school. Children with ADHD do not fit in easily with their peer group. In the younger grades, children with ADHD do impulsive acts such as hitting another child, grabbing a crayon from someone, or blurting out inappropriate remarks or insults. These behaviors make other children mad and less inclined to play with the child with ADHD.

As they reach adolescence and acceptance by the peer group becomes more important, their isolation becomes more problematic. Adolescent children with ADHD stand out as different during a developmental phase when all children want to blend in with the group.

Inattentive Behavior

A child's inattentive behaviors affect him at home and at school. One father describes his frustration in dealing with his son's inattention at home:

> I can't understand why he won't listen to me. I've told him a million times to wash his hands before dinner, but he finds a hundred other things to do instead. I can't tell you how many times I yelled at him to clean his room, but he just doesn't listen. I go in to check on him, and I find him reading a comic book. If he would just listen, he wouldn't be getting himself into trouble all of the time.

The youngster's mother expressed a different view:

> I wish I could make things better. Sometimes I just want to cry at how unhappy
> my son is at home. He is a good kid, but it seems that I am the only one who
> sees it. He is a kind, sweet boy, and it really pains me to hear his father and
> brothers yell at him all the time. He really is getting beaten down.

Some children recognize that they have a hard time staying on task, but still
have a difficult time in controlling their behavior. They can become as frustrated
at their parents.

> When I get home from school, my Dad knows I like to have a snack. He even
> keeps stuff in the house for me to eat. Sometimes while I'm eating something,
> the phone rings, or the cat comes into the room. I answer the phone or start play-
> ing with the cat and I forget to put the cookies back in the closet. This really ticks
> off my Dad. He comes home and yells at me. I tell him that I just forgot, but he
> thinks that I do it on purpose because I want to tick him off.

Inattentive behavior can also cause problems in school. In managing a group
of children in the classroom, teachers frequently have some children working at
their seats alone. The child who is constantly distracted and can't stay on task is
at a great disadvantage. Often his work doesn't get done because he became distracted by some extraneous stimuli in the classroom.

Hyperactivity

Hyperactive behavior is often a problem at home. Because of Jeremy's hyperactivity, his mother was surprised at the amount of energy she needed to parent
her first-grader.

> He takes ten times more work than my other kids put together. He stays up un-
> til 11:00 o'clock and requires me to constantly monitor his behavior. I never have
> any rest. Just when I relax, it seems that all hell breaks loose in the house. Home-
> work with the other kids is a snap. With Jeremy I have to constantly stay on him
> to finish his work. I'm exhausted when I finish with him.

This mother felt tired, overburdened, and greatly worried and concerned about
her child.

Teachers, too, have a challenging time in dealing with a hyperactive child in
their classrooms. It is often difficult to keep a hyperactive child in control when
you have 24 other children to manage. Many teachers leave at the end of the
school day feeling exhausted from having managed a hyperactive child.

Self-Concept

Low self-esteem is a characteristic of children with ADHD. These kids constantly do things that call attention to themselves and frequently get them in
trouble with their parents, teachers and peers.

It is hard to like yourself when your parents, peers, and teachers are constantly reminding you that you are not performing up to expectations. Ten-year-
old Sarah's comments are typical of many children with ADHD:

I can't seem to ever do anything right. I'm constantly being yelled at by my mother and my teacher. Nobody wants to be my friend either. I wish I were like the other kids in my class and didn't have a messed-up brain.

Life can be a struggle for children with ADHD. Everything is hard—home, school, the neighborhood. The constant negative feedback from family, school, and peers can wear away the confidence that is necessary for success in life.

TREATMENT OF CHILDREN WITH ADHD

There are various treatment options available to help a child with ADHD, ranging from medication to behavioral therapy and other forms of family therapy. We will focus on drug therapies.

The use of medications is perhaps the most controversial therapy approach. Psychostimulants such as Ritalin (methylphenidate) work as calming agents in people with ADHD. The mechanism by which a drug that usually causes hyperactivity can calm children with ADHD is currently unknown (Gainetdinov et al., 1999). It is estimated that as many as 5 million children in America are being medicated with psychostimulants for ADHD (Widener, 1998).

Like most drugs, psychostimulants have side effects. These are some of the side effects that have been reported (Barkley, 1990):

- Insomnia
- Reduced appetite
- Headaches
- Stomachache
- Irritability

Physicians who prescribe drugs will often ask teachers to give them periodic reports on the child's behavior in school, in order to help them adjust the dosage of the medication.

Not everyone agrees with the use of drugs with children. Panksepp (1998) raises some provocative questions about the use of psychotropic medications. For example, he wonders if what is diagnosed as ADHD is simply a natural variant of human personality. He also questions the long-term effects of these medications.

THE TEACHER'S ROLE IN HELPING CHILDREN WITH ADHD

The classroom teachers play a multifaceted role in the education of children with ADHD. Teachers can help these children by doing the following:

- Identifying the problem
- Advocating for these children with school and medical officials
- Collaborating with other professionals to coordinate care

- Creating a good environment in the classroom
- Using good classroom management skills

Identifying the Problem

Teachers are often the first to identify ADHD in a child. Teachers are quick to spot a child who behaves differently and can point out these behavior to parents. Most often, parents will be relieved to have the problem identified. Arcia and Fernandez (1998) found that once mothers classified their children's behavior as atypical, they actively sought assistance from professionals. One mother, who talked about how she felt when her daughter's teacher suggested that there was a problem, illustrates the point:

> I thought that something was different. She is my only child, so I don't have any others to compare her to, but I know that she is different than my friends' kids. My friends don't seem to be as tired with their kids. I thought that maybe it was me. Now I know that there is a real problem and I have to get her help.

A formal diagnosis of ADHD can be made by several kinds of professionals—psychiatrists, psychologists, pediatricians, family physicians, and neurologists. Neurologists are physicians who work with disorders of the brain and nervous system. In terms of treatment, only medical doctors can prescribe medications.

Advocating for the Child

Once you have a suspicion that something is wrong, it is your job to make sure that the child gets the appropriate help. Every public school has a procedure to identify children who qualify under the Individuals with Disabilities Education Act (IDEA). The teacher's job is to collect data in the form of classroom observations (i.e., dates, times, and descriptions of activities that were problematic), and present it to the school team. As the teacher, your job is to advocate for the children by persuading your colleagues to give them the services they need to help them be successful.

Collaborating with Other Professionals

Another role for the teacher is to work with outside therapists and physicians who are treating the child. This might involve monitoring the child's behavior and reporting weekly to a physician, or having conferences with the mental health person who is working with the child. Mental health strategies often include a cooperative plan between the teacher and the outside therapists in which both agree to a consistent, unified way to deal with the child's behavior.

Creating a Good Work Environment

Children with ADHD are a challenge for teachers. These children demand a great deal of attention, and they require constant monitoring. When dealing with these children, teachers need to be consistent and clear in their expectations.

One positive step you can take is to give the child an environment free of distractions in which to do work. Teachers also need to encourage children to be their own advocates and ask for a distraction-free environment rather than working at a desk clustered near other children. Children need to know that it is permissible for them to tell the teacher that they are being distracted and need to move. Yu Jin is a successful example of this policy. When Yu Jin, a second-grader, had to do independent reading, she preferred to read under her desk. Her teacher had encouraged her to find a place to work where she would not be distracted. The teacher's goal was to have Yu Jin reading, and she didn't care if it was at her desk or under her desk as long as she did not disturb anyone else.

Provisions can be made for middle and high school students to be able to go to quiet, nondistracting places to work. A special education resource room is one option. Another is a quiet corner in the school library. If this is not possible, teachers can set up a corner of the classroom that is shielded by a visual barrier, in which a child can work without distraction.

Other techniques can be taught to children with ADHD to help them monitor and control their attention to their schoolwork. For example, Mike frequently interrupted his fourth-grade teacher to ask him what he should be doing. His teacher taught Mike several techniques to find out what he should be doing without interrupting the class. They included looking on the chalkboard where his teacher writes the assignment, quietly asking another classmate, or raising his hand.

Peers can be helpful to children with ADHD. DuPaul and others (1998) investigated the effects of classwide peer tutoring on the performance of students with ADHD. They found that peer tutoring appears to be an effective strategy for addressing the academic and behavioral difficulties associated with ADHD.

Managing the Classroom

The key to managing any group of children is to be consistent, respectful, and fair. Even though children with ADHD might do things without thinking due to no fault of their own, they still must uphold certain standards in the classroom. Carla, a sixth-grader, pushed one of her classmates into a desk for no apparent reason. Her teacher took her aside and spoke to her privately. After asking Carla and finding out that she had no reason to push her classmate, her teacher talked to Carla about what she had done and the consequences of her act.

> Carla, I know that you just pushed Jamal and didn't mean to do any harm. But you know that pushing someone else is not an acceptable behavior in this classroom. You are a good person, and I know that sometimes you have difficulty in controlling what you do, but pushing is an unacceptable behavior. You will earn no points today.

Behavior modification schemes are good strategies to use with children with ADHD because they are concrete. You can set up an agreed-upon reward in advance, perhaps extra time on the computer, and you can give out a concrete symbol for this reward, such as a ticket, when the child is behaving appropriately.

Teachers need to go out of their way to catch the child at being "good" or behaving in a socially acceptable manner in the classroom. Once the child has an appropriate number of tickets, he earns the reward. The goal of this procedure is to reinforce the positive behavior and ignore the negative. Of course, certain negative behaviors such as pushing and hitting cannot be ignored, but other negative behavior like staring out of the window can be ignored.

Children with ADHD have a lot of energy and are often restless. Children can be taught socially acceptable ways to be restless. For example, swinging your foot under the table and kicking the table makes noise and distracts other children, but swinging your foot out of sight and not hitting the table or making noise bothers no one.

A high school student can be taught that when she is overwhelmed with the stimulation in the classroom, she can get a drink of water, take a deep breath, and then return to the classroom. The key is to allow the youngster to displace her energy in a way that will not get her into trouble.

Children with ADHD are targets for bullies and are easily victimized. These children need to be taught how to protect themselves from this harassment. A primary weapon they can learn is how to ignore the teasing so as to not let the bully get the attention he wants.

Summary

Children with ADHD have a biological condition that causes them difficulty in school, at home, and with their peers. Teachers can play a key role in helping children with ADHD by identifying the condition and working with parents and other professionals to get the child help.

Although children with ADHD are a challenge in the classroom, you can best deal with them by making adjustments to your classroom routine. Even though children with ADHD have difficulty controlling their behavior, you still have to make them accountable to your normal class rules.

RESEARCH IDEAS

Questions to Investigate

1. What causes ADHD?
2. Do school procedures make it harder for active boys than for active girls?
3. Do children outgrow ADHD?

Resources to Explore

Children and Adults with Attention Deficit Disorder
   http://www.chadd.org

National Center for Learning Disabilities
   http://www.ncld.org

The Menninger Foundation
   http://menninger.edu

References

AMERICAN PSYCHIATRIC ASSOCIATION. (1994). *Diagnostic and statistical manual of mental disorders* (4th ed.). Washington, DC: Author.

ARCIA, E., & FERNANDEZ, M. C. (1998). Cuban mothers' schemas of ADHD: Development, characteristics, and help-seeking behavior. *Journal of Child and Family Studies, 7,* 333–352.

BARKLEY, R. A. (1990). *Attention-deficit hyperactivity disorder: A handbook for diagnosis and treatment.* New York: Guilford Press.

BUSSING, R., ZIMA, B. T., PERWIEN, A. R., BELIN, T. R., & WIDAWSKI, M. (1998). Children in special education programs: Attention deficit hyperactivity disorder, use of services, and unmet needs. *American Journal of Public Health, 88,* 880–886.

DUPAUL, G. J., ERVIN, R. A., HOOK, C. L., & MCGOEY, K. E. (1998). Peer tutoring for children with attention deficit hyperactivity disorder: Effects on classroom behavior and academic performance. *Journal of Applied Behavior Analysis, 31,* 579–592.

FARAONE, S. V., & BIEDERMAN, J. (1998). Neurobiology of attention-deficit hyperactivity disorder. *Biological Psychiatry, 44,* 951–958.

GAINETDINOV, R. R., WETSEL, W. C., JONES, S. R., LEVIN, E. D., JABER, M., & CARON, M. G. (1999). Role of serotonin in the paradoxical calming effect of psychostimulants on hyperactivity. *Science, 283,* 397–401.

KENDALL, J. (1998). Outlasting disruption: The process of reinvestment in families with ADHD children. *Qualitative Health Research, 8,* 839–857.

PANKSEPP, J. (1998). Attention deficit hyperactivity disorders, psychostimulants and intolerance of childhood playfulness: A tragedy in the making? *Current Directions in Psychological Science, 7,* 91–98.

RHEE, S. H., WALDMAN, I. D., HAY, D. A., & LEVY, F. (1999). Sex differences in genetic and environmental influences on *DSM-III-R* attention-deficit/hyperactivity disorder. *Journal of Abnormal Psychology, 108,* 24–41.

SEARIGHT, H. R., & MCLAREN, A. L. (1998). Attention-deficit hyperactivity disorder: The medicalization of misbehavior. *Journal of Clinical Psychology in Medical Settings, 5,* 467–495.

WIDENER, A. J. (1998). Beyond Ritalin: The importance of therapeutic work with parents and children diagnosed ADD/ADHD. *Journal of Child Psychotherapy, 24,* 267–281.

PART FOUR

Social Conditions

CHAPTER 12

Children and Poverty

OBJECTIVE

After reading this chapter, you should be able to explain how poverty can precipitate both physiological harm and social hardships for children. You should also be able to discuss steps teachers can take to be sensitive to children who are poor.

CHAPTER OUTLINE

WHAT IS POVERTY?

Once I asked my father what it was like growing up in the 1920s with five siblings, living on the second floor of a Baltimore rowhouse with just a coal stove in the kitchen for heat and an outhouse in the backyard. "How did it feel being poor?" I asked. He replied, "Food was skimpy. We always went away from the table hungry. Everybody around us lived the same way. I didn't know anything different. I thought we were just like everybody else. Everyone was in the same boat."

Nowadays there are not many poor people who don't know that they are poor. Television has given everyone a window into the lives of affluent Americans. Everybody knows about nice cars, expensive athletic shoes, leather coats, and all of the other signs of conspicuous consumption that we have in the United States. If you are poor in the United States, you know that you are poor.

"Poverty" is a political designation. The magic line between income levels called the "poverty line" is an arbitrary distinction set by politicians. It can arbitrarily be raised, creating fewer poor people, or it can be lowered, creating more poor people. Many people who are living above the arbitrary poverty line are still not well off.

Teachers need to be less concerned about whether children fall into the legal category of "below the poverty line" and more concerned about how their families are doing economically. Zill and others (1991) point out that life in near poverty is almost as detrimental to a child's health as living just below the poverty line. If the family is struggling financially, teachers need to be sensitive to their economic situation and make the appropriate adjustments.

Brooks-Gunn and Duncan (1997) point out, "In recent years, about one in five American children—some 12 to 14 million—have lived in families whose income failed to exceed official poverty thresholds." The National Center for Children in Poverty (1999) at Columbia University looked at poverty rates for children under age 6 from 1975 to 1994. Their findings are disturbing:

- One in 4 young children are in poverty.
- 50 percent of American young children are near poverty or in poverty.

Poverty is not limited to one group. White, African American, and Native American children, children of single parents, and children of two-parent families are all represented on the poverty roles.

These numbers do not include the "working poor" in the United States. If you are reading this on a college campus, look around at all the support people who clean up your campus, prepare and serve food, and clean and maintain your classroom buildings. Many are contract employees with few, if any, health benefits or retirement plans. Many have children and struggle to provide them with athletic shoes, medical care, money for field trips, and all of the other needs children have.

EFFECTS OF POVERTY ON CHILDREN

These are some of the effects that growing up in poverty can have on children:

- Poor prenatal growth
- Poor nutrition in the early years
- Lead poisoning
- Limited access to health services
- Living in unsafe neighborhoods

Prenatal Growth

Poverty can put the child at a physical disadvantage right from the start. Poverty can compromise essential factors related to proper parental growth of a child, including these:

- The health of the pregnant mother
- The mother's nutrition during pregnancy
- The mother's ability to obtain regular prenatal care to monitor fetal growth and treat potential medical problems

The pregnant mother's diet and lifestyle directly influence the development of her child in utero. Sufficient protein is necessary for the fetal brain to develop to its maximum. Substances such as tobacco, alcohol, prescribed medications, over-the-counter medications, street drugs, and other environmental factors can have detrimental effects on the developing fetus. A pregnant woman's use of many of these substances is correlated with delivery of a low-birthweight infant.

Birthweight is a predictor of infant survival and subsequent healthy development. Newborns who weight 5½ pounds or less (2,500 grams) are considered low-birthweight. This condition is related in childhood to frequent illness, deficits in motor coordination and school learning, as well as problems with inattention (Hack et al., 1994; Liaw & Brooks-Gunn, 1993; McCormick, Gortmaker, & Sobol, 1990).

In effect, the child will be coming to school with the "damage" already done. As teachers, we need to work on a remedial level to try to deal with the problems these children present in school.

Poor Nutrition

Brooks-Gunn and Duncan (1997) point out that it is rare to see overt signs of starvation and malnutrition in poor children in the United States, but poverty is associated with deficits in children's nutritional status. The World Health Organization (1999) reports how malnutrition affects all age groups:

Effects of malnutrition on the embryo

- Low birthweight
- Brain damage
- Neural tube defect
- Stillbirth

Effects of malnutrition on the neonate

- Growth retardation
- Developmental retardation
- Brain damage

Effects of malnutrition on the infant and young child

- Developmental retardation
- Increased risk of infection

Effects of malnutrition on the adolescent

- Delayed growth spurt
- Stunted height
- Delayed/retarded intellectual development
- Increased risk of infection

Lead Poisoning

Children in poverty most often live in older, unkept housing. Lead poisoning is a threat to many of these children. Children can ingest lead by eating the chips of lead-based paints that flake off of painted surfaces in older houses, and they can be exposed to lead in contaminated soil.

Lead damages the central nervous system. These are some of the clinical symptoms of lead poisoning (Louria, 1988):

- Irritability
- Lack of coordination
- Memory lapses
- Inappropriate expression of emotions
- Sleep disturbances
- Restlessness
- Listlessness
- Paranoia
- Headache
- Lethargy
- Dizziness

Although the condition is serious, lead poisoning can be treated medically. Many school systems and cities have lead-screening programs. As a teacher, you need to be aware of the symptoms of lead poisoning so you can quickly refer a child with symptoms for a screening. Many teachers are on the front lines in detecting this condition.

Limited Access to Health Care

The Secretary of Health and Human Services, Donna Shalala, pointed out that although health in America continues to show record progress, Americans with low income are not as likely as the more economically advantaged to share in the good news ("Health in America Tied to Income and Education," 1998). According to her report:

- Socioeconomic status has a direct influence on insurance coverage and access to care for both preventative services and regular visits.
- Insurance coverage makes a real difference for poor children in terms of access to health care.

When children have adequate access to health care, their health problems will be detected by health-care providers earlier and the child will receive timely treatment. Conditions like lead poisoning and impaired vision or hearing can be caught early and treated if the child has access to health-care services. Regular health care also ensures that a child will be immunized against harmful, but preventable, childhood diseases.

Dangerous Neighborhoods

Many children are forced by poverty to grow up in substandard housing in areas that are hazardous for children. In cities without playgrounds, children tend to play in streets. Some children live in violent, drug-infested neighborhoods where going outside to play involves the risk of being shot in a gunfight between two rival drug dealers.

The Centers for Disease Control and Prevention (1999) conducted a school-based survey of children in which they found that fear of violence affected a child's school attendance. Children missed school because they felt unsafe at school or when traveling to or from school.

THE ROLE OF THE TEACHER
WITH CHILDREN IN POVERTY

Provide Experiences

Teachers can play a key role in helping children who are in poverty have a more meaningful school experience. You can do this by making sure that students

- are provided with life experiences,
- are provided free learning materials,
- have after-school programs,
- are covered for their school expenses by subsidies when necessary, and
- have teachers who treat them with respect.

Teachers who work with children in poverty can anticipate that these students will not have the experiences that are available to wealthier children. Public school teachers can learn from the experience of Project Head Start, which is an attempt to deal with this gap in experiences. Children in Head Start are given many opportunities for educational activities that they would normally not be able to participate in. Field trips can feature hands-on experiences, and they need not be elaborate. A trip to the local fire station or bakery can be very exciting for children whose horizons have been limited by poverty.

Provide Free Learning Materials

Knowing that the parents of some of her students did not have the money to buy many children's books, Ms. Jacob discussed this problem with the local library and was given many of their old children's books. She distributed these books to the parents so they too would have something to read to their children.

Poor parents can still be interested in the progress of their children in school. School conferences might need to be scheduled early in the morning or in the evening so these parents, who might not have the clout and flexibility to take time off from work, can attend.

School activities can cost a great deal of money. Before you hand out lists of school supplies, make sure they are affordable for your students' families. Many merchants are glad to give pencils or notebooks to a teacher to give to children in her class.

Field trips, although educationally wonderful, can also be expensive. When your class includes children in poverty, either schedule field trips that take ad-

HACK, M. B., TAYI
    MINICH, N. (1!
    New England J
HEALTH IN AMERI
    1998 in *Health*
    tober 26, 1999:
LIAW, F., & BROOK
    development.
LOURIA, D. B. (198:
    Cecil textbook o
McCORMICK, M. (
    children: Beha
    Pediatrics, 117,
NATIONAL CENTI
    //cpmcnet.co
WORLD HEALTH
    http://www.
ZILL, N., MOOR, K
    development of
    ington, DC: C

vantage of free, local resources, or make sure that the school has sufficient money to cover the expenses of children who might be poor. As a teacher, you can always lobby a commercial venture for pro bono service. It is surprising how many local businesses will give things free to teachers who ask. Become an active advocate for your children to get them the resources they need in order to flourish as learners.

Facilitate After-School Programs

School might be the only safe place in the neighborhood, and many students might not want to leave at the end of the school day. Many secondary schools provide clubs and sport teams as after-school activities. Elementary schools also can provide after-school activities. Most elementary school teachers stay after class for some period of time, perhaps 45 minutes to an hour. Why not invite students (with parental permission) to stay with you after school to work on their homework or work on the computer?

Subsidize School Expenses

School activities can be expensive. Dances, sports, and other events can be costly. If a student is not participating in these activities, it might have nothing to do with their motivation, or their commitment to education—it might simply reflect the fact that they don't have the money to participate. As a teacher, you need to lobby the other faculty members and the administration at your school to focus on low-cost or no-cost dances, including having the "dress code" be normal school attire so that students won't stay away for want of dressy clothes. For students who want to play musical instruments, make sure that your school has a program to loan instruments to these students so that they won't lose out on this experience because they don't have the money to rent an instrument.

Treat Students with Respect

For many children school can be the only place that is an oasis of safety. Unfortunately, many children have to worry about violence at school as well. Teachers can work hard to make their classrooms places of emotional and physical safety for all children. Elementary school teachers can use a peaceful discipline policy that emphasizes consequences for misbehavior, yet is gentle and fair.

Secondary teachers also must have a discipline strategy, but they need to temper it with respect. Poor children often get very little respect in their violent environment. Respect is so important to many of these youngsters that they will fight over it, being forced to act to save face when they are "dissed."

It might sound strange to hear a teacher calling a student "Mr. Jones" instead of "Jones," but addressing students formally is a good way to demonstrate the respect that you want the students to give you. Discipline can be administered respectfully. Mr. Morgan, a tenth-grade teacher, had reason to be concerned about Adam, who had not brought his textbook to class, in violation of school rules.

Mr. Morgan spoke
did not bring you
you to bring the b
that he hadn't felt
need your book ir
The penalty for th
morrow." In this i
be respectful and

Summary

Poverty can precip
need to make our s
spect and dignity r
sitive to the monet
work with colleag
sidies and supplie:
not so costly, so th

Questions to

1. How can we ir
2. Can the school
3. What help can

Resources to

Centers for
http://w

Child Welfɑ
http://v

National Cı
http://c

UNICEF
http://v

World Hea
http://v

References

BROOKS-GUNN,
Children, 7,
CENTERS FOR DI
[Online]. Av

CHAPTER 13

Children Who Are Homeless

OBJECTIVE

After reading this chapter, you should be able to discuss the parenting and living conditions experienced by children who are homeless. You should also be able to identify steps you can take to help these children in your classroom.

CHAPTER OUTLINE

Problems of Children Who Are Homeless
Parenting of Children Who Are Homeless
Shelter Living
    Consistency
    Discipline in the Shelter
    Lack of Control Over the Child's Daily Life
    Constant Proximity to Other Children
    Other Shelter Residents
The Teacher's Role in Discussing Homelessness in the Classroom
Homeless Children in the Classroom
    Cognitive Assessment
    Play
    Homework
    Supplies and Trips
    Emotional Needs
Summary

PROBLEMS OF CHILDREN WHO ARE HOMELESS

Children who are homeless bring a unique set of experiences to the classroom. The literature notes an array of problems experienced by children who are homeless. These include environmentally induced problems, such as poor health, hunger, and inadequate nutrition, as well as emotional problems such as anxiety and depression (Bassuk & Gallagher, 1990; Edelman & Mihaly, 1989; Kozol, 1988; Molnar, Rath, & Klein, 1990; Rafferty & Shinn, 1991; Rosenman & Stein, 1990). Teachers need to know about the special environments of children who are homeless so that they can develop effective approaches to working with these students who enter their classrooms.

PARENTING OF CHILDREN WHO ARE HOMELESS

Children who are homeless often come into the classroom confused, overwhelmed, and insecure. For some of these children, the safety of a homeless shelter is a respite from a violent home situation. The regularity of meals, a bed to call one's own, and the absence of physical violence can make shelter life an improvement over a child's previous situation. Some shelters also have programs to help children. Intellectual enrichment programs in shelters have been found to restore age-level functioning and help children with their basic school needs (Grant, 1991; James, Smith, & Mann, 1991).

On the other hand, effective parenting, a hard task under the best of conditions, is extremely difficult for parents who are living with their children in emergency shelters. Families who are homeless have pressing immediate needs—finding a permanent place to live, getting a job, and maintaining physical health. Many of the parents in shelters are young, single parents, the great majority having had their children when they were teenagers (Bassuk, 1990). They came to the shelter with relatively few material goods and no source of income.

Young parents often don't have sophisticated parenting skills. For example, one homeless parent, Pam, a 19-year-old mother, inappropriately expected her 2-year-old son, Jeff, to "sit down and be quiet" during the day. When Jeff moved around and was "not being good," Pam thought that she should spank him.

Compounding the obvious stressors, such as a lack of money and no place to live, are the dysfunctional family backgrounds of most of the parents in shelters. Many women have fled abusive relationships, often with men who are involved with alcohol and drugs (Martin, 1991).

In addition, many shelter parents have survived horrible childhoods. For example, at age 6, Carol, now a 17-year-old mother, was left alone with her four younger siblings for 2 days while her mother "chased after a man." It is difficult to find a parent in a shelter who was not physically or sexually abused as a child, or raised by alcoholic parents.

Shelter mothers often display many of the scars common among women who have been in abusive relationships. Jane's case is not unusual. Jane was married when she was 14 and had her son 1 year later. Her husband was abusive to both her and their child. As a consequence, Jane, like many other abused women, had general feelings of inadequacy, particularly in terms of dealing with her child.

Shelter mothers are so preoccupied with their own problems that they have little energy left to parent their children. Caroline, a mother in one shelter, expressed it well when she said, "It's hard to care about your own child when you are so angry."

Lucille, the mother of two, was candid when discussing her children. "They drove me nuts when I was in situations I didn't want to be [in]. I took it out on them." As a consequence, the emotional needs of children take second place to the parent's primary needs to find a job and a permanent place to live. Thus, many children who are homeless enter the classroom with insecurities, fears, and a poor self-concept.

SHELTER LIVING

Consistency

Shelter living can be chaotic. New people come in every day. Children don't have the security of constant routines or a private space that they can organize and maintain in a predictable way. Inconsistent living conditions contribute to the feelings of fear and insecurity that children who are homeless can bring into the classroom.

Consistency is important for the healthy emotional development of children. Regular rituals help young children feel secure. Bedtime, for example, might be an unsettling event for a child unless his favorite stuffed toy or blanket is in its familiar place. Routines at home and in school serve to help the child feel secure.

A teacher can often compensate for the chaos of the shelter by maintaining a consistent classroom environment and providing children who are homeless with a special space, such as a desk, that they can call their own. From the predictable start of the school day in the morning until the lining up at the end of the day, schools give children familiar benchmarks that assure them that everything is all right.

Discipline in the Shelter

Several things contribute to the lack of stability in a shelter. One is that many shelters have strict rules governing how parents can discipline their children. As a consequence, many parents have experienced discipline problems with their children in shelters. The main problem is that many of these parents discipline their children using physical punishment, something that is prohibited by most shelters. Often the penalty for continually using corporal punishment is to be "exited" from (thrown out of) the shelter.

Sabrina spoke for many mothers when she said, "When I was in my own place, I smacked my child when he got out of line. He learned to listen. Here they have a rule that you can't hit your child. If I hit my child, I'll get written up. He knows that I can't smack him. He tells me, 'If you hit me I will tell.' He knows I can't do anything." Physical punishment is the only discipline tool these parents know, and they feel powerless without it.

Mothers in shelters also feel that their children misbehave because they see so much "bad" behavior from other children. Carol Ann summed up the frustrations of many shelter parents when she said, "Nobody disciplines their children. How can I teach my child when all the other children run wild?"

Lack of Control Over the Child's Daily Life

Another factor contributing to the lack of stability in the shelter is the lack of control parents have over their children's day-to-day lives. Parents at the shelter have no say over when and what their young child eats.

The dining room is open only during certain hours. This presented a problem for Darla: "My daughter is a slow eater and we like to talk. But here we have to eat quickly." Mothers accustomed to feeding their kids between meals cannot get snacks for their children when the kitchen is closed.

Constant Proximity to Other Children

Another problem with shelter living is that shelter parents never get a break from their children. There is no privacy for a parent in a shelter. Mother and children, as well as all of their worldly possessions, are housed in the same small room. An angry Marsha reported, "Since my kids are under ten, they can't be in a room alone. So that means when they nap I have to be in the room with them."

This proximity also creates negative feelings in the children. As Mitchell put it: "My mother is always in my face." When Mitchell was unhappy with being confined to his room, he didn't react by venting his anger at the people who set policy and ran the shelter, but instead yelled at his mother.

Other Shelter Residents

Some shelter residents hate children. Children in shelters must learn to stifle their normal childhood exuberance so as to not anger these very vocal residents. Children learn which of the adults really like them and which adults have to be avoided. When working in a shelter, I was warned by 5-year-old Lara to "stay away from the mean lady."

THE TEACHER'S ROLE IN
DISCUSSING HOMELESSNESS IN THE CLASSROOM

The following are some things the teacher can do to help make the school experience for homeless children more positive:

- Confront the negative stereotypes about homeless people.
- Discuss various family living arrangements with the children.
- Help all children understand the experience of homeless children.
- Encourage children to see the child behind the old clothes.
- Help sensitize the community at large to the situation of people who are homeless.

Many children have a stereotype of homeless people as defective and undesirable, and many children who are homeless entering the classroom are rejected and isolated from their classmates. If the classroom teacher is going to facilitate the acceptance of the child who is homeless, he or she will have to take an active role in confronting the negative stereotypes.

This can be accomplished by dealing with the issue of homelessness as you would deal with any issue in the classroom—in an objective and open manner. The goal is to have the children in the class realize that people who are homeless are individuals.

When doing a unit on families or the community, teachers need to point out that not all families live in houses or apartments, but some live temporarily in homeless shelters. At the same time, the teacher needs to be aware of children's fears about their own situations and reassure them that most American children are not homeless, and that most will never be without a home.

American children, particularly those who have so many "things," need to be sensitized to the fact that not all of the people in our society share their good fortune. To do this, teachers can try the "paper bag" exercise. The children are told to pretend that they have to leave their house. Each child in the classroom is given a paper grocery bag. The children are told to draw life-size pictures of all of the things they would choose to take with them if they could only take what they could carry in this one bag. The discussion after the exercise could focus on what items the children chose to take. This exercise should give the children a concrete image of how few things homeless children have.

Children might be upset to hear that other children have no toys or clothes. Teachers can channel these concerns into a community action project. Children can "adopt" a shelter in their community. They can collect clothes, share some of their toys, and even make toys and books for children in the shelters. It is important for all donations to be made anonymously so that the dignity of the homeless children will be protected.

If a child who is homeless enters the classroom, children need to be encouraged to look at the whole child. Clothes are an important point of social discrimination, even among young children. Children need to be taught to look beyond the clothes to find the person. Many schools are requiring children to wear uniforms in order to minimize status distinctions caused by clothes. Helping children to focus on the commonalities of other children rather than their differences is often helpful. This approach can often be combined with a discussion of commonalities of children from other cultures.

Sometimes children have the capacity to be remarkably kind and sensitive to children who are homeless. The story of Lisa, a 15-year-old resident of one shelter, is an example. Lisa didn't tell any of her new high school classmates where she lived. This secret became difficult to keep because she was invited to spend the night at classmates' houses and was expected to reciprocate by inviting her classmates home after school. After a while, she told her classmates that she lived in the shelter, but added that she lived there because her mother was a counselor. Her friends in the school eventually found out the truth and let the young girl know that they still wanted to be her friend and didn't care where she lived.

Involving parents of the other children in the class in activities to help them understand the homeless will help sensitize the community at large to the needs of children who are homeless. Parents can become vital allies in helping to meet the needs of homeless children in the community as well as in the schools. With the proper preparation, classrooms can become more hospitable places to a homeless child.

HOMELESS CHILDREN IN THE CLASSROOM

Cognitive Assessment

The homeless child who enters the classroom in the middle of the year usually brings no records. The child just shows up in class. There are inherent problems in educating a child who just pops into a classroom for perhaps 8 weeks and is then moved on to another school. Assessment needs to be done quickly so that you can immediately start to meet the needs of the child.

It would be a mistake to automatically place a new child in the lowest ability group. Homelessness is not a measure of intelligence. When assessing the child's ability, push them to their highest possible level of achievement.

Teachers can best cope with this situation by informally testing the child. This can be done in reading, for example, by having the child read and asking the child comprehension questions. In mathematics class, problems for the average student can be selected and used as a start to evaluate the child's mathematic ability. To assess writing ability, ask the child to write a story, spelling the words the best they can.

Secondary education teachers can meet with homeless children individually and ask them questions to get a feel for how much they know about their discipline. This discussion need not be an interrogation, but can feature open-ended questions such as these:

- What topics have you discussed in history?
- Did you discuss photosynthesis in your biology class?
- How did your teacher in your other school teach this topic?
- What books did you read in English literature in your other school? Tell me about the one you liked the best.

Play

Play is the work of children, and their toys are their tools. Toys facilitate the cognitive and emotional development of young children. Cognitive development is enhanced by providing children with vehicles to use their imagination; emotional development is enhanced by providing children with "confidants" and objects to love.

Shelter children have few toys. When I asked 5-year-old Sandy to tell me about her favorite toy, she responded meekly, "I don't have any toys." Teachers need to provide opportunities in school for these children to play, perhaps on the playground or during lunchtime. Teachers of children in the early grades can borrow toys from the school kindergarten and loan them to the children to play with at the shelter.

Homework

Teachers need to adjust their expectations for out-of-school time to fit the realities of the shelter. Most homeless shelters provide no place to do homework. Teachers should try to arrange a time before or after school when these youngsters can do their homework in the classroom or the school library.

Older shelter children are not going to have access to computers to do word processing. A teacher can discretely arrange for these children to have access to school computers after school.

Supplies and Trips

Children in shelters have no money to pay for the incidentals schools require. Buying paper might be routine for most children, but it might be impossible for a homeless child. All supplies that the child needs to do assignments must be provided by the school. Often PTA groups will provide funds for field trips and other out-of-class activities.

Emotional Needs

Coming into a new classroom in the middle of the year under the best of conditions can be traumatic for any child. One can expect children who are homeless to be self-conscious and angry. In addition, they often feel defeated and embarrassed about being homeless (Lines, 1992).

A lot of attention needs to be given toward building up the wounded self-concept of the child who is homeless. Teachers must provide many opportunities for children to feel good about themselves. You can also give the child recognition in the classroom—for example, by making the child a team leader in a group project, or by choosing the child to be the "line leader."

Being a member of a peer group is an essential developmental task for adolescents. Children who enter school in the middle of the year can find it difficult to fit in with a group. A child who is homeless might be encouraged to join a team, musical group, or club; at the high school level such groups function as peer groups. You can facilitate this by talking to the teacher in charge of the various activities and paving the way. This might be the most expedient way to make sure a child gets connected.

Summary

If teachers understand the parenting and living conditions experienced by homeless students in their classroom, they will be better able to meet the needs of these vulnerable children. Preparing the regular class to understand the experience of homelessness will also facilitate the smooth integration of a homeless child into the classroom. Teachers can help homeless children in their classrooms by doing an informal assessment of their cognitive level when they enter the classroom, and making provisions for them to get needed school supplies, connect with school activities, and have a place where they can do homework. By dealing with the problem of homelessness in America in an open manner, the classroom teacher will sensitize all children to one of the most important social problems facing our country.

RESEARCH IDEAS

Questions to Investigate

1. How can you teach parents of shelter children how to be better parents?
2. Should shelter parents be required to work while they are in the shelter?
3. Should children stay in their old neighborhood school even if the shelter is in a different part of town?

Resources to Explore

Council of Homeless Persons
http://www.infoxchange.net.au/homeless

International Homeless Discussion List and Archives
    http://csf.colorado.edu/homeless

National Coalition for the Homeless
    http://nch.ari.net

U.S. Department of Health and Human Services
    http://aspe.os.dhhs.gov/progsys/homeless

References

BASSUK, E. L. (1990). Who are the homeless families? Characteristics of sheltered mothers and children. *Community Mental Health Journal, 26,* 425–434.

BASSUK, E. L., & GALLAGHER, E. M. (1990). The impact of homelessness on children. *Child and Youth Services, 14,* 19–33.

EDELMAN, M. W., & MIHALY, L. (1989). Homeless families and the housing crisis in the United States. *Children and Youth Services Review, 11,* 91–108.

GRANT, R. (1991). The special needs of homeless children: Early intervention at a welfare hotel. *Topics in Early Childhood Special Education, 10,* 76–91.

JAMES, W. H., SMITH, A. J., & MANN, R. (1991). Educating homeless children: Interprofessional case management. *Childhood Education, 67,* 305–308

LINES, S. (1992). Educational disadvantage in the primary school: Children living in temporary accommodations. *Support for Learning, 7,* 8–13.

MARTIN, J. (1991). The Trauma of homelessness. *International Journal of Mental Health, 20,* 17–27.

MOLNAR, J. M., RATH, W. R., & KLEIN, T. P. (1990). Constantly compromised: The impact of homelessness on children. *Journal of Social Issues, 46,* 109–124.

RAFFERTY, Y., & SHINN, M. (1991). The impact of homelessness on children. *American Psychologist, 46,* 1170–1179.

ROSENMAN, M., & STEIN, M. L. (1990). Homeless children: A new vulnerability. *Child and Youth Services, 14,* 89–109.

CHAPTER 14

Children and Violence

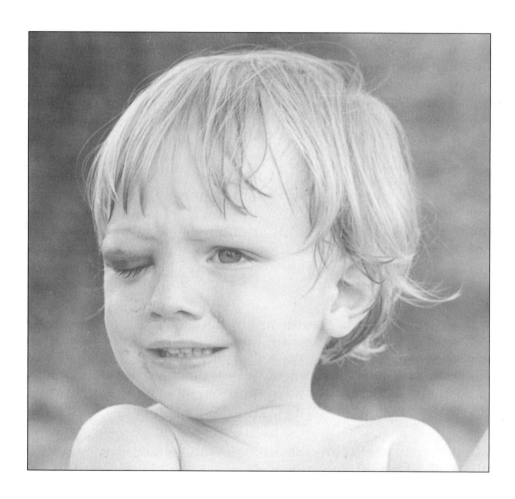

OBJECTIVE

After reading this chapter, you should be able to explain the teacher's role in identifying children who might be abused. You should also be able to discuss ways teachers can help students deal with conflict in a nonviolent manner.

CHAPTER OUTLINE

Violence in the United States
Why Are Children Violent?
Types of Family Violence Children Experience
    Child Abuse
    Violence Between Parents
The Teacher's Role in Dealing with Child Abuse
    Identifying Abuse with Younger Children
    Identifying Abuse with Older Children
Teaching Prevention
    Peer Abuse
    Preventative Classroom Actions
    Conflict Resolution
    Dealing with Bullies
    Peaceful Classrooms
Summary

VIOLENCE IN THE UNITED STATES

Violence is a staple of American society. Children are exposed to or experience violence at home, in school, and in the community. Many children are the victims of violence; others are bystanders, observing others commit violence either in person or on television, video games, or the movies.

In their families, children might be the targets of parental violence or witness violence between their parents. Handsnet (1998) reports that from 1992 to 1996, almost 1 million people a year were victims of violence at the hands of a current or former spouse or intimate partner. It is believed that an even larger number of women experience abuse but do not report it to the police. Reports from battered mothers indicate that 87 percent of their children witness the domestic violence.

The National Committee to Prevent Child Abuse (1996) cites some disturbing statistics for the United States:

- In 1995, more than three children per day died as a result of parental maltreatment.
- In 1995, more than 3 million children were reported as abused.

School is not a safe haven from violence for children either. According to data from the National Crime Victimization Survey (1991), nearly 3 million crimes occur in or near the 85,000 U.S. public schools every year. Bullies have always had a presence in school, but today's bullies are far more violent than their predecessors.

In the community, children are exposed to violence both directly and indirectly. Indirectly, children are exposed to secondhand violence when watching television. In fact, children spend more time watching television than they spend in school (Singer & Singer, 1990). Tuchscherer (1988) points out that between the ages of 5 and 15, children will witness more than 13,000 killings on TV. Many movies, video games, music videos, and music lyrics also have violent themes.

Depending upon where they live, children might or might not be exposed to community violence on a daily basis. Many children must walk past drug dealers to get to school. Dave described what happened during his routine stop at the local convenience store for a soda on his way home from high school:

> I was about to go into the store, but for some reason things looked strange. There was a guy in a big, black car parked right in front of the store. I hesitated for a minute and in that instant the guy got out of the car and began shooting at a guy who was at the counter, right where I would have been. He killed him. It could have been me.

Too many American schoolchildren have witnessed violence firsthand.

WHY ARE CHILDREN VIOLENT?

There are different views as to why children are violent. The *DSM-IV* (American Psychiatric Association, 1994) describes conduct disorder as a "repetitive and persistent pattern of behavior in which the basic rights of others or major age-appropriate societal norms or rules are violated" (p. 85). Children with conduct disorder would have a psychological disturbance that manifests itself in violent behavior.

Another view suggests that many children are living in a violent society and respond to violence with violence. In this view, violence is not a pathological behavior but a logical adaptation to living in a violent environment. Chang, a student teacher working in a high school chemistry class, frequently asked his students to respond to questions he raised. Chang described a disturbing situation in class:

> I asked a question, and the best student in the class raised his hand. When his hand went up, his shirt pulled up a bit and I saw that he had a gun tucked into his belt. I talked to him after class and asked him what he was doing carrying a gun to my chemistry class. After all, he was an A student and headed to college. He said that he lived in "a tough neighborhood" and that as long as he had the gun, people would leave him alone and not get on him about doing well in school. "If I didn't have a gun, my life wouldn't be worth anything," he said.

TYPES OF FAMILY VIOLENCE CHILDREN EXPERIENCE

Some children are directly subject to family violence in being physically and/or sexually abused. They are also bystanders to domestic violence between their parents. Both forms of violence can have a detrimental effect on children.

Child Abuse

There is probably no way to get an accurate count of the number of children who are abused by their parents. Statistics indicate only the number of reported cases. Child-friendly laws in most states mandate the reporting of suspected child abuse by teachers, social workers, physicians, nurses, and other professionals. These reporting laws have helped bring child abuse into public consciousness and have increased the reporting of abuse. An example of a child-abuse law is found in the Maryland statute. Maryland state law defines abuse as follows:

> Abuse means the sustaining of physical injury of a child by any parent or other person who has permanent or temporary care or custody or responsibility for supervision of a child, or by any household or family member, under circumstances that indicate that the child's health or welfare is significantly harmed or at risk of being significantly harmed; or sexual abuse of a child, whether physical injuries are sustained or not. Neglect means the sustaining by a child of significant physical or mental harm or injury from: the absence of the child's parents, guardian, or custodian; the leaving of a child unattended or other failure to give proper care and attention to a child by the child's parents, guardian, or custodian under circumstances that indicate that the child's health or welfare is significantly harmed or placed at risk of significant harm. (Annotated Code of Maryland, "Family Law" §5-701-710)

The line between physical abuse and corporal punishment is often vague. Many people argue that corporal punishment is a legitimate discipline tool for parents to use with their children; others argue just as strongly that it is harmful in any circumstance. In a practical sense, child abuse ends up being defined by its consequences. If a parent hits a child and causes the child physical injury that requires medical care, one would be more likely to define that act as child abuse. A parent who hits his child and leaves no marks would probably not be reported as an abuser.

As we've mentioned, corporal punishment has its advocates and critics. These are some of the arguments given for corporal punishment:

- My parents used it on me and it worked.
- It teaches children a lesson.
- It's called for in the Bible.

Opponents of corporal punishment reply:

- Research indicates that reward is a better way to change behavior than punishment is.
- Parents who model violence teach their children that violence is permissible.
- Spanking can get out of control if a parent is angry, and the child can be seriously hurt.
- Why would you want to hurt someone you love?

Violence Between Parents

Many children witness violence between their parents, and this can scare them. Children depend upon their parents to be in control. When parents are out of control, children lose the rock of stability that most children can count on to always be there. A physical battle between parents can easily escalate to target the children as well, putting them in danger of harm.

THE TEACHER'S ROLE IN DEALING WITH CHILD ABUSE

Teachers have a role in dealing with physical and sexual abuse of children. You will need to be able to identify abuse in children in the age group you teach, and take appropriate action to get them help. The first goal for the helping teacher is to identify the problem and help rescue the child from the abusive situation. To do this, one has to know what the identifying signs of abuse are and recognize them when they are there. If you suspect abuse, you must report it to the appropriate authorities in your state, usually the child protection agency or the local police.

Reporting abuse is not pleasant. Who wants to testify in court? Who wants to face angry parents? But what is the alternative? When I have to deal with abuse, I always think of a 7-year-old girl who was in the hospital where I had a group of students. She had been put in scalding water by her father and was badly burned and in a great deal of pain. If someone had stepped up to protect her, maybe she wouldn't have had to suffer. You can be the person who saves a child from suffering and perhaps saves her life.

The second goal is to support the child who has been abused. You are going to be dealing with a wounded child who is perhaps undergoing therapy with a mental health professional. Your role is not to be the child's therapist, but to be the steady, caring teacher.

Identifying Abuse with Younger Children

Certain behaviors you observe in school might cause you to suspect that a child might have been abused. The behavior will vary depending upon the age of the child. Your job is to identify children who you suspect might have been abused and report your findings to the police or the child protective services agency in your community. You do not have to prove that abuse is taking place; if you just suspect abuse, you must report your suspicions. Our colleagues who are trained to investigate such matters are charged with determining if abuse actually occurred.

Sometimes teachers will notice bruises, burns, welts, abrasions, or scars while working closely with a child who is doing seatwork. Don't ignore what you see. Ask the child directly and privately about the mark the first time you observe it. You need not wait for a pattern of bruises and marks before you take action.

Your best recourse is to lead with an open-ended comment such as "Tell me about your bruise." If the child comes up with an explanation that is suspicious, such as "My mother said to say that I fell off my bike," you should report your suspicions to the appropriate authorities.

There are often less obvious indicators that something is wrong with younger children. Observing a child playing in the housekeeping area, the teacher noticed that the child was yelling at the doll she was holding, "You spilled the milk, you idiot! For that you are really going to get beat!" The child proceeded to beat the doll with a wooden spoon while making the doll say, "I'm sorry! It was an accident! Please don't beat me anymore! It hurts!" This behavior led her teacher to suspect that the child was being abused at home. The teacher reported the behavior to the appropriate agency for further investigation.

Instances of sexual abuse are often identified through play as well. When a young child plays in a sexual way that is developmentally more typical of an adolescent, one should be concerned. A day-care director reported the following case:

> I was concerned because I observed a 5-year-old lying on another classmate during playtime. When I asked her what they were playing, the youngster replied that "they were sexing." One would not expect a 5-year-old child to be experimenting with sexual intercourse.

This behavior was reported by the director as suspicious to the local child protective services agency.

Young children can also communicate their feelings to teachers through artwork and stories. A kindergarten teacher came upon the following incident:

> Samantha drew a picture of a big person beating a smaller one with a large stick. I looked at the picture and said to Samantha, "Tell me about your picture." Samantha replied, "It's a mother and she is really hurting her little girl and the girl is really scared."

Children often communicate their pain between the lines. Teachers need to learn to listen.

Child protective services professionals are trained to get information from children in a legal way. They are careful not to put words in a child's mouth, but instead to get children to talk about what is happening to them. Questioning a child about abuse in a way that will stand up in court is best left to our specially trained colleagues.

Identifying Abuse with Older Children

Children often seek out a trusted teacher to tell about their abuse. Depending upon the age and style of the child, they might tell the teacher in a direct way or in an indirect way. The teacher's job is to pick up on the indirect "hints" that children often drop. Adolescents often drop these hints in their writing. For example, Ms. Jefferson had her English class keep journals. Students were to write in their journals every week, on topics of their own choice. One entry by Theresa described an encounter between a teenage girl and her father, in which the father punched her in the stomach. After class, Ms. Jefferson asked Theresa who the story was about, and she confided that it was about herself. On other occasions teachers will notice sudden, unusual behaviors that seem to indicate that something is wrong. These behaviors might include

- withdrawal from other students,
- depression,
- crying, or
- an unkept appearance.

If the teacher has established a rapport with the student, it is appropriate to gently talk to the student and say something like, "I'm worried about you. Your behavior has changed. Is there anything you want to talk about?" Using this technique, you will not back a child into the corner by suggesting that they have been abused, but will instead give the student an opening to talk to you.

These are signs of child abuse and neglect that you should be aware of:

- Unexplained injuries such as bruises, welts, abrasions, blisters, and lacerations
- The presence of a significant number of injuries that are at various stages of healing
- Scars or wounds that could have been caused by cigarette burns or belt buckles
- Explanations for wounds that don't make sense
- Coming to school dirty and in dirty, unkept clothes
- Falling asleep constantly in school
- Playing in a sexual manner that is inappropriate for one's age
- Direct or indirect communication to you that something is wrong

TEACHING PREVENTION

Young children need to be taught that they have the right to control their own bodies. They can be taught that their body is private and that no one has a right to touch them where they don't want to be touched. (There are exceptions, such as when they are being treated by a physician.) Early assertiveness training teaches children to say no to a behavior that makes them uncomfortable, and empowers them to tell their parents or other trusted adults about behaviors that scare them.

Similarly, teachers have a multiple responsibilities in dealing with peer violence. You must work on a preventive level to create a classroom atmosphere of tolerance and acceptance of people who are different. On a day-to-day level, you need to confront and stop any inappropriate peer behavior. Teachers need to establish a zero-tolerance policy for any demeaning racial, sexual, or nationalistic talk or action.

You will need to be able to do the following:

- Identify and protect children from peer abuse.
- Take measures in your classroom to prevent violence.
- Teach children conflict resolution skills.
- Teach children how to deal with bullies.
- Create a peaceful classroom.

Peer Abuse

Students are also exposed to violence at the hands of their peers. Bullying goes on in both elementary and secondary schools. Bullies have been around for a long time, taunting and intimidating other children, but bullying might be a far more serious problem today—today bullies carry automatic weapons.

Some children are easier to pick on than others. Vulnerable children are usually children who are different. Gay children often must endure harassment, contempt, and physical assault from their peers. A gay teacher reflected on his elementary school experience:

> As a child, grades three through six, I was perceived by classmates to be a sissy. I was labeled a sissy when the other kids noticed that I didn't move or talk like the other boys. I was rejected, harassed, humiliated and insulted by them every day for four years. My classmates took my most personal possession from me, my name, and gave me a girl's name. My teachers did nothing. One day, two boys with whom I never talked attacked me as I tried to pass them on my bike and beat me up, breaking my clavicle. I walked my bike home, ashamed to tell my mother what had happened. (Frieman, O'Hara, & Settel, 1996)

The damage done to this young gay boy is obvious. Aside from the physical damage inflicted by bullies, the child had to endure the damage done to his self-esteem.

Other victims of bullies include children who stand out as different from the rest. These include children who are

- learning disabled,
- in special education programs,
- recent immigrants,
- physically awkward, or
- of a minority religion and wear some symbol that makes them stand out.

These children might appear fearful in class or on the playground or be withdrawn from the other children in the class.

Preventive Classroom Actions

Teachers can work to prevent a violent atmosphere in their classrooms by fostering a climate that celebrates diversity, and by teaching children peaceful methods to solve disputes. Elementary school children can see difference as threatening or as interesting, depending in part upon the environment of the classroom. Ms. Corso, an elementary school music teacher, taught the children in her music class to "sign" one of the songs they performed for their winter concert. All of the children in the fourth and fifth grades learned how to communicate the lyrics using American Sign Language. Before this experience, I had noticed some of the same kids at the local mall making fun of people who were communicating with sign. After they learned to sign their song, I observed another group of children from the same class. Their reaction was completely different. They were talking about how good the hearing-impaired people were at using American Sign. They saw people who were deaf in a positive light, not a negative, threatening one.

There are many other ways elementary teachers can celebrate diversity. Children's backgrounds can be highlighted. Students can learn where new citizens came from, locating their former countries on the map. Relatives of new children can be invited to the classroom to share characteristic foods and display artifacts from their home country.

A sensitive approach to religious holidays is also a good way to encourage diversity. Of course, teachers should discuss Christmas. But they also should discuss Ramadam, Rosh Hashana, and other religious holidays.

Secondary teachers can also include a discussion of diversity in English courses, history courses, and in other places in the curriculum. A wonderful source of information on diversity for teachers is the Teaching Tolerance project of the Southern Poverty Law Center (4100 Washington Avenue, Montgomery, Alabama 36104).

Conflict Resolution

Disputes will occur between children. If you teach the children skills to resolve disputes, they will have alternatives to violence. Conflict resolution is one such technique. Children need to be taught how to settle disputes in a civil manner.

The first step in teaching conflict resolution skills to children is for the teacher to model them. How do you react when a child takes issue with what you say? Children will challenge teachers all the time.

"Why do we have to have homework on the weekend?"

"Can we go outside for recess?"

"Do we have to do more math now?"

"Sally took my eraser."

In these test cases, the goal of the teacher is to model how to resolve conflicts. The first step is to actively listen to the other point of view. Next, you would present your point of view. Then see if there are points of agreement. For example, in the homework case, both sides might agree that it is important to learn math and that practice helps. Finally, look for a position that permits both persons to win.

Of course, not all things are open to negotiation. It might be a given that there will be a test in the biology class. Whether the test is on Monday or Tuesday might be negotiated, however.

Children can learn to engage in this process at a very young age. When two children have a dispute, they can be asked to sit at the "conflict resolution table." Once they are seated, there will be certain rules. Only one person can speak at a time. A ball can be put on the table and only the person who is holding the ball can speak. The other person has to listen. After the speaker talks, she asks the listener to summarize what she has said. Cards with stem phrases such as:

When you do . . . it makes me feel . . .

I would like you to . . .

We can solve this problem by . . .

can be available to remind children what to say during the mediation process. When the original speaker is finished, the second speaker gets the ball and has his say. Often, another impartial child can be present to mediate by asking questions. True, this process takes more time than having the teacher making a decision, but it is worth the effort because it teaches children skills to solve future problems.

Older children can also be taught conflict resolution skills. The same principles apply (e.g., only one person speaks at a time and the other one actively listens).

Dealing with Bullies

Many bullies are unhappy children. Teachers have to view bullies as children with problems rather than as thugs, even though bullies' behavior is problematic. These are children one has to work really hard to reach. When working in an elementary school in a tough neighborhood, I had a group of four boys. From their point of view they were the toughest kids in the school. From the point of view of their classmates they were bullies. Underneath the bravado these fifth-graders projected, I found them to be like the other kids. They were tough. Most of them were on their own for a good part of the day and night. After hanging out with their friends after school, they usually came home to an empty house where they had to put together something if they wanted dinner. The kids started spending time with me because it was preferable to sitting in the principal's office.

I told them that because they were the toughest boys in the school, I needed them to protect some kindergarten kids. Each one was assigned a kindergarten kid to mentor. Their assignment was to read to their child. Even though their reading skills were not great, they were able to read a picture book. Jimmy, who was the biggest, toughest kid in the group, got really attached to his partner. He treated the kindergarten child with a degree of tenderness and kindness that none of his teachers had seen from him before. I talked to him about this, and he told me that his kindergarten pal really liked him. "My mother thinks I'm a jerk, but Bobby really likes me. He calls me his big brother."

Once we start to look at bullies as children, we might find that many of them are just scared kids who need our help. However, scared as they might be, they still need to follow the rules of the school. The one criterion for Jimmy and his "gang" to stay in the group was that they stay out of trouble.

Sometimes children can tell their teachers how to help them. Paul had incredible problems with his temper. He would frequently fly off the handle and go after other children in his middle school class, attacking them verbally and sometimes physically. He told his teacher that when people yelled at him, it just made him worse and feel out of control, and she worked with him to find an effective method to help him keep his temper under control. He described how his teacher helped him:

> I can tell when it's coming. I feel agitated. Anything will set me off, but my teacher can calm me down. She talks calmly to me and reassures me that I am in control and that everything is all right. My old teacher used to yell at me. That didn't work. It just made things worse. This teacher knows what to do to help me.

Peaceful Classrooms

As teachers we cannot control what goes on in the community. Many children in our country live in violent neighborhoods. It is not uncommon to find that when urban school children are asked "Who has seen somebody getting shot?" almost all of the children in the class raise their hands.

We can, however, control our classrooms and make them safe places. Your classrooms can be an oasis of safety in a dangerous world. No child should have to worry about anything bad happening to them when they are in your classroom. You can have strict rules governing how children must behave with each other, beginning with respect for every person in the classroom. Children cannot be permitted to hit each other, nor should they be permitted to assault each other verbally. As a teacher, you cannot ignore the seemingly innocent racial, ethnic, or sexual joke. You must have a zero-tolerance policy for verbal harassment.

Summary

Violence is part of the life of most children. We have a role in identifying children who are being abused and in making sure that we take action to stop this destructive behavior. Abuse between children in our classes is best dealt with by an aggressive prevention program that stresses teaching tolerance and conflict resolution skills to our students regardless of age.

RESEARCH IDEAS

Questions to Investigate

1. Should the United States join other countries, such as Sweden, in banning all corporal punishment of children?
2. If you teach children how to be peaceful in the classroom will they be able to transfer these skills to their life at home and in the community?
3. How can we teach parents alternatives to corporal punishment?

Resources to Explore

Family Violence Prevention Fund
  http://www.fvpf.org

National Committee to Prevent Abuse
  http://www.childabuse.org

Safehouse Denver
  http://www.safehouse-denver.org

Texas Youth Commission
  http://www.tyc.state.tx.us

The UNESCO International Clearinghouse on Children and Violence on the Screen
  http://www.nordicom.gu.se/unesco

References

AMERICAN PSYCHIATRIC ASSOCIATION. (1994). *Diagnostic and statistical manual of mental disorders* (4th ed.). Washington, DC: Author.

FAMILY LAW. The Annotated Code of the Public General Laws of Maryland. §5-701-710 (1988). Cumulative Supplement.

FRIEMAN, B. B., O'HARA, H., & SETTEL, J. (1996). What heterosexual teachers need to know about homosexuality. *Childhood Education, 73*, 40–42.

HANDSNET HEADLINE (1998). What child care providers need to know on domestic violence. http://www.igc.org/handsnet2/Articles/art.906739472.htm.

NATIONAL COMMITTEE TO PREVENT CHILD ABUSE (1996). Prevention of child abuse and neglect fatalities: Fact sheet number 9. http://www.childabuse.org/fs9.html.

SINGER, D. G., & SINGER, J. L. (1990). *The house of make-believe: Play and the development of imagination.* Cambridge, MA: Harvard University.

TUCHSCHERER, P. (1988). *TV interactive toys: The new high tech threat to children.* Bend, OR: Pinnaroo Publishing.

UNITED STATES DEPARTMENT OF JUSTICE. (1991). *National crime victimization survey: U.S. Department of Justice.* Washington, DC: Author.

CHAPTER 15

Children and Divorce

OBJECTIVE

After reading this chapter, you should be able to describe how you can help children in your class whose parents are divorcing.

CHAPTER OUTLINE

WHO'S GETTING DIVORCED?

Divorce will be part of the life experience of many of the children in your class. This powerful family event will affect children whose parents are just separating as well as those whose parents have been divorced for years. The many children of divorce I have worked with both in individual counseling and in group counseling have been my teachers. Their stories are told in this chapter.

EFFECTS OF DIVORCE ON CHILDREN

Separation and divorce have a powerful emotional effect on children (Hetherington, Stanley-Hagan, & Anderson, 1989; Keith & Finlay, 1988). Young children are often confused about the part of divorcing called the "separation," which happens when their parents live apart before they go to court and obtain a legal divorce decree.

Elementary school children often bring into the classroom the powerful feelings they experience over these major changes in their lives. These feelings of anger, sadness, anxiety, abandonment, being out of control, and being overburdened at having to take the responsibilities of an absent parent will need to be dealt with by the early childhood educator in the classroom.

Adolescents are also affected by their parents' divorce. Like younger children, they experience the loss of the absent parent. They also have to deal with the lifestyle changes and hostility in the family that frequently are the by-products of divorce. Divorce can be particularly troubling to adolescents, who are trying to carve out their own love relationships with peers.

Children might act out their feelings concerning separation and divorce in disruptive ways, or they might, alternatively, become extremely passive and withdrawn. Teachers who are aware of the changes these children are going through can provide some support to the children and can also be prepared to deal with some of the disruptions that would impede the normal flow of classroom activity.

CHILDREN TELL TEACHERS HOW TO HELP

Clues about what teachers can do to help children can be discovered by listening to the children themselves. One of the most consistent points children make is that they want their teachers to know about their family's situation. The children feel that they will do better work in school if their teachers understand what is going on in their lives. They hope that if teachers know about the pressures they are experiencing, teachers will be more tolerant of occasional lapses in their performance at school.

Margaret, a fifth-grader, illustrates this point when she says, "I'm thinking about the divorce sometimes in school and not doing my work. I don't want my teacher to think that I don't care about my work." Margaret is a good student who wants her teacher to see her distraction as a reflection of her concern about her family's problem rather than as a lack of interest in school. Scott, a first-grader, expresses a similar concern: "I want her to know so that when I'm feeling sad she will know the reason and not yell at me."

Children additionally hope that their teachers will be able to provide them with extra emotional support. Effective teachers have already established a warm, trusting relationship with the children they teach. A child will look to a trusted teacher in time of need, as 6-year-old Anton does: "If I have a problem, I can go to her and she will know what I'm talking about." Likewise, 5-year-old Tim says, "I want my teacher to know, because if I become sad and my teacher knew about the separation I could talk to her."

Francesca, a first-grader, expresses the confidence she has in her teacher: "If I say something weird about the divorce, she would make me talk about it." Francesca has the confidence that her teacher will hear and help her deal with any fears she has about her parents' divorce.

Sometimes teachers do not directly learn about a pending separation or divorce from students or parents, but are aware only of an abrupt change in the child's classroom behavior. For example, Todd, was a kindergartner who used to separate easily from his parents when he was dropped off in the morning at school. Suddenly, Mr. Bernstein, his teacher, noticed that Todd began to cry when his parent left him at the school. Mr. Bernstein took the initiative and called Todd's house to share his perception of Todd's classroom behavior and spoke to his mother, who answered the phone. This was an important first step for the teacher in helping the parent understand that Todd was reacting to the home situation in school.

Mr. Bernstein asked Todd's mother, "Is there anything going on in your family that I should be aware of in order to help your son?" The women was guarded in her response. Parents are often reluctant to discuss family problems with a teacher. In such a situation, the teacher needs to explain to parents that he or she needs to know personal family information in order to better help their child, and that they do not mean to pry into the family's private life.

It is more difficult for adolescents to inform their teachers about their personal lives. They might not come right out and tell their teacher what is going on, but instead might drop hints. Instead of telling their teacher outright that their dad has moved out of the family house, they might drop a hint like, "I don't have my book today. I left it at my dad's house."

If a secondary education teacher gives a journal-writing assignment, the adolescent might drop in a few lines about her current family situation and give the teacher a hint as to what is going on at home. Other times, teachers have to pick up clues along the way. When a good student all of a sudden misses assignments, becomes disruptive in class, or does poorly on tests, teachers can assume that something is going on in the home. A conference about grades can start with the stem "Tell me about what is new at home."

THE TEACHER'S ROLE IN HELPING CHILDREN COPE WITH DIVORCE

Teachers play an important role in helping their students to cope with divorce. These are some things you can do to help these children:

- Accept their unusual behavior
- Allow them to focus on their feelings
- Understand and compensate for their new home schedules
- Monitor and control their potentially disruptive behavior in school

A teacher who is knowledgeable about the child's family situation will be able to more accurately assess the academic performance of the child. One should expect that children in these situations sometimes will not be able to concentrate and will be sad. Children who sometimes seem "spaced out" in class might be preoccupied with their "problems" (Bisnaire, Firestone, & Rynard, 1990; Frieman 1993, 1997, 1998).

Knowing that a child is in the middle of a separation or divorce, a teacher can be more accepting of the child's unusual behaviors. The teacher might also be able to regain the child's academic focus by modifying an assignment to concern the issues with which the child is preoccupied. For example, a teacher who notices a student drifting during a free reading time can go over to him and say, "Chris I know it is difficult to concentrate when you are concerned about your parents' separation. Instead of reading, why don't you write in your journal about how you are feeling right now?"

Teachers also need to be sensitive to how a child's normal schedule can be disrupted by a separation or divorce. Home projects, which formerly were conscientiously done and turned in on time, might suddenly start appearing late because the child was staying with the noncustodial parent in another house and that parent wasn't involved in the project or didn't know about it. In addition, participating in a home learning project is low on the priorities of a noncustodial parent who is trying to catch up with 6 days of missed parenting. In these situations, the teacher needs to be understanding about why the home project was not done and provide a special time before or after school when the child can complete the assignment.

A teacher who is aware of the child's situation will also be better prepared to monitor and control the child's potentially disruptive behavior in the classroom. Some classroom behavior is unacceptable under any circumstances. Even if a child is experiencing problems related to the separation or divorce, he or she cannot hit another classmate. The teacher still needs to set appropriate limits and offer a socially acceptable outlet for the child's feelings. Thus, for example, a teacher might privately tell a fifth-grader who had just started a fight with another child, "I understand that you are angry about the separation of your parents. It is fine to be angry, but you cannot hit another person. If you feel angry, go over and punch the bag in the corner, or sit by yourself for a few minutes to think and get your anger under control. When you are ready to talk about how you feel, let me know and I will be happy to listen." This teacher instituted kind, respectful, but firm disciplinary measures.

Talking to Children

Children often share important personal information, sometimes indirectly, with their teachers. One of the teacher's most important tools for being supportive is to let the young child know that she or he is willing to listen. Special techniques can be helpful in getting children to talk about what is on their mind.

Once the child gives the teacher an opening, it is important for the teacher to actively reply in a way that shows the child that he or she cares and is willing to listen. The teacher can make comments such as these:

"How you are feeling right now?"

"Tell me about it."

"That must have been difficult for you."

"How did that make you feel?"

"What did that make you think about?"

These comments encourage children to talk about their feelings. Suppose a student comes up to the teacher and tells her, "I'm really tired this morning. I couldn't sleep because of all the noise." The teacher might respond, "Tell me about all the noise, Eunni." Her open-ended reply invites Eunni to talk about the fact that her parents were fighting and the fighting made her frightened.

Once children begin to open up about their bad feelings, the teacher should not agonize about saying the "right" thing to make it all better. Unfortunately, there is no one thing that a teacher can say to alleviate pain. The teacher can be most supportive by offering comments such as these:

"It's hard, isn't it?"

"That must have made you feel bad [sad, scared]."

"Could I give you a hug now?"

These comments demonstrate to children that the teacher cares about their feelings.

Older children respond to some of the same stem comments. The secondary education teacher who establishes a record of listening to students and taking their problems seriously has a better chance of getting adolescents to open up than does the one who trivializes their concerns.

Isolated Children

Some children have a difficult time expressing their feelings directly, particularly young children who have isolated themselves from their friends. These young children can be reached through the use of developmentally appropriate materials for young children, such as clay, water, paint, crayons, puppets, books, and housekeeping props. Teachers can encourage children at the easel to paint a picture about their family. Angry children can be given clay to pound and shape and water to manipulate.

Rhonda was an angry and isolated 4-year-old who seemed to be having problems coping. Her teacher, Ms. Herston, was having a difficult time reaching her through art or housekeeping play materials. Noticing Rhonda sitting alone during play time, Ms. Herston picked up a tiger puppet and approached her.

Although Rhonda would not talk to her teachers or any of the other children in the class, she was quick to talk to the tiger puppet on Ms. Herston's hand. The tiger learned that Rhonda was extremely angry at her mother for leaving the house. Through the puppet, Ms. Herston was able to help Rhonda understand that she was not bad if she was angry at her mother. Ms. Herston used the tiger to help Rhonda practice talking to her mother about how she felt.

Older children also can be encouraged to express themselves through art and writing. Teachers can facilitate writing by giving the children prompts like these:

If I could change anything, I would change . . .

I would like to tell my Dad (or Mom) . . .

I wish my mother (father) . . .

Sometimes I wish . . .

Classroom Activities

By providing activities in which children can play out their concerns, the teacher can help them to express their feelings. Unfortunately many children in the early grades are not given the chance to play. Dress-up materials, readily accessible art supplies, music experiences, and movement activities often are not included as they should be as an integral part of the classroom.

Teachers in the primary grades, working in such systems, should strive to weave more creative art, music, and movement experiences into their classroom day. If this is not possible, primary teachers can borrow materials from kindergarten teachers and provide them for use during breaks in the day or during recess and lunch.

THE TEACHER'S LIMITS

Unfortunately, teachers cannot solve the problems of the children experiencing divorce. They can only help them cope. Many children whose families are involved in divorce are concerned about abandonment. As teachers, we want to reassure children that no matter what happens we will always be there for them, but this is a promise that we often cannot keep. One of the common consequences of divorce is that the parents sell the family home or move into different housing, and the child has to go to a different school. If the child is changing schools, you can make yourself available, with the parents' permission, to talk to the child's new teacher to ensure an orderly transition to the new school.

During a divorce, children sometimes feel a loss of control. Their world is turned upside-down, and is often changing quite rapidly. The teacher can be helpful in this area by being consistent, particularly in setting limits.

Divorced children are often dragged into the struggle between their parents. Tommy, an 8-year-old, was concerned because his father was depressed. He explained that he didn't want to leave his father because "Dad will become lonely, and get sad again and cry." Therapeutic intervention outside of the school was aimed at helping Tommy's parents keep him out of the middle, but the teacher also had a role in helping. The teacher gave Tommy the time he needed to be an 8-year-old, and play without having to deal with his parents' problems. A time for play, even in the primary grades, is an essential part of a developmentally appropriate curriculum for just this reason.

HELPING PARENTS

Providing help for parents who are not on good terms with each other can be difficult. If teachers are to be effective in supporting a child during a separation or divorce, they must make an effort to communicate with both parents, not just the custodial parent.

Both parents are important people in the child's life, and both play an important role in shaping the child's behavior. A teacher who must ask parents to set limits on the child at home should send a note to each parent, not just one.

It is also critical that the teacher avoid getting herself in the middle of the parents' dispute. If a parent tries to involve the teacher in the ongoing conflict, the teacher should refer the parent to an appropriate social service agency in the community that specializes in counseling services. The teacher can tell the parents that for her to be of help to their child, she needs to stay out of the parental dispute. She can ensure both parents that she will work to be the advocate of their child, report individually to both of them, and stay neutral.

Summary

It is clear that through understanding and the use of selected communications skills, teachers can improve the academic performance and facilitate the emotional well-being of the children in their class whose parents are separating or divorcing. Teachers can talk to children to find out their situations. Once identified, these children can be helped in the classroom. Teachers can also work with parents to ease the children through this family transition. In this way, teachers can help children cope with the powerful emotions they experience during a separation or divorce.

RESEARCH IDEAS

Questions to Investigate

1. Should parents stay together for the sake of the children?
2. Can the legal divorce process be made less adversarial?
3. What do adolescents whose parents are divorced think about marriage?

Resources to Explore

American Bar Association
   http://www.abanet.org

Center for Divorce Education
   http://www.divorce-education.com

University of Minnesota Extension Service
   http://www.mes.umn.edu

References

BISNAIRE, L. M. C., FIRESTONE, P., & RYNARD, D. (1990). Factors associated with academic achievement in children following parental separation. *American Journal of Orthopsychiatry, 60,* 67–76.

FRIEMAN, B. B. (1993). Separation and divorce: Children want their teachers to know. *Young Children, 48,* 58–63.

FRIEMAN, B. B. (1997). Two parents, two homes. *Educational Leadership, 54,* 23–25.

FRIEMAN, B. B. (1998). What early childhood educators need to know about divorced fathers. *Early Childhood Education Journal, 25,* 239–241.

HETHERINGTON, E. M., STANLEY-HAGAN, M., & ANDERSON, E. R. (1989). Marital transitions: A child's perspective. *American Psychologist, 44,* 303–312.

KEITH, V. M., & FINLAY, B. (1988). The impact of parental divorce on children's educational attainment, marital timing, and likelihood of divorce. *Journal of Marriage and the Family, 50,* 798–809.

CHAPTER 16

Grandparents Raising Children

OBJECTIVE

After reading this chapter, you should be able to discuss the challenges faced by grandparents who are raising their grandchildren. You should also be able to report how you can help involve grandparents in the children's school experience.

CHAPTER OUTLINE

WHO IS THE PARENT?

As I chatted with Ms. Brown in her second-grade classroom after school, Jason, one of her students, brought his grandmother into the classroom to see his drawing on the bulletin board. His teacher, Ms. Brown, was surprised when Jason introduced her as his "mother." Her look of disbelief must have showed, because Jason's grandmother quickly explained, "That's right, I'm his grandmother, but I'm the one who is raising him."

Odds are, you will have some children in your class who are being raised not by their parents but by their grandparents. These grandparents have raised their own children and are now taking a second turn at parenting by raising their grandchildren—commonly because the parents have died or have abused, abandoned, or are otherwise incapable of taking care of the children, often because they are either on drugs or in jail.

This parenting arrangement has its effects both on the grandparents raising the children and on the children themselves. Teachers who are aware of this parenting arrangement can help both children and their grandparents cope with this situation.

WHY ARE GRANDPARENTS TAKING OVER?

The Administration on Aging (1999) estimates that 4 million children now live in households headed by a grandparent. In over 1.5 million of these households, grandparents are the sole caregivers. As Bond (1999) points out, the number of grandparents caring for grandchildren has increased by almost 40 percent over the last 10 years. Grandparents take on the responsibility of raising their grandchildren for many reasons—mainly because the parents are unavailable. Following are the most common reasons parents are unavailable to their children.

Death

One reason grandparents take over is because one of their own children, the child's parent, has died. The death of a child is an emotional blow to a parent, and one can expect to see a period of mourning in which the parent experiences a myriad of emotions, ranging from anger to depression. To help the surviving grandchildren cope, grandparents will often have to put their own emotions on hold while they tend to their grandchildren.

As I talked to Mrs. Everson, a longtime volunteer at a school where I supervised student teachers, I marveled at how well she was coping with the death of her daughter. She explained: "What choice did I have? I had to care for the child. My grandchild was the most important thing. I didn't have the time to cry and be depressed. He needed me to be strong. When I got him to bed at night and he was all settled in, I had time to be by myself and cry for my daughter. I had to think of the child first."

Drugs

When a child's parents are addicted to street drugs, grandparents often enter the picture to take over the parenting role. In many cases, grandparents just step in when it is apparent that their child is unwilling or unable to parent properly. One parent told me her fears. Mrs. Washburn cared for her grandson while her daughter, Danielle, worked during the day. As Danielle became involved with drugs, she started neglecting to pick up her daughter at the end of the day. Finally she just drifted off and left her child with her mother. When Mrs. Washburn tried to talk to her, Danielle threatened to take her daughter away and never let her mother see her again: "There are a lot of people who would want a little girl. I will give her to one of them. You will never see her again." Mrs. Washburn took care of her grandchild, but lived in fear that her daughter would return and take her granddaughter away.

Like many grandparents, Mrs. Washburn took over the responsibility of parenting without going through any legal process. Many grandparents fear reprisal from their children or children-in-law if they try to win legal parenting rights. As a consequence, these grandparents have no legal standing as parents and face difficulties when enrolling their grandchildren in school and seeking medical treatment for them.

Incarceration

When parents are sent to jail, grandparents can step up to take care of their children. Depending upon the jail sentence, this arrangement can be temporary or permanent. Although the birth parent is not present physically, they are often emotionally present. Children retain the bonds and attachment to their parents regardless of the label *criminal* attached to them by society.

Teenage Mothers

Grandparents frequently become the de facto parents of their teenager's child. After the novelty of being a parent wears off, the teenage mother often begins to depend more and more on her mother to raise the young child as the child's father often drops out of the picture. As time passes, the grandmother can become the mother figure to the child, and the one in charge of making the day-to-day decisions regarding the child's life, even though the child's mother still lives in the same house.

This process can be a gradual transition, starting with the grandmother taking partial responsibility for her grandchild and ending with the grandmother taking primary responsibility for the child's care. Musil (1998) noted that this transition has an effect on the grandmother, as grandmothers with primary responsibility reported greater parenting stresses and less instrumental and subjective social support than did those who had partial responsibility for their grandchild's care.

This role reversal can be confusing for children. In effect, grandmother becomes mother and mother becomes big sister as both mother and child have the status of being the grandmother's child.

EFFECTS OF SECOND-TIME PARENTING ON GRANDPARENTS

Many American subcultures, such as the African American culture, place strong value on caring for children within the extended family (Timberlake & Chipungu, 1992). But this choice often is not a choice. The grandparents take care of their grandchildren because that is the way it is, it is something they must do. This creates a conflict. On the one hand, the grandparents feel a strong bond to their grandchildren. They love them and want to step in and take care of them. On the other hand, the grandparents want to live out their years in a relaxed manner, having worked hard their entire lives to raise their own children. Caring for young grandchildren can bring great difficulties to the grandparents. To better understand these children, teachers will find it helpful to understand what their primary caregivers, their grandparents, are experiencing. Sixty-two-year-old Mrs. Miller told me her story, which is typical of many:

> I'm tired. I worked for all these years raising my kids. It wasn't easy. Now I thought I would be able to look after myself—take some trips, tend to my garden, do things at the church. I love my grandchild and would do anything in the world for her, but it's really hard now. I'm not as young as I used to be, and I have a hard time keeping up with her. I feel like I worked so hard and now I deserve my time to enjoy life, but I can't.

It is not easy for grandparents to become parents again. They pay a price, experiencing many feelings that can get into the way of successful parenting.

Stress and Depression

Grandparents face an array of things to be depressed about. After all, many have had to put their own dreams and plans for retirement on hold. Many are disappointed with their own children for not doing a better job of parenting and perhaps feel a little guilty for having raised a child who turned out to be such an ineffective parent. Some are thrust into the role of parenting a teenager, a difficult job in the best of conditions, while others worry about having to return their grandchild to the parent. All of this is done without much legal, social, or financial support.

In a national longitudinal study, Minkler and others (1997) found that undertaking the primary care of a grandchild is associated with increased depression. Hayslip and others (1998) found that custodial grandparents raising grandchildren reported experiencing emotional problems.

Isolation from Peers

Another feeling that is prevalent with grandparents is a sense of isolation from their peers. Most of their peers have long since passed out of the stage of child rearing and are more involved in retirement activities. Custodial grandparents who are busy raising children don't have much time for leisure activities. As they become more involved in child rearing, they move farther away from the interests of their peers. Mrs. Campbell explained to me: "I used to go on short trips with my girlfriends. Since I have been taking care of my grandchild, I can't just go away when I want. After a while of me turning them down, they stopped asking me. I don't blame them. They are carrying on with their lives."

Compounding the isolation from their peers is the fact that grandparents don't really fit in with the parents of their grandchild's playmates. These younger parents are not quick to link up with these grandparents, due to the generational difference.

Health Concerns

Some grandparents are struggling with ill or impaired health, which limits their stamina. Advanced age brings a real concern: "Will I still be there to see the job of raising this child through to the end?" Many grandparents who begin caring for their infant grandchildren while in their sixties will be very old by the time the children reach high school age.

Financial Concerns

Raising a child is expensive. Many grandparents are retired and living on a fixed income that is severely taxed by the considerable expenses involved in raising a child. Unless legal steps are taken to transfer guardianship and custody, grandparents have difficulty accessing the government programs that might provide financial assistance. Health insurance coverage can also be a problem. The pressure of providing for a grandchild can put a significant strain on grandparents' resources.

Legal Issues

Many grandparents raising children avoid legal arrangements in order to keep their relationship with their grandchild private. Child welfare benefits and protection from the child's parent are thus sacrificed. Grandparents often have a tenuous relationship with their own children and do not want to threaten their contact with their grandchildren by taking their own children to court to win formal parenting rights.

If they went to court, grandparents would face several options. One is guardianship and custody, which would given them parental authority while still giving the child's biological parents rights. The second choice is an adoption, in which the grandparent would have all rights and the natural parent would relinquish theirs. A third option could be putting the children in the foster care system.

Martha was afraid to use the court system: "I've seen how the courts work. They don't care about the kids. They won't give custody to me. I'm 68 years old, but I will still take better care of my grandson than his mother. If I go to court, I will lose my grandchild." Feeling that the deck is stacked against them, many grandparents avoid the legal system.

EFFECTS ON CHILDREN OF BEING RAISED BY A GRANDPARENT

Children who are being raised by their grandparent must deal with many unique issues. Children both young and old have to deal with having been abandoned by their biological parents. This is a very powerful issue that haunts many children. Children often tend to blame themselves for their parents' abandonment. They feel that they were somehow unworthy or that they did something wrong. Grandparents frequently don't help the child deal with this issue because they don't want to tell their grandchildren the real truth about their parents for fear of "badmouthing" their own child.

Another concern is confusion about who their mother really is. Very young children might only know grandmother as their mother figure and might see their biological mother as a big sister.

Older children often feel that their grandparents don't understand "modern" issues. Grandparents seem to have come from a different world, where the dating patterns, music, and clothing styles of their grandchildren are alien.

Other children can present a problem for youngsters who are being raised by grandparents. Having to explain that your grandmother is your "mother" might necessitate a discussion of why your mother left and what she is like. Adolescents might want to avoid all of these topics. Adolescents want to be like everyone else and fit in unnoticed. A "mother" who looks like their grandmother can be a cause of shame and embarrassment for them.

THE TEACHER'S ROLE IN HELPING GRANDPARENTS WHO ARE RAISING CHILDREN

The teacher's role in helping grandparents who are raising grandchildren is twofold. One task is to help the grandparent learn how to deal with a child of an "alien" generation, and the other task is to work with the child in the classroom. These are some things you can do to help:

- Teach contemporary parenting to the grandparents.
- Approach the grandparents in a respectful manner.
- Be careful to preserve the dignity and status of the grandparents.
- Help the grandparents understand the modern school curriculum.
- Help get the grandparents involved in the school.

Teaching Skills for Parenting Today's Children

Not having peers who are raising children, grandparents can learn to depend upon you, the teacher, to help them learn how to parent in today's times. A teacher cannot assume that just because someone has raised children, they know how to do it well, just as the teacher cannot assume that just because someone was successful in raising children in the past, they will be successful raising a child in today's world.

Many grandparents might have had a difficult time of raising their own children. If their own children have turned to drugs and abandoned their responsibilities as parents, grandparents can feel unsure about whether they themselves are competent to raise their grandchildren.

Teachers of young children are more often called upon to give input on general child-rearing questions than are high school teachers. With some sensitivity a teacher can offer to help a grandparent become aware of what's going on now without suggesting that they lack parenting skills. Grandparents can be introduced to discipline techniques that stress rewarding positive behaviors instead of corporal punishment. Teachers of young children can share with grandparents the techniques they use in their classrooms to discipline children.

Of course, grandparents, like all parents, must be approached in a respectful manner. Many of these grandparents have made great sacrifices to care for their grandchildren. Building upon this bond of love, teachers can let grandparents know that they respect and admire how they have stepped in, and they can offer the grandparents support and help.

Parenting suggestions should be made with great care to preserve the status and dignity of the grandparent. Young teachers might find it intimidating to tell an older person what to do. Ms. Megan, a second-year teacher, approached a grandmother to offer help:

> Mrs. Williams, I know you can teach me a few things about children. Do you mind if I come to you if I have a problem? I would really like to tap into your years of experience. You can really help me. By the way, maybe I can help you understand what is "in" with the kids now. You might have noticed that Reshida is coming home with stickers. In class, I give her a sticker whenever I catch her being good. Maybe you could help me out and do the same thing at home. It makes my job a lot easier if things are consistent at home. I will send the chart and some stickers home, and you can add stickers when you catch her doing good things at home, like be polite, cleaning up her toys, being nice to her sister, and things like that.

In this conversation, Ms. Meagan gave advice without appearing to tell Mrs. Williams what to do.

Grandparents can frequently use help in understanding what their grandchild is doing in school. Ways of doing math have changed over the years, and many grandparents will not have up-to-date skills to help their grandchild with homework. Some teachers have held mini workshops to teach grandparents how to do math the contemporary way.

Work in the Classroom

When studying families in elementary grades, be sure to include books and stories about children being raised by their grandparents. Treating this parenting constellation as just another parenting alternative helps normalize this situation.

Most often grandparents are not working outside the home and are available to volunteer in the classroom. Having a child's grandparent working as a parent helper enhances the prestige and standing of the youngster with his classmates.

Summary

Without legal, financial, or social support, many grandparents have taken over the role of parenting their grandchildren. Life is not easy for these grandparents. They face legal, financial, health, and lifestyle pressures.

Teachers can work to reduce the isolation of grandparents who are raising grandchildren by involving them in the total school experience. Teachers can serve as the bridge to help grandparents understand their grandchild's contemporary culture. Grandparents face many obstacles, but their presence as the functional parent attests to their love and devotion to their grandchildren.

RESEARCH IDEAS

Questions to Investigate

1. Should school start support groups just for grandparents?
2. Can grandparents be used to mentor younger mothers?
3. What role do older people play in our society?

Resources to Explore

Administration on Aging
http://www.aoa.dhhs.gov

American Association of Retired Persons—Grandparent Information Center
http://www.aarp.org

Senior-Site
http://www.seniors-site.com

References

ADMINISTRATION ON AGING (1999, October). Grandparents raising grandchildren. [Online] Available http://www.aoa.dhhs.gov/Factsheets/grandparents.htm.

BOND, C. (1999, March). Staying young at heart: Grandparents raising grandchildren. Family Education Network. [Online] Available: http://www.familyeducation.com/article/0,1120,1-3209,00.htm.

HAYSLIP, B., SHORE, J., HENDERSON, C. E., & LAMBERT, P. L. (1998). Custodial grandparenting and the impact of grandchildren with problems on role satisfaction and role meaning. *Journals of Gerontology: Series B. Psychological Sciences and Social Sciences, 53B*, 164–173.

MINKLER, M., FULLER-THOMPSON, E., MILLER, D., & DRIVER, D. (1997). Depression in grandparents raising grandchildren: Results of a national longitudinal study. *Archives of Family Medicine, 6*, 445–452.

MUSIL, C. M. (1998). Health, stress, coping, and social support in grandmother caregivers. *Health Care for Women International, 19*, 441–455.

TIMBERLAKE, E. M., & CHIPUNGU, S. S. (1992). Grandmotherhood: contemporary meaning among African American middle-class grandmothers. *Social Work, 37*, 216–222.

CHAPTER 17

Children Who Are Members of a Racial, Religious, or Sexual Minority

OBJECTIVE

After reading this chapter, you should be able to identify the children who are at risk because of others' intolerance and be able to discuss the teacher's role in creating a nonbiased classroom.

CHAPTER OUTLINE

Why Are Minority Children at Risk?
Experiences of Children Who Are Members of Minority Groups
    African Americans
    Native Americans
    Hispanic Americans
    Religious Groups
    Lesbian, Gay, and Bisexual Children
The Teacher's Role in Creating a Nonbiased Classroom
    Positive Feelings
    Role Models
    Intergroup Contact
    Curriculum
    Teasing
Summary

WHY ARE MINORITY CHILDREN AT RISK?

In most American classrooms, teachers will have children from racial, religious, or sexual minority groups. An understanding of what these children face in school can help teachers not only best meet the needs of minority group members but also sensitize the entire class to people who are different.

Why is Langston at risk just because he is African American? Why is Rachel at risk just because she is Jewish? Why is Perry at risk just because he is homosexual? Why are they at risk when there is nothing wrong with these children? They are at risk because of other people's intolerance. Sometimes this prejudice is expressed by individuals, and other times it comes out in an institutional practice.

Individual prejudice is easy to spot. The student who calls one of his classmates a "fag" is displaying individual prejudice. Institutional prejudice is more subtle and harder to recognize. It involves an institutional practice that perpetuates or creates an unfavorable perception or practice that has an adverse effect on one group. Using representations of Native American people as mascots, official symbols, emblems, and namesakes for football teams, such as the professional football team in our nation's capital, the Washington Redskins, is an institutional practice that is offensive and demeaning and perpetuates negative racial stereotypes.

Where does prejudice come from? As Allport (1954) points out in his classic work on prejudice, young children are wholly free from racial bias. Somewhere along the line—from parents, family, friends, the media—many children learn how to prejudge people. From watching the Washington Redskins play football on television, children learn that all "redskins" are warriors who wear warpaint, ride around on horses, and carry spears. Going to movies, children learn that all Italian Americans are gangsters. Listening to their parents telling "Polish" jokes, children learn that all Polish Americans are unintelligent. Our social environment is filled with many opportunities for children to learn negative stereotypes about minority groups. Our challenge as teachers is to counter these by presenting a bias-free classroom as a model for children to emulate.

Prejudice works because many people are threatened by difference—they need everyone to be like them and think like them, in order for them to maintain their own feelings of self-worth. The feeling is that if everybody around me looks like me, eats the same food as I do, and believes in the same things as I believe in, then I must be all right.

Children need to be comfortable with who they are. Children who are members of minority groups need to grow up with the same things that most white Christian children learn in school and from society. Minority children need to learn

- that they are as good as any other American,
- that they deserve to be treated the same as everyone else,
- that people like them have made and are still making contributions to society, and
- that people like them are successful.

Parents and teachers need to help children who are members of minority groups realize that, like all Americans, they come from valuable cultures that have helped enhance America.

EXPERIENCES OF CHILDREN WHO ARE MEMBERS OF MINORITY GROUPS

All children who are members of minority groups need to be valued and respected. Members of groups, however, have unique experiences.

African Americans

There is a long history of discrimination against African American children in the United States, but our nation has come a long way in dealing with our past practices of legal discrimination. Although racial discrimination is now illegal in the United States, it still occurs. Comer and Poussaint (1992) point out that policy making and attitudes are controlled by whites who are often antagonistic or indifferent to the needs of African Americans. As a result, African Americans have to fight for the respect that whites take for granted.

African Americans have a unique culture derived from their own history and languages. The people who promoted and prospered from slavery actively worked to destroy the culture of the newly arrived African slaves. After slavery was abolished, people interested in segregation actively worked to eliminate any mention of African Americans in history books and to keep African Americans as an underclass, out of positions of power and influence. The fact that African Americans have overcome these considerable obstacles speaks to the resolve and strength of their culture.

Parents of African American children have to work hard to make sure that their children grow up with racial pride. The primary way parents teach their children pride is by example. An African American parent who has pride in her skin color and in the contributions of her ancestors can impart those feelings to her children. Pride is also transmitted to children by parents when they celebrate holidays such as Martin Luther King's birthday, or actively participate in and support ethnic organizations.

Native Americans

There are only 300,000 to 400,000 Native American children of school age, and most of them are educated in public schools (Charleston & King, 1991). They face many obstacles to achieving success in school. One obstacle is the lack of visibility of the positive aspects of their cultures.

Native American cultures are not positively presented in mainstream society. Most American children know of Native Americans from cowboy movies and mascots of athletic teams, images that are distortions of Native American cultures.

Another obstacle is that students who identify themselves as Native Americans are often subjected to taunts and racial slurs that make them feel threatened and ashamed. When they defend themselves against harassment, they often are suspended or expelled. Alienation is a key contributing factor in the high dropout rates of Native American children (Charleston & King, 1991).

Finally, many of the cultural values these children have grown up with are at odds with school practices. For example, Native American values stress cooperation rather than competition, and this can put these students at a disadvantage in a school that emphasizes competition. Relay races, spelling bees, rewards for the highest grades in the class—all are competitions that do not reflect the values of many Native American cultures.

Hispanic Americans

Hispanic Americans (Latino Americans) share common cultural origins and language, although they come from diverse nations and backgrounds with distinctive histories and distinctive socioeconomic and political experiences. According to the report of the President's Advisory Commission (1996), in 1994 there were 26.4 million Hispanic Americans living in the continental United States; this large group had the following subgroup divisions:

64 percent were Mexican Americans

Almost 11 percent were Puerto Ricans

13 percent were from Central and South America and the Caribbean

5 percent were Cuban Americans

7 percent were classified as "other"

Recent Hispanic immigrants have come primarily from Central and South American countries that have been experiencing political unrest.

The unique problem that Hispanic American children face is that their bilingualism is often treated as a liability rather than as a rich culture resource. Because of poverty and poor housing, many Latino students are being segregated into schools that are "resource poor."

The main task in dealing with children who speak only Spanish is first to teach them to speak English. The other tasks include providing Hispanic American children with role models and a strong sense that people of their culture are valuable and have contributed to the world's culture. Teachers also must be creative in searching for interpreters to make sure that they will be able to communicate with these children's parents.

Religious Groups

We are a nation of many religious groups and a tradition of religious tolerance. Although the Constitution of the United States calls for separation of church and state, the Supreme Court has been called upon to make many rulings on the appropriate barriers that should exist between public schools and religion.

Although we are legally a pluralistic society when it comes to religion, in reality the dominant religion is seen by many as the standard to follow. It is assumed that all children will follow the main religion in one form or another, and if they object they are often viewed poorly by the majority group.

Many children of Moslems, Jews, Jehovah's Witnesses, and other religions and atheists face conflicts when they are called upon in school to engage in an activity that is not part of their family's religious tradition. If school celebrations are structured around traditional Christian holidays such as Easter and Christmas, children of minority religions will be excluded.

These children all feel like they are the objects of a tug-of-war. The school is pulling one arm to get them involved in the mainstream religious celebrations, and their parents are pulling on the other arm to keep them true to their family religious traditions. The loser in this contest is the minority group child, who faces a no-win situation.

Lesbian, Gay, and Bisexual Children

A number of studies suggest a possible genetic basis for homosexuality (Frieman, O'Hara, & Settel, 1996). Gay children often must endure harassment, contempt, and acts of physical violence. The effects can be psychologically as well as physically damaging. As a result, the child's self-esteem and self-confidence can deteriorate and the child can suffer from self-directed homophobia (Pharr, 1988).

This type of discrimination is often not recognized by teachers. Teachers first need to examine their own feelings about homosexuality. They can start by asking themselves if they feel just as comfortable comforting a gay or lesbian child who is being teased by classmates on the playground as they feel comforting a heterosexual child. The first step in ensuring that you meet the needs of gay children is to examine and deal with your own biases, and learn to treat all your students with the same care and respect.

THE TEACHER'S ROLE IN CREATING A NONBIASED CLASSROOM

The following are some positive steps teachers can take to ensure that their teaching strategies establish harmony in their classrooms:

- Help all children feel positive about themselves.
- Introduce the children to successful role models.
- Promote intergroup contact.
- Implement a curriculum that supports the contributions of all groups.
- Have a zero-tolerance policy for teasing.

Positive Feelings

The first step is to help children develop high positive regard for themselves. People who feel good about themselves are less likely to feel threatened by someone who is different. All children prosper if they feel good about themselves.

You set a positive tone when you respect all students in your class. When disciplining a child, never attack the child's personality; instead, focus on the aspect of the child's behavior that needs changing. A seventh-grade teacher saw Johnny Smith throw a spitball at another classmate. She responded: "Mr. Smith, that behavior is inappropriate in this classroom and violated a school rule. The penalty for throwing a spitball is 15 minutes of after-school detention. Now will you please continue the good job you are capable of doing with your social studies seatwork."

Role Models

All children like to see people like themselves who are successful. It is important to include important people of all genders, religions, cultures, races, and sexual orientations in your lessons. It is a way of saying to a child, "See that person. They are famous. They have achieved great things. They are like you. You can achieve great things too."

Teachers might have to do some research to identify these minority contributors, who frequently are not identified in history texts. Displaying a picture of a female U.S. Supreme Court justice on the wall can say to every female student that they too can become a member of the U.S. Supreme Court. Reading a story by James Baldwin can suggest to African American children that someone like them has become a great author and that, by implication, so can they.

Intergroup Contact

The U.S. Army provides a good example of how intergroup contact can reduce prejudice. In the army, men and women are trained together to support and protect each other. The most important aspect of fellow soldiers is whether they will protect your back, not their gender or skin color.

When students of different persuasions are together in the classroom, they have the time to learn to see each other as individuals. When people are together, they can learn to focus on what they have in common rather than what sets them apart.

As a teacher in a multicultural classroom, you can make sure when you structure cooperative group activities that you intentionally pair children who come from different backgrounds. Giving these children a common task will focus them on cooperating and working in harmony.

If you have a homogeneous class, you might have to be a bit more creative. One technique to broaden your class is to pair with another teacher in another school that has a culturally different population. The children can write to each other or communicate over the Internet, and begin to know each other as people. Often teachers who pair like this culminate the experience in a shared field experience where the children can meet and interact in person.

Curriculum

Highlighting the accomplishments and events of all cultures helps broaden your students and give them a wider worldview. When studying religions, why tie your discussion to the major Judeo-Christian groups? Your job is to bring in material about all the major religions of the world. You might need to draft guest speakers or make use of the Internet to collect information.

Part of your task will be to replace inaccurate information with more current facts. When children see the effects of discriminatory behavior dramatized, they can experience what it is like to be a member of a different group.

Teasing

In your classroom, you need to adopt a zero-tolerance policy for teasing based on minority group membership. No matter how innocent it appears, teasing reinforces prejudices. It is much easier for teachers to ignore this type of teasing than to deal with it, but you must confront it. Use these opportunities to focus the class on their similarities and point out how bad people are made to feel when they are teased.

Summary

Some children are at risk only because of other people's intolerance. Children who are African American, Hispanic American, Native American, Moslem, Jewish, gay or lesbian, and so on have suffered at the hands of others. A teacher's job is to end this discrimination by having a zero-tolerance policy for teasing, working to help all children have a positive self-concept, providing role models for minority group children, and providing curriculum and intergroup contact that put all children together.

RESEARCH IDEAS

Questions to Investigate

1. What measures can we take to ensure that all schools will have a diverse student body?
2. How can we help parents of diverse cultures learn about each other?
3. How can you use the Internet to make your class more diverse?

Resources to Explore

Anti-Defamation League
http://www.adl.org

Chicano/Latino Net
http://www.latino.ssnet.ucla.edu

Diversity Resource Center
http://www.civilrights.org

Jewish Christian Relations
http://www.jcrelations.com

Native Web (Native American Information)
http://www.nativeweb.org

Museum of Tolerance
http://www.weisenthal.com

References

ALLPORT, G. W. (1954). *The nature of prejudice.* New York: Addison-Wesley.

BAUMRIND, D. (1995). Commentary on sexual orientation: Research and social policy implications. *Developmental Psychology, 31,* 130–136.

CHARLESTON, G. M., & KING, G. L. (1991). *Indian nations at risk task force: Listen to the people* (ED 343 754). Washington, DC: U.S. Department of Education, Indian Nations At Risk Task Force.

COMER, J. P., & POUSSAINT, A. F. (1992). *Raising black children.* New York: Penguin Books.

FRIEMAN, B. B., O'HARA, H., & SETTEL, J. (1996). What heterosexual teachers need to know about homosexuality. *Childhood Education, 73,* 40–42.

PHARR, S. (1988). *Homophobia: A weapon of sexism.* Little Rock, AR: Chardon Press.

PRESIDENT'S ADVISORY COMMISSION ON EDUCATIONAL EXCELLENCE FOR SPANISH AMERICANS. (1996). *Our nation on the fault line: Hispanic-American education* [Online]. Available: http://www.ed.gov/pubs/faultline.

CHAPTER 18

Children New to the United States

(WITH IDEAS FROM MARCIA MINDEL,
Special Education Resource Teacher, Montgomery County, Maryland)

OBJECTIVE

After reading this chapter, you should be able to discuss how you can promote the adjustment of children whose first language is not English and who have recently arrived here from a country with a different culture.

CHAPTER OUTLINE

WHO ARE CHILDREN NEW TO THE UNITED STATES?

More and more classroom teachers are going to be having students in their class who are new Americans. They are either immigrants or the American-born offspring of immigrants to the United States. These children will present classroom teachers with a unique set of challenges, from dealing with language barriers to issues related to parents who have different cultural values.

Almost 20 percent of American children are the children of immigrants. The number of children who are either immigrants or the American-born offspring of immigrants grew to 13.7 million in 1997, up from 8 million in 1990, making them the fastest-growing segment of the U. S. population under the age of 18 (Dugger, 1998). California, Texas, Florida, and various eastern states have larger clusters of children whose parents are immigrants than do others. For example, nearly one-third of the total student population in New York City schools are immigrants (Rivera-Batiz, 1996). Many of these children are from Central American countries, Asian countries, such as Korea and Vietnam, as well as from Russian and other Eastern European countries.

Historically, immigrants to the United States have not been readily accepted by the resident population. As Simcox (1997) points out, many citizens who favor controls on immigration perceive immigrants as a threat to the dominant culture and society's fiscal health. The fact that immigrant children and the children of immigrants are considered at risk is a statement about how resident Americans feel about them and subsequently treat them. The lack of sensitivity to an immigrant's culture contributes to her sense of isolation, which of itself can lead to adjustment difficulties.

THE SCHOOL SYSTEM AND IMMIGRANT CHILDREN

In the early 1900s, children in our schools were expected to learn English without any intervention. Many children learned English on their own, as Chavez (1998) points out, practically by osmosis, but many others fell behind and dropped out of school.

In *Lau v. Nichols* in 1974, the Supreme Court required schools to give students who speak and write very little English an education that meets their language needs. The Court, however, did not spell out how this should be done, so school districts across the United States have followed several different strategies.

One of the strategies some school districts adopted is bilingual classes. Using this strategy, children are taught in their native language until a gradual transition to English instruction is made. Bilingual education is a strategy that lends itself to places like California and Texas, where there are large groups of Spanish-speaking children. Bilingual education has always been the most politically controversial strategy, having its articulate opponents and proponents. In 1998, California voters prohibited this bilingual approach when they passed Proposition 227.

Another strategy used by other districts is special English as a Second Language (ESL) classes where English is taught using small groups or one-on-one tutoring. This technique requires teachers with special training who may or may not have fluency in the language of their students.

A third strategy is an immersion approach, where the teacher instructs only in English regardless of whether the students can fully understand the language. This technique gives the regular classroom teacher the primary responsibility in helping children who have limited English skills.

CHALLENGES FACED BY IMMIGRANT CHILDREN

Children who are immigrants and children whose parents are immigrants face several challenges in America's schools. The first challenge is learning to speak English. Not only must these children learn to speak, they also must learn to read, write, and spell words in this new language.

Other challenges faced by these children include keeping a healthy ethnic identity while developing an American identity. The children of many of America's earlier immigrants wanted so badly to become Americans that they kept their ethnic identity hidden. My father was a child of immigrants. I went to visit him once when he was hospitalized and heard a conversation in another language coming from his room. As I peeked in, I was shocked to discover that my father was fluent in another language. When his guest left, I asked him why he had never taught the language to me and my siblings. He explained that when he was growing up in the early 1900s it was important for him to be an American. He said he didn't learn English until he went to school, and that his parents spoke the "old language" at home. Faced with discrimination against immigrants, he quickly realized that he had to throw off all of the markers of the "old country" in order to get a job and be accepted as an American.

Although today's children are still faced with the challenge of dealing with racism and discrimination, they have civil rights laws to protect them now. Nonetheless, children who are immigrants are still faced with covert racism and discrimination. They face a challenge in developing a pride in their ethnic identity while dealing with the prejudice that exists in the minds of many people.

American ways are often foreign to people coming from different cultures. When working with some children who had just come to the United States from the then Soviet Union, I was surprised when one high school girl asked me if her phone conversations with her friends were monitored by the school. She expected things to be like they were in Odessa, her old home. Other parents who come from countries where it is traditional never to question authorities, and where school officials are considered authorities, find it very difficult to deal with American school officials. They are not used to speaking up and asking for what they want.

Children from war-torn countries can need time and nurturing before they realize that they are safe. You need to be patient with their initial untrusting behaviors and realize that they will change in time.

CULTURES IN CONFLICT

By understanding the child's native culture, teachers will gain an invaluable understanding of why the child does what he does. Often living in two worlds, immigrant children frequently find that their old world culture and values conflict with those of their new country. This clash can have an adverse effect on children.

James, Kim, and Moore (1997), when examining the racial and ethnic differences in Asian American adolescent drug use, found that the transition to Western culture disrupted the hierarchal family structure, interdependence, and self-identity of young Asian Americans. Kim, Kim, and Rue (1997) note that traditional cultural influences are still operating in the conscious or unconscious minds of Korean American children, especially in the areas of child rearing. I saw Kyung, a 17-year-old Korean American young man, when he came to a community mental health clinic at the suggestion of his school counselor. Kyung was in deep conflict because he wanted to join his classmates and go to after-school dances, but his father would not give him permission to date. Kyung's struggle was in dealing with his "American" values of dating at 17 and his father's "old world" values. Compounding the problem was Kyung's value of not disrespecting his father by questioning his decisions. This clash put him in a very uncomfortable position.

Espinosa (1995) points out the need for teachers to develop a greater understanding of the features of the Hispanic American culture that influence parents' child-rearing and socialization practices, communication styles, and orientation toward formal education. She points out that in many Latin American countries it is considered rude for a parent to intrude into the child's life at school. Parents believe that it is the school's job to educate and the parent's job to nurture, and that the two jobs do not mix. This value can cause a teacher to misinterpret a parent's unwillingness to take an active role in communicating with their child's teacher.

The issues can be even more complicated for teachers because Americans tend to think of Hispanic American culture as a homogeneous entity. As Haycock and Duany (1991) remind us, differences among Hispanic American subgroups in communication styles and socialization practices are often greater than the overall differences between Hispanics and non-Hispanics. We have to be careful not to think that all children who have Spanish as a native tongue have the same culture.

Cultural ignorance can often lead one to make false conclusions about a child's behavior. When I was in a clinical training program run by a university mental health clinic, I was taught that it was important to notice if the client made eye contact with me during our interview sessions. Lack of eye contact was considered an unhealthy sign. In interviewing a young Asian American girl, I observed that she didn't make eye contact when she talked to me. When I mentioned this to an Asian American colleague, she pointed out that according to this young child's tradition, to have looked me in the eye would have been a measure of disrespect, in that I was her elder and in a position of authority. In this example, what could have been viewed as a mental health problem was actually a sign of respect for the authority figure. Teachers need to study the native cultures of the children they teach in order to discover such cultural characteristics.

THE TEACHER'S ROLE IN MEETING THE CHALLENGES TO HELP CHILDREN NEW TO THE UNITED STATES

When you work to help children new to the United States, you will be faced with many challenges, including these:

- Learning about the child's culture
- Having to communicate, yet not knowing the child's language
- Helping a non-English-speaking student survive in the classroom
- Teaching American customs
- Working with the child's parents
- Designing special school activities to help new children adjust

Learning About the Child's Culture

Teachers face many challenges in dealing with immigrant children. One challenge is to learn as much as possible about the child's native culture. One can learn about other cultures by many means, including these:

- Books from the library
- Documents available from the ERIC Clearinghouse
- Talking to other parents from the culture
- Talking to people from a community cultural center

You can also ask the child questions about her culture. Have her share a special holiday or custom with the class. She can invite her parents to help. In this way, all of her classmates will be able to learn about her native culture.

Not Knowing the Child's Language

You will probably not know how to speak most immigrant children's native languages. This of course makes your life more difficult, particularly if the child's English-language skills have not yet been developed. You should try to find within your school system or within your community someone who speaks both the child's first language and English. Searching the phonebook for community centers or trade centers is a good place to start, if you have no one in your school system who is available to help. Many local universities have scholars who specialize in languages and know community speakers of the language who can help interpret.

Once you find a person, get her to teach you several words and phrases in the child's native language. Include these:

- "Hello."
- "Welcome to the class."
- "My name is . . . and I am your teacher."
- "What is your name?"

This basic vocabulary will make an important statement to the child about your value and respect for his language.

A Non-English-Speaking Student

It is always an adventure to have in your classroom a student who doesn't speak fluent English. In the best of conditions the child will be getting English instruction from a special teacher. This specialist can also help you deal with the child in your classroom.

The first step is to involve the entire class in helping the new child. You can tell the class that the new child already speaks another language and is also learning English. In effect you are giving the children a positive view of the new child—as not a dumb child who can't speak English but a bright child who is learning to speak a second language.

You can appoint one child who can serve as the new student's class buddy. The buddy's responsibility can be to just befriend the new child and help them with class and school routines. Care should be taken in selecting the buddy. Be sure to choose a child who is a patient, accepting, and kind.

If there is more than one child in the bilingual family, you can train the older children to read to the younger ones. Provide the older children with appropriate books to read to the younger ones. In this way, the older students benefit from reading and the younger students can practice their listening comprehension skills.

In Marcia Mindel's school, each family is given a bilingual picture dictionary as well as alphabet cards and vocabulary games that can be played at home. Parents too can learn from the picture dictionary. All older children are also given an English dictionary.

Teaching English has its amusing aspects. Our American English is peppered with slang and idioms that are baffling to many children just learning the language. Marcia Mindel cites a funny experience.

> I told an upper elementary student, who was a native of Central America, to "knock it off" when he was talking during my instruction in English. He diligently dumped his desk, knocking off all of his pencils, papers, and books to the floor. He sat there and smiled at me respectfully, because he thought he had demonstrated his skills in English by following my directions.

Teaching American Customs

Most new children will learn American customs by watching the other children. Again, classmates need to see the child's native customs not as wrong, but as different. Most native children find it a fun experience to teach a new child how to behave, dress, and gesture like an American. Children quickly learn how to give a "high five" to their classmates. Boris was a high school student in my daughter's class who had come to America from Russia and was quickly learning English. His classmates dove in and taught him all of the expressions used by the teenage culture. When Boris repeated one of the expressions to the teacher in a class discussion, his classmates quickly silenced him and explained that what they taught him was best not said at home, school, or in church.

Imagine how strange pizza must look to a child who grew up in Vietnam and has eaten a diet of mainly rice. It's no wonder that they might not know what to do with the pizza on their lunch tray. Marcia Mindel helped a young Vietnamese child by eating lunch with him and explaining what they were both eating. Other classmates were invited to join the group and share tastes of their lunch. In this way the youngster got to sample foods in a pleasurable, nonthreatening way.

Respecting the Old Customs

The new child is trying to fit in and become like everyone else, but she might dress differently, have a different hairstyle, and eat different foods for lunch. Teachers need to help the other class members to see the child's native behaviors as good rather than as an object of teasing. Teachers have to work hard to adopt a policy of respect for all students and to have a zero-tolerance policy for any teasing. As a model, you might want to try the same "exotic" foods that the child is eating, to model that different can be good.

Meeting these challenges can help teachers successfully integrate immigrant children into American society. The presence of children of other cultures gives us an opportunity to look at our own culture through fresh eyes and rediscover the great values and attitudes that we as Americans have toward cultural diversity. The presence of an immigrant child can be a very positive experience for all involved.

WORKING WITH PARENTS

Because of the language and cultural differences, it takes special skills to deal with parents of immigrant children. Before teachers can deal with these parents, they must know how the parents view things.

Language

Obviously it is a problem to talk with parents who don't speak your language. Many immigrant parents might speak a basic form of English, but might be uncomfortable talking and trying to understand you in a conference. Often, as teachers, you need to find a native speaker of the parents' language to help you when you talk to parents. A school employee is best, because she or he will be required to adhere to professional ethics in regard to privacy.

If a school person is not available, the second choice might be an older member of the community who speaks the appropriate language. Before you start, you must discuss with the translator the ethical implications of hearing another person's private business. The translator needs to agree to abide by the privacy ethics of teachers. This concept of privacy can also be explained to the parent before the interview.

In a pinch, a teacher might have to use an older student who is bilingual. If one uses a student, one must be careful not to say anything of a personal or private nature during the parent-teacher conference. The last choice for a translator is the child herself. The child should be used only in an emergency or to communicate the most public of information.

Marcia Mindel encourages parents to send her notes in their primary language if they have concerns or questions. She is always able to find someone in the school or the community to translate the note. Her school translates the school's weekly bulletin into Spanish for their many Spanish-speaking parents. When a child in her class does something well in school, a short note or certificate is sent home to the parent in their primary language. Field trip permission forms also are also sent home in the parent's primary language.

As the child masters English in school, he might become the most English-proficient person in the family. Children might have to miss school in order to translate for their family at doctors' appointments, appointments for financial aid, or with the immigration authorities. Even though the parents have access to a translator, the child is needed to hear any comments in English that the translator might not choose to share. Parents see this as the child's duty to the family, and it is sometimes more important than coming to school.

As the teacher, you have to understand this issue and be supportive. Prepare work for the child who has had to miss school, and make sure that he gets some time during or after school to make up the work he missed.

Poverty

Many immigrants are poor. You can expect that many of these parents will be working several jobs and will be hard-pressed to help their children with homework. You can expect a house that has few English books lying around to read. One of your first activities might be to make sure that the new youngster gets her own library card and learns how to use the local public library.

Many children come to school without the necessary school supplies. Their families might be on a tight budget and not have enough money to buy all of the items used in school. Teachers can ask area merchants to donate some supplies for these children. (Refer to chapter 12 for more information about poverty.)

Dealing with Authority

Although we might not think of ourselves in these terms, we are authority figures. In a true sense, as public school teachers we represent "the government." Many people come to the United States to flee repressive situations. These people have learned to view authorities as their enemies, and sometimes bring this attitude with them.

Parents who do not have their green cards can become frightened when the school calls. They might not want to get involved with the school and might not attend parent conferences. Just because a parent does not come to a school conference doesn't mean that they don't care about their child's education. Marcia Mindel reports that many of the immigrant parents in her school are working two jobs to make enough money to support the family. The time between jobs is for being with the children or sleeping. For many of these parents, day-to-day living is very difficult.

You can help by sending a lot of notes home in the parents' primary language. When the parent gets a steady stream of messages that show you really care about their child, they will begin to slowly build up a trusting relationship with the school.

I was helping one family who immigrated from a country where members of their religious group were persecuted by the government. Our relationship included frequent phone calls in which I tried to keep contact on a friendship level. They were very guarded and didn't say much when I called, even though their English skills were very good.

When we were alone and outside, my new friends asked me, "Who is listening in when we talk on the phone?" I explained to them that people are not allowed to listen in on conversations, under our system of law, without a court order. They were surprised. Their reluctance to talk was not personal distrust of me, but rather a transferred suspicion of authority. Unfortunately, this suspicion can also apply to public school people and can be difficult for teachers.

Respond to suspicious parents with understanding, explanations, and patience. After a while, you will prove that you care about their children and will establish your own level of trust with parents.

Rearing Children in a New Land

Parents often feel that they cannot control their children as they experience the culture shock of raising children in America. One parent told me:

> My daughter is fifteen. She talks on the phone constantly, and I cannot understand what she says. She wears makeup and short skirts, which is in direct conflict with our ways. I don't understand the school. The high school seems like a social place with lax rules. It's not a serious place for learning, and the children do not have the hours of homework that I did in the old country. I feel out of control.

Some parents feel unable to help their children academically in any language. Many parents' own schooling was interrupted by civil war; many other parents lived in rural areas where there were no schools. Parents might even be illiterate in their primary language and not be able to understand anything sent home from the school even if it is in their native language. Life might seem very much out of control for them.

Special School Activities

The following activities have been used by Marcia Mindel in her school to help the Spanish-speaking children practice their language skills and feel connected to the elementary school. Similar activities can be useful with other children new to the United States.

Homework Club

Marcia Mindel has set up a Homework Club at her school. The club meets on a regular basis, and children are given individualized help. Volunteers are recruited from the community to assist. To encourage a feeling of belonging, each Homework Club member is given a membership card.

Friendship among the students grows as they realize they are not alone and that there are others who share their same concerns and challenges. Each club member is given a dictionary and taught how to use it so that they can become more independent. The children also have access to computers and reference books that they might not have at home.

School supply materials are also provided for the members of the club, many of whose parents don't know what kind of supplies to buy for their children.

Reading Buddies

Children in an upper grade are paired with a lower-grade class in Marcia Mindel's school. The older children read to the younger ones, and they do activities together. For example, the younger child might draw a picture from the story and the older child might write several sentences about the picture. Younger children also are able to read stories to the older children.

All of these activities are opportunities for these children to learn in an emotionally safe, supportive atmosphere. Every activity is designed to help the children take pride in their school accomplishments. To build a sense of pride in school, Marcia Mindel likes to frame a child's essay and present it to the parents. The child's essay is in English and the child also translates it into the parents' primary language. Mindel has found that many parents put this framed essay in a place of importance in the home to share with family members and friends.

Summary

Children who are new to the United States face the regular challenges of school, but in a different language and strange culture. By understanding and respecting the child's culture, we can begin to build a working relationship between the child, the child's family, and the school. With some special effort, teachers can help these children grow, learn, and prosper in their new country.

RESEARCH IDEAS

Questions to Investigate

1. What would America be like if we had no immigrants?
2. How much of one's mother culture should a child retain?
3. How do you teach an appreciation of diversity if your school has no new Americans?

Resources to Explore

American Civil Liberties Union
   http://www.aclu.org

American Immigration Center
   http://www.us-immigration.com

Culturally and Linguistically Appropriate Services—Early Childhood Education Institute
   http://clas.uiuc.edu

References

CHAVEZ, L. (1998, June 10). We have a ways to go in the bilingual war. *Jewish World Review* [Online]. Available: http://www.jewishworldreview.com/cols/chavez061098.htm.
DUGGER, C. W. (1998, March 21). Report: English favored by kids. *San Jose Mercury News* [Online]. Available: http://www-rcf.usc.edu/~cmmr/SJMerc_March21.htm.

ESPINOSA, L. M. (1995). *Hispanic parent involvement in early childhood programs.* Washington, DC: U.S. Government Printing Office. (ERIC Document Reproductive Service No. ED382412.)

HAYCOCK, K., & DUANY, L. (1991). Developing the potential of Latino students. *Principal, 70,* 25–27.

JAMES, W. H., KIM, G. K., & MOORE, D. D. (1997). Examining racial and ethnic differences in Asian adolescent drug use: The contributions of culture, background, and lifestyle. *Drugs: Education, Prevention and Policy, 4,* 39–51.

KIM, W. J., KIM, L. I., & RUE, D. S. (1997). Korean American children. In G. Johnson-Powell & J. Yamamoto (Eds.), *Transcultural child development: Psychological assessment and treatment* (pp. 183–207). New York: Wiley.

RIVERA-BATIZ, F. (1996). *The education of immigrant children in New York City* (ERIC Digest No. 117). New York: ERIC Clearinghouse on Urban Education. (ERIC Document Reproductive Service No. ED 402 399.)

SIMCOX, D. (1997). Major predictors of immigration restrictionist. *Population and Environment: A Journal of Interdisciplinary Studies, 19,* 129–143.

CHAPTER 19

Children of Substance-Abusing Parents

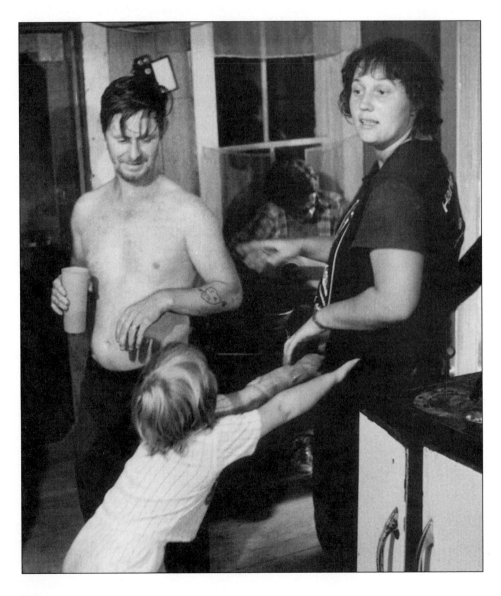

OBJECTIVE

After reading this chapter, you should be able to discuss the physiological effects of maternal drug use on children in utero, and describe techniques to help children of substance abusers so they will not suffer for the behavior of their parents.

CHAPTER OUTLINE

Who Are Children with Substance-Abusing Parents?
The Lifestyle of the Substance Abuser
    Abuse While the Child Is in Utero
    Abuse During Childhood
Effects on the Child of Substance-Abusing Parents
The Teacher's Role in Helping Children Whose Parents Are Substance Abusers
    Expect the Child to Perform at a High Level
    Have a Consistent Learning Environment
    Keep in Control
    Hold Children Responsible for Their Own Behavior Only
    Set Limits When Necessary
    Provide a Quiet Place to Work
Working with Parents
Summary

WHO ARE CHILDREN WITH SUBSTANCE-ABUSING PARENTS?

Through no fault of their own, many children are being conceived and raised by parents who abuse illegal drugs (such as cocaine) or legal ones (like alcohol). By understanding the experiences of these children, teachers can provide them with help and support.

    Drug abuse is widespread in the United States. According to data from the National Association for Children of Alcoholics (1999), approximately 11 million U.S. children under the age of 18 have alcoholic parents. State surveys indicate that 8 to 12 percent of women delivering in their hospitals had used illegal drugs at some time during the pregnancy, including just before delivery (Chasnoff, 1992; Vega et al., 1993).

THE LIFESTYLE OF THE SUBSTANCE ABUSER

The life of a substance abuser revolves around the abused substance, whether it is alcohol or an illegal drug such as cocaine. The most important thing in the abuser's life is to satisfy the need for this substance. Everything else is of secondary importance.

For the addict, the drive to satisfy the addiction supersedes the needs of the addict's children. This dysfunctional priority affects everyone in the family in a negative way.

The drug lifestyle is not physically healthy. Substance-abusing women have a higher incidence of infections, especially hepatitis B, AIDS, and other sexually transmitted diseases. Addicted people usually take poor care of their bodies and often do not eat properly.

Abuse While the Child Is in Utero

Illegal drugs

The effects of maternal substance abuse on the child begin in utero. It is difficult to do research on the effects of the addiction because these mothers not only are taking drugs, but are also eating poorly, engaging in risky sexual behavior, and generally living "on the edge." Many of these women get little, if any, prenatal care and live in poor housing conditions. Researchers find it hard to control for the sole variable of drug abuse. Nonetheless, whether or not the alcohol or drugs are the only causes of the problems, substance abuse during pregnancy creates a multitude of complications.

The fetus in utero pays the price for all of the substances consumed by its mother. Virtually all drugs that the mother takes while pregnant will be passed to her developing fetus. These drugs reach the fetal circulatory system by crossing the placenta and can cause direct toxic effects on the fetus, as well as fetal and maternal drug dependency (Robins & Mills, 1993). The newborn child of an opiate-addicted woman will experience withdrawal after birth when the mother's drugs no longer are directly passed to the newborn. Symptoms of opiate withdrawal in a newborn are similar to those found in adults.

Cocaine-exposed infants have an increased incidence of premature birth, impaired fetal growth, and neonatal seizures (Chasnoff et al., 1985; Chasnoff et al., 1989; Bingol et al., 1987). The early thought was that "crack babies" suffered irreversible damage due to their mother's addiction. Later research has been less fatalistic. Hurt and others (1997) found that they were unable to detect any difference in performance, verbal, or full-scale IQ scores between cocaine-exposed and control children at age 4.

Fetal Alcohol Syndrome (FAS)

Maternal alcohol consumption can have a detrimental influence on the developing fetus. Although scientists do not agree on how much alcohol is harmful, they do agree that excessive use of alcohol is detrimental and can cause fetal alcohol syndrome (FAS). Fetal alcohol syndrome involves a pattern of delayed growth, intellectual and behavioral difficulties, and distinctive facial characteristics that are present in children born to women who abused alcohol while pregnant. FAS is the main cause of mental retardation in the United States, affecting about 7,500 infants each year (Martini, Welch, & Newsome, 1995, p. 201).

Children with FAS are likely to have learning disabilities and attention deficit hyperactivity disorder (ADHD). They also have other behaviors that can interfere with learning and behavior in the classroom, including these:

- Difficulties with sequencing
- Difficulty with memory
- Difficulty understanding cause-and-effect relationships
- Weak generalizing skills
- Outbursts or other acting-out behaviors
- Severe temper tantrums
- Difficulty adjusting to change
- Difficulty predicting and/or understanding the consequences of behavior
- Difficulty making and keeping friends
- A tendency to be easily manipulated and led by others
- Difficulties with visual/spatial perception and balance

These behaviors make the child a challenging task for any teacher. Depending upon the degree of the condition, the child could be placed in a regular classroom but will surely need special services. Thus, a great deal of damage can be done to the child before birth by the mother's alcohol and drug consumption.

Abuse During Childhood

During their years growing up, children face the consequences of their parents' substance abuse. One trauma is that these children often witness violence in their family, typically by seeing their parents battering each other. Witnessing an abusing father battering their mother is a powerful event for a child. Frequently the abuser uses the child's behavior as an excuse for battering the woman, which can cause children to blame themselves for their mother's abuse. At other times children can feel guilty because they have been unable to help their mother avoid a beating.

Other traumas are caused when children themselves are directly abused. These children often suffer physical violence from a drunken or "high" parent (Redden, 1999; Regan, Ehrlich, & Finnegan, 1987). The consequences of child abuse range from psychological damage to death.

EFFECTS ON THE CHILD OF SUBSTANCE-ABUSING PARENTS

Children who live with substance-abusing parents carry burdens. One burden is feeling responsible for their parents. Eleven-year-old Dana felt that it was his responsibility to stop his mother's substance abuse. Dana was reunited with his mother after he had been out of the house for several months in foster care, following a child-abuse incident. As part of the condition for his return home, the court ordered him into counseling, where I met with him. He was very articulate and very mature. Said Dana:

> My whole family is drowning in a bottle of wine, and I want to stop it. I search the house when my mother is at work and find her drugs. I flush them down the toilet. She was given this medicine to stop her from drinking, but she never takes it. If you drink when you take it, you throw up and get really sick. When

she gets home from work, she likes a soda. I slip the medicine into her soda. Last night she went out drinking and did she get sick. I was scared that she would find out and let me have it, but she didn't.

I did talk to Dana about not secretly slipping medicine to his mother again, because there can be harmful consequences to taking this medication and drinking alcohol. But it is hard enough being responsible for yourself as an 11-year-old child; to be responsible for your parent as well is too much.

Another burden is that these children are often left alone, both physically and emotionally. Parents who are concerned with meeting their own substance needs frequently neglect their children. They do not prepare meals, they do not wash the clothes, and they leave their children alone for long periods after dark. These children are also psychologically alone. They have no parent to comfort them, provide them with security, and help them through the normal hurdles of childhood.

Growing up too fast is another burden for children of substance abusers. Children need a gradual transition from dependence on parents to independence. Children of substance abusers have too much responsibility too soon and never have the experience of just being a dependent child. A typical example is Rose, a 5-year-old I worked with in an urban Head Start center. She lived with her addictive mother and her younger sister, who was also a student in the center. Rose nurtured her younger sister. She made her snacks, comforted her when she was scared, made sure her coat was buttoned, and held her hand as they walked home. Rose always gave to her sister, but never seemed to need anything for herself. One morning Rose was helping me fix the morning snack. As we were walking together, she stubbed her toe ever so gently. She began to cry in a manner that was way out of proportion to her slight bump. As I held her and comforted her, I realized that it wasn't her toe, but her feelings, that needed comforting. For once, she was being able to be a child and get comforted by her teacher. She didn't have to be the grown-up in control.

Children of substance abusers never experience what it is like to grow up in a normal family where parents are there to take care of them. As a consequence, these children face an array of troubling feelings, including guilt, anxiety, embarrassment, and depression. Their school performance is impaired. When they get older, they are more likely to drop out of school (American Academy of Child and Adolescent Psychiatry, 1999; McGrath, Watson, & Chassin, 1999; Post & Robinson, 1998).

THE TEACHER'S ROLE IN HELPING CHILDREN WHOSE PARENTS ARE SUBSTANCE ABUSERS

These are some things you can do to help children whose parents are substance abusers:

- Expect the child to perform at a high level
- Have a consistent learning environment
- Keep in control

- Hold children responsible for their own behavior only
- Set limits when necessary
- Provide a quiet place to work

Expect the Child to Perform at a High Level

There are many steps that classroom teachers can take to best meet the needs of children whose parents are substance abusers. The first step is to expect the child to perform at a high level. Do not prejudge the child. Much has been written about self-fulfilling prophecy, in which children perform up to a teacher's expectations. There is a danger that people will prejudge these children and not expect them to perform well (Thurman et al., 1994). Fortunately this is not a problem with a good teacher.

Have a Consistent Learning Environment

Another step is to pay close attention to the learning environment in your classroom. Children who live in chaos are helped by finding some predictable order in their lives, and your classroom can provide that anchor of stability. As the teacher, you can be consistent and predictable. You can have clear expectations for appropriate behavior and enforce those expectations in a consistent manner.

Keep in Control

As the teacher and authority figure, you are always in control of the classroom. Your demonstration of control is often in sharp contrast to the child's experience in growing up with a parent who is out of control. You control how the lessons are taught and how the children in the classroom behave. Because you are in control, these children will not have to worry about being responsible for an adult, as they are at home, and can concentrate on their work.

Hold Children Responsible for Their Own Behavior Only

Holding children responsible only for their own behavior is another step you can take in the classroom. Frequently children of substance abusers have an inordinate amount of responsibility for the care of younger siblings and maintaining the household. You can help by involving them in projects where they are responsible only for their own behavior. Try not to put them in group situations with a weak group member who might let these already overburdened children assume the responsibility for the entire task. Make sure when they work in groups that they do only their share.

Set Limits When Necessary

Don't be reluctant to discipline these children if they need it. As much as you might feel compassion, considering their home lives, you must still be consistent and appropriate in monitoring your school and classroom rules. If necessary, you can tell the child that his behavior is inappropriate and he has to pay a penalty, but that you still respect and value him. It is basically a message that says, "I like you but I don't like what you are doing."

Provide a Quiet Place to Work

Finally, you might provide a quiet work area for the child who has a problem focusing. Children who are distracted by auditory and visual stimulation will prosper from being able to work in a corner of the room or otherwise private work area. You might arrange a special signal with the youngster so that she can discretely inform you that she is experiencing sensory overload and needs to withdraw to a more private place to work. This signal can be private so the child will not be embarrassed in front of her classmates.

WORKING WITH PARENTS

Working with parents who are substance abusers can be a maddening experience. When they are sober or not high, they can behave like normal parents, but when they are drunk or high they can be impossible. It is never productive to talk to a parent who is drunk or high. If approached by a parent in this condition before or after school, find a way to end the interaction before it starts. A discrete comment such as "I can't talk to you now, but I will call you to set up an appointment time when we can talk" can work. If you are concerned that a parent might be drunk or high when they come in for a scheduled appointment, never meet them alone. Have another teacher or administrator sit in on your conference.

Teachers must make sure that children do not suffer in school because of their parents' irresponsibility. Parents who are substance abusers often do many things that have a negative impact on their children. Because of the chaos in the house, the child might not be able to do his homework. He might be kept up late or have to care for his siblings when his parents are out. The Homework Club described in chapter 18 would be a vehicle to give children of substance abusers a safe, quiet place to do their work.

Substance-abusing parents often don't pay attention to issues of importance to their children. Their child might be the one who didn't bring in the money for the school trip even though her parents are not poor. The provisions for providing for these children are the same ones as noted in chapter 12.

Children are often kept out of school by abusing parents. The parent might be hung over and unwilling or unable to get out of bed in the morning to take the child to school, or the parent might be going out to drink and leave the child in charge of younger siblings. This is not a situation that a teacher can deal with alone. You need to monitor the attendance of these youngsters very carefully. If they miss school, you have to mobilize the outreach workers from your school system, perhaps social workers, to intervene with the family. Your job is to make sure that your outreach people act promptly. Sometimes teachers have to be nags and pests in order to get prompt service for the children in their class.

Finally, teachers must be alert for signs of child abuse and neglect. As we noted earlier, many substance-abusing parents abuse their children. Refer back to chapter 14 for the signs of abuse and appropriate teacher actions.

Summary

Children who have substance-abusing parents are in a difficult position. By being aware of the situation, we can provide these children with a consistency and stability in school that is lacking in their home life. Although we cannot end the destructive behavior of their parents, we can try to make sure that these children do not suffer in school because of the irresponsibility of their parents. We also need to work to mobilize school and community resources to help these children.

RESEARCH IDEAS

Questions to Investigate

1. How early should drug education start in the schools?
2. Should drug-addicted parents be allowed to retain custody of their children?
3. Would supervised group homes for older adolescents be an alternative to foster care?

Resources to Explore

British Columbia Ministry of Education
  http://www.bced.gov.ba.ca

National Association for Children of Alcoholics
  http://www.health.org/nacoa

National Clearinghouse for Alcohol and Drug Information
  http://www.health.org

National Institute on Alcohol Abuse and Alcoholism
  http://silk.nih.gov

National Institute on Drug Abuse
  http://nida.nih.gov

Schaffer Library of Drug Policy
  http://www.druglibrary.org/schaffer

References

AMERICAN ACADEMY OF CHILD AND ADOLESCENT PSYCHIATRY. (1999). Children of alcoholics [Online]. Available: http://www.cmhcys.com/facts/fam/alcoholic.htm.

BINGOL, N., FUCHS, M., DIAZ, V., STONE, R. K., & GROMISCH, D. S. (1987). Teratogenicity of cocaine in humans. *Journal of Pediatrics, 110,* 93–96.

CHASNOFF, I. J. (1992). *Epidemiological study of the prevalence of alcohol and other drug use among pregnant and parturient women in Illinois.* Chicago: National Association for Perinatal Addiction Research and Education.

CHASNOFF, I. J., BURNS, W. J., SCHNOLL, S. H., & BURNS, K. A. (1985). Cocaine use in pregnancy. *New England Journal of Medicine, 313,* 666–669.

CHASNOFF, I. J., GRIFFITH, D. R., MACGREGOR, S., et al. (1989). Temporal patterns of cocaine use in pregnancy: Perinatal outcomes. *Journal of the American Medical Association, 261,* 93–96.

HURT, H., MALMUD, E., BETANCOURT, L., BRAITMAN, L. E., BRODSKY, N. L., & GIANNETTA, J. (1997). Children with in utero cocaine exposure do not differ from control subjects on intelligence testing. *Archives of Pediatric and Adolescent Medicine, 151,* 1237–1241.

MARTINI, F. H., WELCH, K., & NEWSOME, M. (1995). *Applications manual: Fundamentals of anatomy and physiology* (3rd ed.). Englewood Cliffs, NJ: Prentice Hall.

MCGRATH, C. E., WATSON, A. L., & CHASSIN, L. (1999). Academic achievement in adolescent children of alcoholics. *Journal of Studies on Alcohol, 60,* 18–26.

NATIONAL ASSOCIATION FOR CHILDREN OF ALCOHOLICS. (1999). Children of alcoholics: Important facts [Online]. Available: http://www.health.org/nacoa/impfacts.htm.

POST, P., & ROBINSON, B. E. (1998). School-age children of alcoholics and non-alcoholics: Their anxiety, self-esteem, and locus of control. *Professional School Counseling, 1,* 36–40.

REDDEN, G. (1999). Violence in the family [Online]. Available: http://www.health.org/nacoa/famviol.htm.

REGAN, D. O., EHRLICH, S. M., & FINNEGAN, L. P. (1987). Infants of drug addicts: At risk for child abuse, neglect, and placement in foster care. *Neurotoxicol Teratology, 9,* 315–319.

ROBINS, L., & MILLS, J. (Eds.). (1993). Effects on in utero exposure to street drugs. *American Journal of Public Health, 83* (suppl), 2–32.

THURMAN, S. K., BROBEIL, R. A., DUCCETTE, J. P., & HURT, H. (1994). Prenatally exposed to cocaine: Does the label matter? *Journal of Early Intervention, 18,* 119–130.

VEGA, W. A., KOLODY, B., HWANG, J., & NOBLE, A. (1993). Prevalence and magnitude of perinatal substance exposures in California. *New England Journal of Medicine, 329,* 850–854.

CHAPTER 20

Youths Who Engage in Antisocial Behavior

OBJECTIVE

After reading this chapter, you should be able to identify youths in your class-rooms who are using illegal substances and those involved in gang activities. You should understand the street terms associated with this antisocial behavior and identify the signs that youth are engaged in this activity. You should also know how best to help these students.

CHAPTER OUTLINE

Youths Who Use Dangerous Substances
Identifying Students Who Are Using Drugs
  Alcohol
  Amphetamines
  Cocaine
  Inhalants
  Marijuana
  Phencyclidine (PCP)
The Teacher's Role in Dealing with Drugs
Youth Involved in Gangs
  Gang Culture
  Gang Activities
The Teacher's Role in Dealing with Gangs
Summary

YOUTHS WHO USE DANGEROUS SUBSTANCES

The reasons for drug use are multiple and complex. There is no way to tell for sure why a youngster decides to use drugs. Drugs help many students escape a reality they find painful. Others use drugs because of peer influences. There are many other reasons why youths choose to use illegal drugs. As teachers, our job is not to try to figure out why a youngster is using drugs. That job is best left to our colleagues in mental health who have the special training to deal with this complicated issue.

IDENTIFYING STUDENTS WHO ARE USING DRUGS

Different drugs have different effects. You will find it helpful to know which drugs are currently being used by your students, and how you might be able to identify a student who is using any of the following drugs:

- Alcohol
- Amphetamines
- Cocaine
- Inhalants
- Marijuana
- Phencyclidine (PCP)

Alcohol

Although alcohol is legal for adult use, in most states it is illegal for middle and high school students to use alcohol. Alcohol is readily available in most parts of the United States, and underage children can gain access to it at home or by purchasing it with false identification or through third parties.

Youth drink beer, wine, or liquor. A 12-ounce glass of beer, a 5-ounce glass of wine, and a 1.5-ounce shot of liquor all contain the same amount of alcohol and have an equal effect on the drinker. Youth who are drunk are often involved in school accidents, violence, and disturbances, and in alcohol-related automobile accidents.

Signs and symptoms of alcohol use and intoxication that a teacher might observe include these (National Clearinghouse for Drug and Alcohol Information, 1999):

- Smell of alcohol on breath
- Irritability
- Euphoria
- Loss of physical coordination
- Inappropriate or violent behavior
- Loss of balance
- Unsteady gate
- Slurred or incoherent speech
- Slow thinking

Amphetamines

Amphetamines are stimulants, or "uppers," that stimulate the central nervous system and produce increased alertness and activity. Stimulants are legitimately prescribed by physicians for short-term appetite control, and to treat ADHD in children.

Youth will take these drugs to feel alert or energetic or to get "high." Consumers of stimulants also report a feeling of well-being. These are some of the behaviors observed in people who take even small, infrequent doses of amphetamines:

- Restlessness
- Anxiety
- Mood swings

- Panic
- Paranoid thoughts
- Hallucinations
- Convulsions and cardiac disturbances

Long-term users often have acne that resembles a measles rash; trouble with their teeth, gums, and nails; and dry, lifeless hair (Students Against Drugs and Alcohol, 1999).

Cocaine

Cocaine is an addictive stimulant that directly affects the brain. It is sold on the street as a fine white crystalline powder, know by various names—*coke, C, snow, flake, blow.* "Crack" is a cocaine that has been processed into a rocklike, smokeable substance. The crack smoker gets an immediate euphoric high. This attribute of the drug, along with its low price, has made it a very desirable form of cocaine.

The user can consume cocaine several ways:

- "Chewing"—taking it orally
- "Snorting"—inhaling the powder through the nostrils
- "Mainlining"—injecting the drug directly into the bloodstream
- "Smoking"—inhaling the vapor into the lungs

The effects of cocaine appear almost immediately after a single dose and disappear within a few minutes or hours. You might observe the following behaviors in a student who has taken cocaine before coming to your class:

- Euphoria
- High energy
- Talkativeness
- Mental alertness, especially to sensations of sight, sound, and touch

If the student has taken a particularly large dose of cocaine, you might observe more disturbing behaviors such as muscle twitches, paranoia, and erratic and violent behavior (National Institute on Drug Abuse, 1998).

Inhalants

Inhalants are breathable substances, some of which are found in common household products packaged in aerosol cans. Products used as inhalants include spray paint, vegetable oil, hair spray, model airplane and other glues, paint thinners, nail polish, gasoline, and nitrous oxide (laughing gas).

Because these products are so readily available, they are easily accessible to younger children. These products are very dangerous—there is a high risk of sudden death from spray inhalation. Observing a user shortly after inhalant use, a teacher might notice the following:

- Motor incoordination
- Inability to think and act clearly
- Sometimes abusive and violent behavior

If you observe any of the following behaviors it might indicate that a youngster is a long-term user of sprays or other inhalants (Students Against Drugs and Alcohol, 1999):

- Drastic weight loss
- Impairment of vision
- Impairment of memory and the ability to think clearly

Marijuana

Marijuana is a dried plant known on the street as *pot, dope, grass, weed,* and the like. It is usually smoked in loosely rolled cigarettes called *joints*. Some users slice open and hollow out cigars and replace the tobacco with marijuana to make what are called "blunts." Marijuana can also be brewed into tea or mixed in baked products such as cookies or brownies.

Marijuana is the most commonly used illicit drug. There is a great deal of controversy over whether marijuana should be legalized, because there is evidence that the drug can be used for medicinal purposes. Nonetheless, at this point in time the drug is illegal.

Marijuana can make the user feel relaxed, loosened up, and giggly. Other signs that a teacher might observe include these (American Council for Drug Education, 1999):

- A feeling of confusion
- An appearance of being "spaced out"
- Memory loss
- Loss of interest and motivation
- Loud talking and inappropriate laughter followed by sleepiness
- Glassy, red eyes
- A sweet burnt scent

Phencyclidine (PCP)

PCP, or "angel dust," is legally used as a veterinary anesthetic and tranquilizer. PCP is produced illegally in labs and is sold on the street in several forms:

- In powder form ("angel dust")
- As tablets and crystals
- In pills ("hogs" or "peace pills")

It is often smoked, usually mixed with marijuana, parsley, and mint leaves.

PCP intoxication can produce violent and bizarre behavior in youth, even those usually not prone to such behavior. The violent behavior can be directed at themselves or at others. You might observe the following behaviors in PCP users (Students Against Drugs and Alcohol, 1999):

- Muscle rigidity
- Loss of concentration
- Visual disturbances

- Delirium
- Feelings of isolation
- Speech impairment
- Fear of death
- Convulsions

THE TEACHER'S ROLE IN DEALING WITH DRUGS

As a teacher you have only one course of action to follow. Your job is to identify youngsters with a problem and make sure that they get professional help. Teachers are not trained as social workers or drug and addiction counselors. Your job is to teach, and you need to trust your professional colleagues to help the youth with a substance-abuse problem.

You might know that a youth is exhibiting signs of drug abuse, but you might not be able to tell which drug is being used because many of the signs noted above apply to more than one drug. You need not worry about being exact. If you see any of the signs, refer the child for help to your school counselor or nurse. It will be up to your fellow professionals to make the necessary contacts within the law to get help for the youth.

YOUTH INVOLVED IN GANGS

Teachers need to be aware of gang activity. You job is to be able to identify:

- Gang culture
- Gang activities

Youth gangs have become a symbol of the alienation many young people feel from mainstream society. Researchers who have studied gangs have noted some of their common characteristics. Members of gangs are usually young teenage males of similar racial or ethnic backgrounds, though researchers recently have found gangs with active members as young as 8 or 9 years old and female gangs. There is now also evidence of ethnic and racial crossover in gangs in multiethnic neighborhoods (Campbell, 1990; Huff, 1990; Lal, Lal, & Achilles, 1993; Taylor, 1993).

Gangs often engage in antisocial, illegal, violent, and criminal behaviors. Many are involved in dealing illegal drugs. Gang members are increasingly violent and are large users of alcohol and drugs. Modern gangs use sophisticated communications devices and automatic weapons.

Recruitment of new members is an ongoing process. School is an especially good place to solicit new members.

Gang Culture

Gang members do things that set them apart from the mainstream. As Lal (1999) points out, these behaviors not only segregate and sustain the gangs, but also add an illusion of mystery and glamour that is sometimes called "the lure of the gangs." Youth who are not gang members but are infatuated with gang culture are said to be "romancing the gang." Gang distinctiveness is most noticeable in the following:

- Attire and paraphernalia
- Identifying marks such as tattoos
- Posturing
- A gang mentality (members call this "being down for the hood" or being "loco" for the gang. It is a willingness to do anything, even die or commit murder, for the gang)
- Activities, particularly recruitment of new members

Gang Activities

As a teacher you can suspect gang activity if you notice any of the following activities:

- Graffiti—used for communicating, warning, and marking turf
- Flashing/slanging—used for claiming affiliation, identifying, threats
- Hanging out—used for marking turf, show of force, protection for members
- Intimidation—used for gaining control, gaining respect, instilling fear
- Recruitment—used for building a power base, establishing loyalties, sustaining membership
- Extortion—used for instilling fear, gaining respect, getting easy money
- Assaults/fights—used for retaliation, gaining respect, show of force
- Drug use/dealing—used for acquiring money, getting high, partying
- Use/sale of weapons—used for protecting self, members, and turf, and for acquiring money

THE TEACHER'S ROLE IN DEALING WITH GANGS

Gangs are a community problem and need to be dealt with by law enforcement persons, social service personnel, and educators working in concert. Solving the gang problem is not a job for a teacher. Our part in the process is to recognize that gang activity is going on, either in your class, on the school grounds, or in the school, and to bring the matter to the attention of the principal. As head of the school, the principal will call in the other professionals to collaborate and deal with the problem.

Summary

Teachers have to be able to identify students who are using illegal drugs and identify those who are involved in gang activity. The teacher's job is to report this activity to the school principal so she can mobilize the appropriate community resources to deal with the problem.

RESEARCH IDEAS

Questions to Investigate

1. Can schools create a socially acceptable alternative to gangs?
2. What should a school do when it catches a student using drugs?
3. Should mandatory drug testing be required of all children in schools?

Resources to Explore

American Council for Drug Education
   http://www.acde.org

National Clearinghouse or Drug and Alcohol Information
   http://www.health.org

National Institute on Drug Abuse
   http://www.nida.nih.gov

References

AMERICAN COUNCIL FOR DRUG EDUCATION. (1999). [Online]. Available: http://www.acde.org/common/Symptom.htm.

CAMPBELL, A. (1990). Female participation in gangs. In C. R. Huff (Ed.), *Gangs in America* (pp. 163–182). Newbury Park, CA: Sage.

HUFF, C. R. (1990). *Gangs in America.* Newbury Park, CA: Sage.

LAL, S. R. (1999). *Gangs: From social groups to violent delinquents.* [Online]. Available: http://eric-web.tc.columbia.edu/monographs/uds107/gang_gangs.htm.

LAL, S. R., LAL, D., & ACHILLES, C. R. (1993). *Handbook on gangs in schools: Strategies to reduce gang-related activities.* Newbury Park, CA: Corwin Press.

NATIONAL CLEARINGHOUSE FOR DRUG AND ALCOHOL INFORMATION. (1999). [Online]. Available: http://www.health.org.

NATIONAL INSTITUTE ON DRUG ABUSE. (1998). *Research report: Cocaine* [Online]. Available: http://www.nida.nih.gov/researchreports/cocaine.

STUDENTS AGAINST DRUGS AND ALCOHOL. (1999). [Online]. Available: http://www.sada.org/stimulants.html.

TAYLOR, C. S. (1993). *Girls, gangs, women and drugs.* East Lansing: Michigan State University Press.

Appendix
Websites of General Interest

American Academy of Child and Adolescent Psychiatry
http://www.aap.org

American Psychological Association
http://www.apa.org

Educational Resources Information Center (ERIC)
http://ericir.syr.edu

Federation of Families for Children's Mental Health
http://www.ffcmh.org

National Child Care Information Center
http://nccic.org

National Institute for Mental Health (NIMH)
http://www.nimh.gov

National Network for Family Relations
http://www.nnfr.org

National Parent Information Center
http://npic.org

The Family Life Development Center
http://child.cornell.edu/fldc

U.S. Department of Health and Human Services
http://www.aspe.os.dhhs.gov

Credits

Author Photo: Deborah Fuller/Towson University
CO 1: © Suzie Fitzhugh/Stock Boston
CO 2: © PhotoDisc/Education
CO 3: © Susan Rosenberg/Photo Researchers
CO 4: © Bob Daemmrich
CO 5: © John Eastcott/Yva Momatuk/The Image Works
CO 6: © Wil and Deni McIntyre/Photo Researchers
CO 7: © Steve Skjold Photo CD
CO 8: © Jeff Albertson/Stock Boston
CO 9: © Mirto Vintonio/Stock Boston
CO 10: © Photodisc/Health and Medicine 2
CO 11: © Bob Daemmrich
CO 12: © Akos Szilvasi/Stock Boston
CO 13: © Arthur Grace/Stock Boston
CO 14: © Jean Claude Lejeune/Stock Boston
CO 15: © PhotoDisc/Education
CO 16: © PhotoDisc/Education
CO 17: © Hazel Hankin/Stock Boston
CO 18: © Bob Daemmrich
CO 19: © Steve Rubin/The Image Works
CO 20: © Steve Skjold Photo CD

Index